THE Muppets™

Big Book of Crafts

Foreword by
Cheryl Henson

Photographs by
John E. Barrett

Illustrations by
Stephanie Osser & Matthew Fox

THE Muppets™

Jim Henson

Big Book of Crafts

by The Muppet Workshop

and Stephanie St. Pierre

WORKMAN PUBLISHING · NEW YORK

Copyright © 1999 by The Jim Henson Company, Inc.

MUPPETS, MUPPET, the Kermit head logo, the JIM
HENSON signature logo, and characters' names, like-
nesses, and personalities are trademarks of The Jim
Henson Company, Inc. All rights reserved. The
MUPPET puppets and characters are exclusive prop-
erty of The Jim Henson Company, Inc., and nothing
herein is intended to authorize any person or entity to
imitate, copy, build, or use in commerce in any form
the MUPPET puppets.

No portion of this book may be reproduced
mechanically, electronically, or by any other means,
including photocopying—without written permission
of the publisher. Published simultaneously in Canada
by Thomas Allen & Son Limited.

Library of Congress Cataloging-in-Publication Data
St. Pierre, Stephanie.
The Muppets Big Book of Crafts / by The Muppet
Workshop and Stephanie St. Pierre ; illustrations by
Stephanie Osser ; photographs by John E. Barrett.
p. cm.
Summary: Includes instructions for creating all kinds
of craft projects, including rugs, placemats, costumes,
masks, jewelry, models, puppets, and more.
ISBN 0-7611-0526-3
1. Handicraft Juvenile literature. [1. Handicraft.]
I. Osser, Stephanie, ill. II. Barrett, John, E., ill. III.
Muppet Workshop. IV. Title.
TT160.S24 1999   99-38606
745.5--dc21   CIP

Workman books are available at special discounts
when purchased in bulk for premium and sales
promotions as well as for fund-raising or educational
use. Special editions or book excerpts can also be
created to specification. For details, please contact
the Sales Director at the address below.

WORKMAN PUBLISHING
708 Broadway
New York, NY 10003-9555
www.workmanweb.com

Printed in the United States

First Printing October 1999

10 9 8 7 6 5 4 3 2 1

CONTENTS

Dipping and Dyeing 169

CHAPTER 12 Costumes and Hats 183

CHAPTER 13 Masks and Disguises 205

CHAPTER 14 Jewelry 221

Foreword
by Cheryl Henson

The place where the first Muppet was born was in the kitchen of my father's childhood home in Maryland. That's where he built the very first Kermit—out of an old green coat that had belonged to his mother, a Ping-Pong ball cut in half (for the eyes), and some felt and cardboard (for the mouth).

The first official Muppet Workshop was created a few years later, when my dad married my mother. Together, they set up a place in the basement of their new home to build puppets for their first TV show, *Sam and Friends.*

Then came five kids, and with them came another kind of workshop. When we were growing up, we lived in a big messy house filled with cats, dogs, rabbits, guinea pigs, friends, neighbors, and all of the stuff we built throughout the years.

Jane and Jim Henson with four of their five children (from left to right): Cheryl, John, Brian, and Lisa.

The stuff was made in the makeshift workshops we set up in the basement and the garage.

At Halloween time, my father made wonderfully frightening monster pumpkins by carving just the outer orange pumpkin skin, allowing candlelight to glow through the white flesh. All of us kids made our own costumes. Sometimes we would piece together leftover puppet fur to make scary old witch masks; other times, we made beautiful princess, animal, or outer space creature costumes. At Christmas, our gigantic tree was covered with all kinds of imaginative homemade decorations. One year my father made hundreds of bread dough monster ornaments to give to his friends to decorate their trees.

Last—but certainly not least—is the "official" Muppet Workshop where all of the puppets of *Sesame Street, The Muppet Show,* and all of the different Muppet television shows and movies are made. The Muppet Workshop is tucked away on a side street in a plain five-story building in New York City. People walk past it every day without having the slightest idea of what's

place—everywhere you look, things are coming to life.

There aren't any set rules or even guidelines on how to build something that has never been built before, and each new puppet is a challenge. Many different kinds of skills are required: Puppet builders have to be able to draw, sculpt, sew, carve, paint, and build. But more than anything else, they need to be able to think creatively.

And that's what they did when they came together to create the crafts in this book. They were asked to invent things they might have made when they were kids. And together with Stephanie St. Pierre, they came up with the following ideas for what I believe are some of the best craft projects ever.

We hope that you are inspired to build some of them—and to come up with some new, unexpected ones of your own!

Heather Henson with a Halloween pumpkin carved by Jim.

going on behind its white brick walls. But once you step inside, there's nothing ordinary about it.

All over the building there are great bags of colorful feathers and bolts of fur fabric. Dozens of drawers bear labels proclaiming things like "WHISKERS," "NOSES," or "USED EYEBALLS." On one floor, someone is sewing silver sequins on costumes. On another, someone else is dyeing fake fur a bright orange color.

A Muppet builder is using curved scissors to cut creatures out of blocks of foam. Others turn puppets this way and that, testing their movements and their facial expressions. In the metal and electrical workshops, still others are creating robotics and animatronics: One holds a pair of Muppet eyes complete with computer-controlled blinking mechanisms. It is a magical

"Now read this!"

The introduction will teach you the basics.
Soon you'll be making great projects like this
Surprise Cupboard (page 114).

Before You Get Started

**Setting Up a
Workshop of
Your Very Own**

The Muppet Workshop has room after room filled with materials and supplies. In one room, you might find a huge bin of foam rubber scraps piled nearly to the ceiling, while next door, boxes filled with scraps of furry fabrics and wrapping paper teeter in stacks. The walls are lined with shelves of bags, bins, and drawers stocked with spools, cans of glue, wire, plastic junk, rolls of different-colored tapes, and much more. There's a lot of stuff, but all of it has been carefully sorted and labeled so that anybody who needs anything can find it right away.

Before you begin any of the projects in this book, it's a good idea to set up a workshop of your own—a place where you can think, draw, and design, and in which you can build your craft projects. It's fun to get started—all you'll need are supplies, tools, a way to organize and store your stuff, and, of course, space to work on your projects. Read on to find out what you'll need in your workshop.

**"Hey!
Someone
filed me in
the wrong
drawer!"**

Stuff You Will Need for Your Workshop

MATERIALS AND TOOLS

There are a number of different tools and materials you'll need to make the crafts in this book. But where can you get all this stuff? Start by looking around your house. Gather up all of the various arts and crafts supplies you've bought or received over the years. Search through drawers and closets for old keys, bits of wire, colored feathers, buttons, sequins, bells, glitter, or pieces of broken toys. Check out the cans, bottles, and newspapers in the recycling bin. Start a scrap bag, and save old clothes, socks, and

"Make your own workstation out of a large cardboard box."

tights that are ruined or don't fit anymore; old towels, tablecloths, sheets, and pillowcases are good to save, too. Keep old shower curtains and plastic tablecloths, and collect pieces of wrapping paper, old greeting cards, and ribbon scraps. Bear in mind that one person's trash is another person's treasure.

If you can't find an item you need, see if you can substitute another item in its place. And, of course, if all else fails, you can most likely find necessary items at your local hardware, craft, or fabric store (in fact, a small number of the projects in this book will probably require such special purchases). Just remember: If you're using items that you've found around the house, always check with the owner of those items *and*

MATERIALS

You might want to keep some of these things handy for your projects:

- aluminum foil, plastic wrap, wax paper (clean and unused)
- balloons
- cardboard: tubes, corrugated boxes, lightweight cardboard, and posterboard
- cellophane
- clay

- coloring stuff: pencils, pens, markers, and crayons
- confetti and glitter
- decorations: baubles, beads, buttons, sequins, feathers, and pom-poms
- fabric dye and food coloring
- fabrics of every description (including felt and fur)
- flour
- foam, Styrofoam, and sponges
- glue (white glue, wood glue, rubber cement, glue sticks)

- masks
- metal stuff: springs, curtain rings, nails, screws, chains, nuts, and bolts
- natural stuff: leaves, twigs, flowers, pinecones, and other things
- paints: poster paint, acrylic paint, watercolors
- paper: newspaper, tissue paper, crepe paper, old greeting cards, neat colored and textured paper, metallic paper
- pipe cleaners
- recycling: tin cans, plastic soda bottles,

small jars (clean and empty)
- ribbons, rickrack, yarn, cotton and nylon thread, cotton string, twine
- rubber bands
- tape (electrical, clear or cellophane, duct, and masking)
- tracing paper
- wax
- wire: hangers, colorful telephone wire
- wood: balsa blocks, scraps, dowels, clothespins, toothpicks, Popsicle sticks

with an adult to see if you can use them. You don't want to turn a pair of ripped jeans into a quilt, only to find out that they were your mom's favorite pants!

On these two pages we've listed most of the tools and materials that you will need to do *every single* project in this book. However, if you're like the people at the Muppet Workshop, you'll probably find that you like some kinds of projects better than others; you may even decide to specialize in one kind of craft. So don't let these lists scare or intimidate you. They should excite and inspire you. If you don't have the required materials, move on to another project—there are plenty of fun, simple things to make in this book.

STORAGE

Once you've collected some stuff, you need to organize it so that you can find what you need when you need it. You can keep your things in a cardboard box or a dresser drawer in your room or in your workshop area. Shoe boxes, milk crates, and shopping bags are handy storage places for fabrics, ribbons, and assorted other things. Old mugs make good pencil holders. Egg cartons and tackle boxes are good places to store tiny things like colored beads or buttons. Zipper-close bags are great for feathers (they tend to float away) and scraps. You can even start an art file of pictures torn from magazines. Put the pictures into big envelopes and separate them into categories like "animals" and "machines."

How you store things will depend on what you have on hand, but keep in mind that containers should have lids or be able to close in some way and every container should have a label that tells you what's inside. At the Muppet Workshop, each weird little scrap is tucked away in a special place. Organize your own workshop in the same way, so the next time you need some round plastic thingies to make a pair of googly eyes, you know exactly where to find them (in the box marked "EYEBALLS" at the bottom of your sock drawer, of course!).

TOOLS

- awl
- buckets, bowls, pans
- hammer
- hole puncher
- knitting needles
- measuring compass, T-square, triangle (for drawing perfect angles)
- measuring cups and spoons
- needles and pins
- paintbrushes of all sizes
- pencil and eraser
- pliers
- pushpins
- rubber gloves
- ruler and tape measures (one soft and one rigid)
- safety goggles
- sandpaper
- scissors (regular and heavy duty)
- stapler
- tacks and paper clips

Adults only:

- iron and ironing board
- low-temperature glue gun
- saw, sandpaper, drill
- utility knife and kitchen knife
- wire cutters

"These tools are heavy!"

Also, make sure that the people around your house are aware of your storage systems, or things could wind up being thrown away.

SPACE

Every project needs its space! Finding a special corner of your own would be ideal, but sometimes you'll need an extra-big space, or a space for projects that require a lot of drying time and cannot be moved until they are finished. This could be a problem if you start a project on the kitchen table after school and it can't be moved until the next day. So keep in mind how long your stuff will be out and how much space you will need before you begin a project (read through each project before you start it!), and always check with an adult before you begin.

Setting up a workshop is a project in itself, so have fun with it!

Muppet Workshop Advice

Before you begin any project, read the directions through *completely*. Oftentimes you will find that you need an adult's help (even if it's just for a minute), and sometimes you'll need an extra pair of hands, which someone your own age can provide. You also have to figure out if you have all of the materials and tools that a project calls for, and if not, you must either get them or figure out a way to substitute something else. You also need to know how long a project will take. Some projects can be completed in less than an hour, but others require time to dry (or freeze, or harden) for a couple of hours or even overnight. If you know this ahead of time, you can plan ahead and avoid being frustrated when you find out that you won't have a project ready by a certain time. (For example, if you're making a craft as a gift for a birthday party and it won't be ready until the next day.)

As you read through this book, you'll notice a few pieces of art that repeat from project to project. These pieces of art let you know at a glance when a certain kind of information is being passed along from us to you. Please be sure to pay attention to these warnings and pieces of advice, because it is absolutely essential that everyone is happy and safe when Muppet Crafts are in progress. These two pages contain an explanation of the icons used throughout this book.

GRAB A GROWN-UP!

When you see this picture in the "What You Will Need" list for a project, it means that you must ask a grown-up to help you handle certain tools and appliances. Sometimes the adult is needed for the whole project, while other times he or she is only needed for a minute to complete a difficult task or a task that's unsafe for kids to complete alone. As always, read through the directions of every project before you begin, so you and your adult can figure out when he or she will be needed. If an adult can't help, just pick one of the many fun and cool projects in this book that you can do on your own.

> **"When you see us, grab an adult to help you."**

THE "BEAR" ESSENTIALS

Many of the crafts in this book call for the following items:

- a pencil and eraser
- a pen
- a black Magic Marker
- a ruler (standard 12- or 18-inch length)
- a pair of scissors (Fiskars or another big, strong kind)
- white glue (Elmer's Glue is good)

So whenever you see this Fozzie mug icon in the "What You Will Need" list of a project, it means that you need all (or most) of this stuff in order to make the craft. We think it's a good idea to store it all together in a cup or pouch, then you can just grab it when you need it.

HOW EASY ARE THE PROJECTS?

  When you see this single Miss Piggy head at the beginning of a project, it means that the project is easy.

When there are two Miss Piggy heads, the project is harder.

When there are three Miss Piggy heads, it means the project is pretty complicated and will require a lot of help from an adult or a few friends. But don't let that discourage you—the hardest projects are lots of fun, and they'll teach you lots of new craft skills. Just get some help!

A QUICK REVIEW:

Adult Icon

Bear Essentials

Difficulty levels:

Easy

Tricky

Challenging

ALWAYS!

Here are some tips to bear in mind:

● Always use oven mitts or pot holders when handling anything hot.

● Always use goggles or other protective eye gear if you are using sharp objects or stuff that sprays or splatters.

● Always ask a grown-up for help when something is too difficult for you or when you see the adult symbol.

● Always read tips.

● Always read projects through from beginning to end before you start.

● Always look for the difficulty level to let you know what you're in for.

● Always check with adults to make sure you've chosen a good location for a project, and make sure

they know how long the project will need to be there.

● Always clear your work area before you begin and cover the work surface with clean newspaper.

"...Always remember to clean up afterward!"

Hot Tips for Making Crafts

As you go through the projects in this book, you'll begin to notice that some projects use the same craft techniques as others. Rather than repeating them time after time, we decided to put the information up front and ask you to refer back to it when needed. Each time a project requires you to refer back to this section, it will tell you which of these pages to turn to.

PAPIER-MÂCHÉ

Papier-mâché is a soft, smushy material made of newspaper and homemade glue. It is one of the most useful tools a craftsperson has, since it can help build strong, solid shapes of any size. You can apply papier-mâché to all kinds of surfaces, from blown-up balloons to plates to wire skeletons known as armatures. With papier-mâché, you can build anything—a teeny bumblebee or a giant seven-foot-high Muppet monster!

"Extra! Extra! Read all about it!"

Crafts Weekly

In this book, we created many things with papier-mâché, including the "Spider Piñata" on page 38 and the "Giant Bird" on page 64. Any project that calls for papier-mâché will refer you back to this page for instructions.

Here's how papier-mâché is made:

● In a bowl, mix 1 cup flour and ¾ cup cold water to form a runny homemade glue. (You may also purchase a papier-mâché mix at some arts and crafts supply stores. If you do, follow the directions on the package.) Make more glue mixture as needed.

● Place the glue mixture into a shallow pan.

● Cut or tear newspaper into large or small strips (depending on the size of your project).

● Carefully dip each newspaper strip into the glue mixture, one at a time. Lift the strip from the pan, pinch it between the thumb and index finger of your other hand, then slide them down the length of the strip to remove excess glue. Now you're ready to apply the newspaper strip to your project, smoothing as you go.

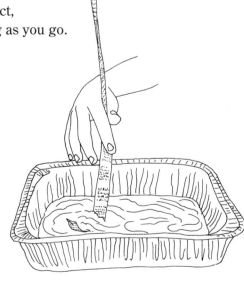

Later, when the papier-mâché has dried, you may decorate the surface of your project in any way you like. Bring on the paint! Sprinkle on the glitter!

PLASTER OF PARIS

A couple of the projects in this book (such as the "Sandy Turtle" on page 56) use a sculpting material called plaster of Paris. It is a powder that, when mixed with water, makes a warm, gooey substance that you can cast into all kinds of shapes. You can buy it at most arts and crafts supply stores. Follow the mixing directions on the box or bag. Usually, the plaster recipe involves adding ⅔ cup water to 1 cup plaster of Paris.

GLUING TIPS

● Don't forget to lay down newspaper on your work surface to keep the furniture from getting gooey!

● White glue can get very gloppy and messy if you use too much—start out with a small amount and add more as you need it.

● A low-temperature glue gun (with glue sticks) can make many of the projects much easier and faster to complete. If you use one, *always* have a grown-up help you!

● White glue sticks are a good substitute for white glue when you're gluing paper to paper— they're neater and cleaner, too.

● When glue gets on your hands or clothes, wash them with warm water.

PATTERNS BIG AND SMALL

Some of the projects in this book require the use of patterns, and while some of our patterns can be directly traced, most of them will need to be enlarged (especially the patterns for things you'll end up wearing). All of our patterns are presented on a grid background, and those patterns that are not marked "actual size" are shown at a smaller scale. The grid background will allow you to enlarge the patterns by copying them by hand onto an enlarged grid (or larger-square graph paper) or by using a photocopier to blow them up to whatever size you need.

"Follow our directions to make your projects big or small!"

SYMBOLS OF MEASUREMENT

This symbol stands for feet: '

This symbol stands for inches: "

So 5'6" would mean five feet, six inches.

The symbol ✕ in between measurements means "by."

So 8½" ✕ 11" means 8½" by 11", or 8½" wide and 11" long (width always comes before length in a measurement).

To Enlarge a Pattern by Hand

All of our patterns indicate the "scale" of the grid they're on, so that you can enlarge the pattern to the correct size for your project. For instance, in the example below, the scale is ½" = 1". This means that each of the boxes in our pattern is ½-inch square. You'll need to make each box in your bigger grid 1-inch square for the project to work. Here's how to do it:

● Draw a larger grid onto a large sheet of paper to the scale indicated. In our example, that means you'll draw a grid in which each square is 1-inch tall and 1-inch wide, with the same number of boxes as our grid.

● Choose a starting point for copying the pattern, say, Kermit's left eye, and begin by

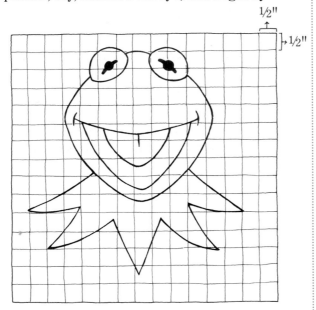

counting up and across to the correct box. Now, begin transferring the design, box by box, onto the new grid by copying the exact same curves, angles, and straight lines shown in each box of the original pattern.

When you've finished enlarging, cut out your new pattern (making sure to cut out any interior spaces that need to be removed) and

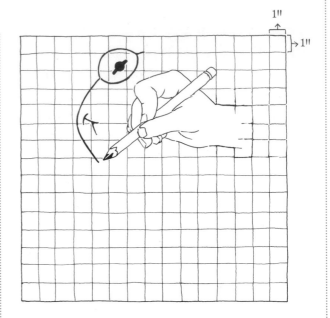

continue following the directions for the project. If you need to trace the pattern, refer to the tracing directions on pages 9 and 10.

To Enlarge a Pattern on a Photocopier

It's faster and easier to use a photocopier to enlarge a pattern, but you must have access to a copier that has a special enlarging feature (often called a *zoom* capability). Just refer to the percentage increase on each pattern page in the back of the book.

Note: Some patterns must be fitted to you! In those few cases, the project's directions will tell you how to do it. You can also alter sizes at the end of a project with a few well-placed stitches or some glue.

TRACING AND TRANSFERRING

Y ou know how to trace! You just put a piece of tracing paper over a drawing you want to copy, and, well, copy it! But what happens when you want to transfer that tracing onto a piece of fabric or cardboard? Here's what you do:

1. You already know the first part. Just grab that piece of tracing paper and a pencil and trace whatever picture you want. Make sure to copy every line in the drawing. (Note: If you are tracing onto a dark material, like black paper or dark fabric, you should use light-colored chalk to do your tracing. That way, it will show up on the dark material when you transfer it.)

2. Turn the tracing paper over. On the back of the paper, shade over the traced lines you just drew, using the side of the pencil point, so that you have a nice, smudgy, thick outline of the shape.

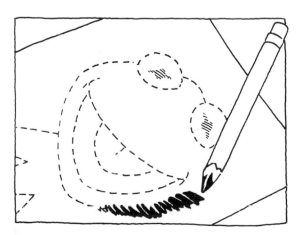

3. Turn the tracing paper back over and lay it on the piece of fabric, cardboard, or whatever you want to transfer the design to. Retrace the lines you drew the first time. This will transfer the smudgy pencil outline from the back of the tracing paper onto your fabric, cardboard, or wood.

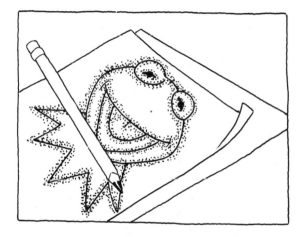

Whew! That wasn't so hard!

Now that you're armed with all of this information, go forth and make Muppet Crafts!

"On your markers! Get set! Scribble!"

Scribbles and Sketches

Artists, architects, engineers, and inventors all use drawing to *visualize* their ideas. Using lines and shading, an artist can sketch a beautiful landscape before beginning to paint, or an architect can design the building she would like to build before the cement is poured. Putting pencil to paper, an engineer can carve out the lines of a bridge, or an inventor can map out his ideas and make sure his invention will actually work before he builds it.

We, the craftpeople of the Muppet Workshop, are no exception. In fact, all of the craft projects in this chapter started as a drawing—or two or three—as did many of the other crafts in this book. It was only after the drawings were looked at and talked about with the book's project director that the crafts in this book were cut, glued, bent, rolled, molded, sculpted, sewn, painted, constructed, built, and . . . well, the list is endless. . . .

On the next few pages you'll learn how to use your drawing and coloring skills to create things to play with, stuff to wear, and decorations to hang on the walls. Don't worry about how "professional" your drawings are. The nice thing about drawings is you can always throw them away and start all over again!

JIM HENSON'S DOODLES

Jim Henson, the creator of the Muppets, started doodling as a kid. By the time he was in high school, he had started to turn his doodles into posters, stage sets for plays, TV shows, movies, and, of course, Muppets. Not all of Jim's doodles turned into something more concrete, but many did. Do you recognize any of them?

Paper Doll Set

How easy is it?

**What You
Will Need:**

- Bear Essentials
- poster board or thin cardboard
- permanent black marker
- colored markers
- glue stick
- crepe paper, wrapping paper, magazine cutouts, construction paper
- glitter, ribbon, lace, or other trims
- giant envelope (or large sheet of paper)

Long before Barbie, dressing up paper dolls was a popular pastime . . . and for lots of good reasons: they're fun, inexpensive, and easy to make; they're portable; they can look like anything you can possibly imagine; and their wardrobes can be updated in the blink of an eye.

For this project, you can use our funny paper doll patterns, or draw paper dolls of your own. Maybe you'll make a group of monsters with fangs and horns who enjoy wearing funny hats! Or perhaps you'll decide on a family of bears who wear firemen's suits and tuxedos. You could even trace figures from books or newspapers or cut out photographs of clothing from catalogs or fashion magazines. After all of this, you can make an envelope to store your creations or send them to a friend as a wacky "Howdy do!"

PROJECT MADE BY APRIL ASHER

1 Draw sketches on the poster board until you come up with creatures you like, or trace figures from books or magazines (see page 9 for tracing instructions) or use our pattern on page 292. Go over the outline with the permanent marker. Be sure to leave enough space between the legs and between the arms and the body. And don't forget to give your creatures broad shoulders—the shoulders are where you'll hang the clothes later.

• • • • • • •

2 Color the bodies of your dolls. They can be furry or scaly, or you can give them underwear.

• • • • • • •

3 Cut them out with scissors.

• • • • • • •

4 The most important thing to remember when making clothing for your paper dolls is to include folding tabs so that the clothing can be attached to the dolls (see the tabs on our outfits on pattern page 293). Here are some clothing ideas:

• Trace the clothing patterns on page 293 and cut them out; then trace them onto other paper to create your own fashions. Add color, glitter, ribbon, lace, or other trims.

• Look through old magazines and catalogs for pictures of clothing that will fit your paper dolls. Trace your dolls over the page and cut out the outfit, including small tabs for folding over (at shoulders, on legs, etc.) to attach the clothes to the paper doll. Or use these catalog cutouts as patterns to create your own fashions.

• Trace the outline of your doll onto pretty origami paper or wrapping paper for ready-to-wear clothing. Or make your own fashion statement by using plain paper and filling in the outline to make your own designs.

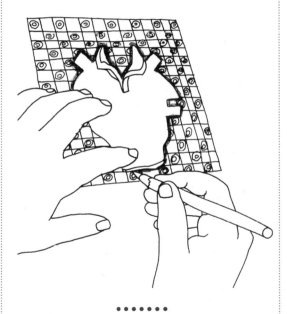

• • • • • • •

5 Keep your dolls and their wardrobe in a giant envelope, or make your own special paper doll envelope. Take apart an envelope you have at home, flatten it on a tabletop, and use it as a pattern. Trace the shape of the envelope onto your chosen paper, cut out, and fold on the same lines. Glue and let dry.

Now, how about staging a fashion show?

A STAND-UP GUY

Cut out a ½-inch-wide strip of thin cardboard or poster board about twice the width of your doll (or you can trace our stand pattern on page 292).

Fold the strip in half to form a V-shape. Snip a small slit in the middle of each side, from the top down. Cut a small slit straight up in the middle of each of your doll's feet and fit these slits into the slits on the cardboard V, as shown.

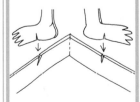

Now your creatures can stand up.

Funny Fruit Card Game

How easy is it?

PROJECT MADE BY MARK ZESZOTEK

What You Will Need:

- Bear Essentials
- thin cardboard or poster board (enough to make all the cards exactly the same size)
- construction paper
- glue stick
- rubber band or ribbon (optional)

Card games are great fun. They're also portable—you can stick them in your pocket and take them almost anywhere. This memory matching game (see the game instructions) uses ten pairs of matching picture cards. If you're feeling ambitious, you can make even more matching pairs. And if you're feeling generous, you can tie the whole deck up with a ribbon and give it to a friend as a present.

"Haven't I seen you somewhere before?"

1 Decide how many pairs of cards you want to make. (Remember: In order for the game to work, you must make two pictures of each fruit. The more pairs you make, the harder and more interesting the game will be.) Carefully cut the cardboard into 5 × 7-inch pieces, one for each card.

• • • • • • •

2 Sketch your fruit patterns on construction paper before you cut them out. Or think about "drawing" the fruit with your scissors—cutting freehand, making curves with your cuts. Cut out the pairs of fruit shapes.

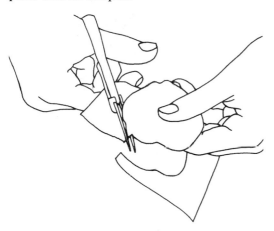

We've also cut out silly features; you can do the same. Arrange these features on the fruit cutouts until you are happy with the way they look; then glue them onto the fruit shapes. Be sure each pair of cards is exactly the same.

• • • • • • •

3 Glue the fruit cutouts onto the cardboard cards. Make sure the glue layer is thin and smooth. Let the cards dry.

Play away—alone or with a friend. To keep your cards together, tie up your deck with a rubber band or pretty ribbon.

"My Granny Smith taught me how to play!"

PAIRS OF PEARS

You've probably played this game hundreds of times. Some people call it "Concentration." To play, you need a deck of cards that contains several pairs of objects—in this case, funny fruit. To begin, mix them all up and lay them face down. (Remember: All the cards must have exactly the same backs so you can't tell which card is which!) Next, turn over the cards one by one, trying to find a pair. Each player gets to turn over two cards at a time. If the cards don't make a pair, the player turns them face down again and lets the next person take a turn. When you find a pair, grab it and take another turn. When all the cards have been picked up, the game is over. Whoever has the most pairs at the end of the game wins.

"This is a 'pear-fect' rainy day game!"

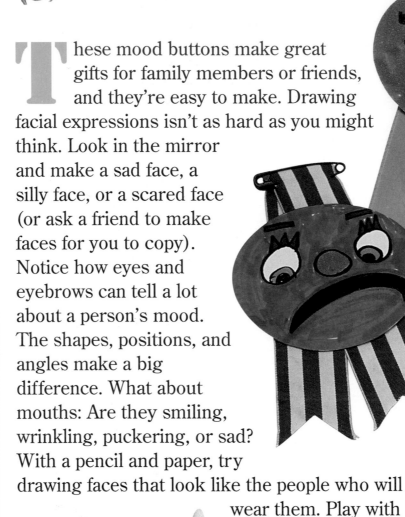

Mood Buttons

How easy is it?

What You Will Need:

- Bear Essentials
- heavy white drawing paper or construction paper
- different-size jar lids, drinking glasses, or other circular-shaped things
- colored markers
- cardboard
- tape
- safety pins
- ribbons (optional)

"I'm in a great mooooooooood!"

These mood buttons make great gifts for family members or friends, and they're easy to make. Drawing facial expressions isn't as hard as you might think. Look in the mirror and make a sad face, a silly face, or a scared face (or ask a friend to make faces for you to copy). Notice how eyes and eyebrows can tell a lot about a person's mood. The shapes, positions, and angles make a big difference. What about mouths: Are they smiling, wrinkling, puckering, or sad? With a pencil and paper, try drawing faces that look like the people who will wear them. Play with different expressions using your observation and drawing skills. You might just end up with a surprised look on your *own* face at how well these mood faces turn out.

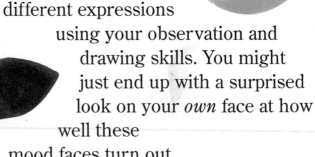

PROJECT MADE BY ELENA PELLICCIARO

1 Using a variety of jar lids and drinking glasses, trace circles of different sizes onto your drawing paper and onto the cardboard. Use your scissors to cut out only the cardboard circles (for now), making them slightly smaller than their outlines.

. . . .

2 Sketch different faces in each of the circles on the drawing paper. When you're happy with one, outline the facial features with the black marker.

. . . .

3 Color in the faces with the colored markers, then pick out your favorite faces and cut those circles out.

. . . .

4 Glue each face onto a cardboard circle that's about the same size. Let them dry.

. . . .

5 Tape a safety pin to the back of each button, as shown.

6 To add ribbons to the buttons, fold a strip of ribbon in half and glue it to the cardboard back. Let the glue dry, then pin a safety pin through the ribbon, as shown. For an "award" ribbon, cut a V-shaped notch in the end of the ribbon.

"Ba-LOONY"

Pin your button on your hat, lapel, or bag and let the world know how you feel!

"Wacky"

"Cheer-y"

Window with a View

How easy is it?

- an adult
- Bear Essentials
- white poster board (14" × 22" minimum)
- colored pencils, markers, crayons
- large piece of corrugated box cardboard (20" × 28" minimum)
- utility knife (for adult use only)
- masking tape
- fabric (24" × 28" minimum)
- string (48" length minimum)

Expand your horizons by making this terrific-looking window with a view. Even if the landscapes outside *your* window are beautiful, another point of view is always welcome.

Try making a day scene and a night scene. Or let your imagination run wild. After all, why should you be stuck with normal scenery? With our window, you can gaze at anything you want! Create an outer-space scene or an underwater seascape.

Scare your friends with a view into your own private monsterland! Look around, get inspired, grab a pencil and paper, and get ready to sharpen your drawing and framing skills!

This window doesn't require you to renovate your room.

PROJECT MADE BY PAUL ANDREJCO

1 Picture your own idea of a perfect view. Use your pencil and eraser to start sketching—mountains, waterfalls, animals, houses, cars, your favorite Muppet characters—directly onto the poster board. When you're happy with your landscape, color it in with colored pencils, markers, or crayons.

• • • • • • •

2 To make the window frame, measure a 20 × 28-inch rectangle on the corrugated cardboard. Ask an adult to cut it out carefully with the utility knife.

• • • • • • •

3 Center your poster board scene exactly in the middle of the cardboard rectangle. Trace the outline of the poster board onto the cardboard. Remove the poster board.

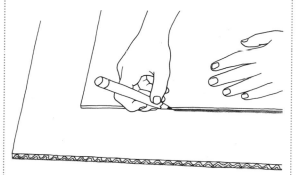

• • • • • • •

4 Draw a second outline ¼ inch inside the outline on your corrugated cardboard. To do this easily, make a dot ¼ inch *inside* each corner, then connect the dots with a ruler. Ask an adult to cut along the inside lines of your window frame with the utility knife.

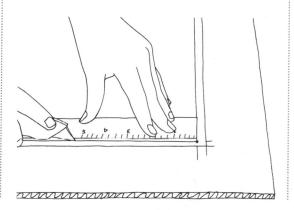

5 Place your window frame on top of the drawing so that the drawing is "framed." When you have it positioned just right, flip both boards over and tape your drawings securely to the back of the frame.

• • • • • • •

6 To make the windowsill, measure a long, thin piece of cardboard (28 inches long × 3 inches wide) and have an adult cut it with the utility knife. Create a triangle pattern in which two 2-inch sides form a 90° angle. Cut it out and trace it onto carboard four times. Cut out the triangles.

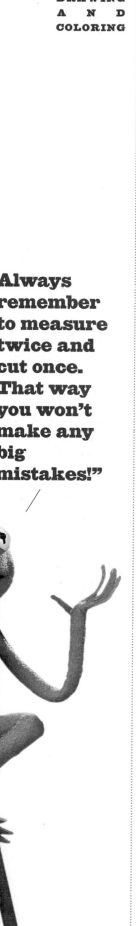

"Always remember to measure twice and cut once. That way you won't make any big mistakes!"

7 Spread glue where you want the windowsill to be placed, approximately 2 inches from the bottom of your window frame. Place the long edge of the windowsill on the glue line and press to attach. Next, spread glue along both 2-inch sides of each cardboard triangle and attach the triangles so they support the windowsill, as shown. Let the glue dry.

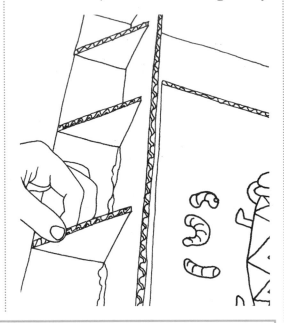

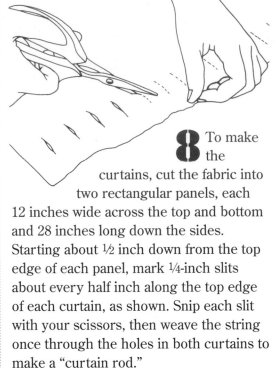

8 To make the curtains, cut the fabric into two rectangular panels, each 12 inches wide across the top and bottom and 28 inches long down the sides. Starting about ½ inch down from the top edge of each panel, mark ¼-inch slits about every half inch along the top edge of each curtain, as shown. Snip each slit with your scissors, then weave the string once through the holes in both curtains to make a "curtain rod."

• • • • • • •

9 Using a sharp pencil, poke a hole through the upper-right corner and a hole through the upper-left corner of your window. Thread one end of the string through each hole and tie the ends of the string together in the back. Use the string on the back to hang your window from a nail on your wall.

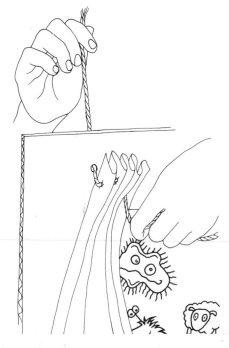

Now sit back and enjoy your view!

SQUINT AT THE PRINT

For this fake magazine cover-girl shot, Miss Piggy's scarf looks as if it has a printed pattern of Kermit heads. Actually, they're drawn on with fabric markers. They're all slightly different.

CHAPTER 2 / COLOR

The Rainbow Connection

"**W**hat's your favorite color?" There's a question you've probably been asked a hundred times! Color is such an important part of our lives that we may find different colors can express our feelings and even alter our moods. The colors of the clothes we wear, the furniture we choose, the flowers we grow can make a big difference in how we feel every day.

Try this experiment: Sit back and close your eyes. (Read this paragraph first, of course!) Imagine yourself in a room that is completely decorated in gray—gray couch, gray chairs, gray curtains, gray walls, and gray carpet. How do you feel? Now, imagine that everything in that room is bright

COLOR WHEEL

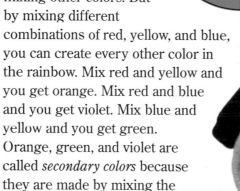

A color wheel shows how the different colors relate to one another. It works like this: Red, yellow, and blue are called *primary colors*—they're the only colors you can't create by mixing other colors. But by mixing different combinations of red, yellow, and blue, you can create every other color in the rainbow. Mix red and yellow and you get orange. Mix red and blue and you get violet. Mix blue and yellow and you get green. Orange, green, and violet are called *secondary colors* because they are made by mixing the primary colors together. The colors in between, like blue-green, are called *intermediaries*.

Make your own color wheel using paints or markers. Start by drawing a circle or *pie*. Then, take your pen and pretend it's a pie cutter. Divide your pie into eight equal *slices*. Using your colored markers (or pie-shaped pieces of color from an old magazine), fill in each pie slice with the primary, secondary, and intermediary colors, blending colors as you move around the wheel.

"Somehow, I've always liked the color green . . . ."

COLOR ME WILD

For the *Song of the Cloud Forest* (above), the Muppet *Workshop* created worlds bathed in eye-popping colors. These distinctive colors give each production its own unique look.

orange! That gave you a jolt, didn't it? Now, try to picture the room in deep, dark blue . . . or pale pink . . . or neon yellow. How would these rooms make you feel? Pretty different, huh? Well, that should give you a hint of the effect of color in *your* life.

As artists and designers, we know how great the impact of color can be. We use color in our work to soothe or to shock; color brings the work to life.

The colors that most artists work with come from pigments. A pigment is a substance—usually a powder—that can be mixed with liquids to form paints, dyes, and inks. Some pigments are made from natural ingredients like blue or red berries, or purple seashells, or even flowers and leaves, while others are made from chemicals.

Color is essential to everything the Muppet Workshop builds, from sets to costumes and props to the Muppet characters themselves. Think about the Muppets' colors: Why do you suppose Animal is a wild and crazy reddish-orange color? How about Miss Piggy? She's pretty in pink, but her appearance can be deceiving—this pig packs quite a punch. This difference between how she looks and how she acts is one of the things that makes her fun. Of course, with Kermit, what you see is pretty much what you get—cool, calm, collected, and green, the most soothing color in the spectrum.

Have fun playing around with the colors of the crafts in this chapter. Use your favorite colors, or experiment with some new ones and make a "Rainbow Connection" of your own.

Stained Glass Butterfly Window

How easy is it?

S tained glass windows were invented hundreds of years ago, and the process of creating stained glass hasn't become much easier since then. The craftsperson begins with an illustration of his or her design, drawn exactly the same size as the window-to-be. With special tools, glass cutters carefully cut many brightly colored glass shapes to fit an overall pattern. The glass pieces are arranged and then bound with molten lead, which hardens into a strong lead structure.

Your window, though made of cardboard and melted crayons, will teach you the basic methods of making a stained glass window and will create a similar effect when light shines through it. A stained glass window might tell a story in pictures, or it may be an abstract design—whatever the pattern, it will always look beautiful on a sunny day!

What You Will Need:

- an adult
- Bear Essentials
- tracing paper
- white chalk
- 2 large sheets of black construction paper
- old crayons
- wax paper
- kitchen knife
- iron
- glue stick
- 2 pipe cleaners
- clear tape or masking tape

1 To make the "lead" frame, trace the butterfly pattern with white chalk and transfer once to each piece of black construction paper (see page 9 for tracing instructions and page 294 for butterfly pattern).

· · · · · · ·

2 Cut out the two butterfly shapes and then cut out the interior spaces for the "glass." When finished, your butterfly shapes should be identical.

PSST! A SHORT-CUT

If you'd rather do a quicker, easier version of this stained glass window, substitute colored tissue paper for the melted crayons! Just glue it in place.

3 To make the "glass," choose your crayon colors and lay out a large piece of wax paper for each. Ask a grown-up to use the kitchen knife to shave a small pile of crayon bits into the center of each piece of wax paper (one color for each piece of paper). Spread the shavings into a thin, even layer and cover with another piece of wax paper.

· · · · · · ·

4 Ask an adult to set the iron on *cool* or *low* and gently iron over each top sheet of wax paper to melt the crayons. *Be careful* not to let the crayons leak over the edges. Work from one side of the paper to

the other until all the shavings are melted and smooth. Set aside to cool. Once the sheets are cool, do not bend them or they may crack.

"Color moi beautiful! "

5 Trace each butterfly wing section onto a colored wax sheet.

· · · · · · ·

6 Use scissors to cut out the "glass" (wax paper and crayon) pieces, making sure to leave *a little extra space* (about ¼ inch) around each tracing line.

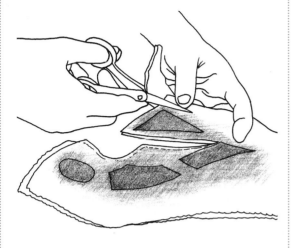

· · · · · · ·

7 Cover the back of one black butterfly sheet with glue. Glue the colored "glass" pieces in the correct positions to one side of the butterfly shape.

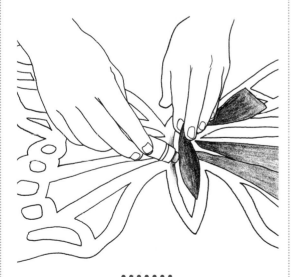

· · · · · · ·

8 Cover the back of the second butterfly sheet with glue. Carefully lay it directly on the "glass"-filled butterfly shape, and when it's in the correct position, *gently* but firmly rub all over to help set the glue. Let it dry. Bend each pipe cleaner and tape them both to the back of the butterfly's head as antennae.

· · · · · · ·

9 Tape the butterfly to a sunny window and enjoy!

COLORED LIGHT

This is a photograph of the installation of a stained glass window in the ceiling of The Jim Henson Company offices in New York. It was created especially for the building, and it shows a "Kermit's-eye view" of his hometown swamp.

Suncatcher Bugs

How easy is it?

PROJECT MADE BY PAUL HARTIS

What You Will Need:

- Bear Essentials
- pipe cleaners
- clear plastic and glass beads and buttons (holes must be large enough to thread with pipe cleaner)
- black felt
- nylon thread
- chandelier crystals (optional)
- colored cellophane
- pushpin
- window suction cups (optional)

Suncatchers are well named—they really do capture light and add pizzazz to a sunny room.

Go on a hunt for wonderful, sparkling, clear (untinted) beads and other small glass or plastic objects to make these sunny creatures. As you search for things, hold them up to the light and see how they look. Do they sparkle and shine? When the light passes through them, does it make rainbows? If the answer is yes, these are good choices for your Suncatchers. If you can't find any crystal beads or buttons around the house (don't forget to check the sewing box!), you can buy them at any craft or bead store.

1 Take a pipe cleaner and fold it in half to find the center. String a bead "eye" on either side of the center.

2 Cut out two small circles of black felt and glue onto each eye.

3 Bring both ends of the pipe cleaner together, then string a larger bead onto the pipe cleaner. This makes the head of your bug. Curl the ends of the pipe cleaner to make antennae.

4 To make the bug's body, thread as many beads as you want onto an 18-inch length of nylon thread. Large crystals (like the ones you find on chandeliers) make terrific tails.

5 Pass the leftover nylon string through the head bead, as shown, and adjust the body so that it hangs *below* the head.

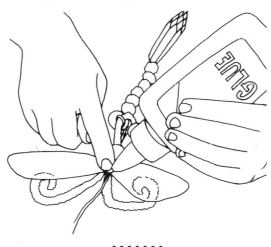

6 With the black marker, draw wing shapes onto the colored cellophane. Cut out the wings and glue them in place at the base of the bug's neck.

7 Hang your bugs in a sunny window by tying a longish piece of thread around each bug's head, then looping it over a pushpin above the window. You can also loop it over a small suction cup (with hook) that's been stuck to the window.

Let in the sunshine and enjoy the rainbows!

"Would you like to dance, honey?"

"Why, I would bee honored!"

Groovy Glasses

How easy is it?

- **Bear Essentials**
- **tracing paper**
- **lightweight cardboard
  (white works best)**
- **colored markers**
- **colored cellophane**
- **clear tape**
- **glitter, fake fur,
  feathers, pipe
  cleaners, or other
  decorations**

How would you like to make a change in your life in the blink of an eye? Just make these groovy glasses and try looking at the world through different-colored lenses. Your glasses can be as elaborate or wacky as you want them to be. Feathers, sequins, or glitter can make them completely silly or turn them into an elegant disguise. Create the look you want and then slip a pair of cellophane lenses into the frames and peer through them. Try mixing colors, too—put a yellow lens over one eye and a red one over the other. Wow! Psychedelic!

Try looking at the world through rose-colored glasses.

PROJECT MADE BY ELENA PELLICCIARO

1 Trace and transfer the patterns for the eyeglass frames, the lens holder, and the lens frames onto the cardboard (see page 9 for tracing instructions and page 295 for patterns).

. . . .

2 Cut out the eyeglass frame, lens holder, and lens frames. Remember to also cut out the *center* of each lens frame where the colored cellophone "glass" will be placed later. Color the eyeglass frame and lens frames with markers.

. . . .

3 Place the lens holder inside the eyeglass frame and fold the eyeglass frame's square tabs in to secure the lens holder in place. Glue tabs to the lens holder and let dry.

4 Trace the basic lens pattern onto the colored cellophane. Use two different colors if you like. Carefully cut out each lens.

. . . .

5 Tape the edges of the cellophane lenses to the lens frames. Decorate the top of each lens frame by gluing on glitter, fake fur, feathers, and so on.

. . . .

6 Slip the lens frames between the lens holder and the eyeglass frame and put on your colorful new shades!

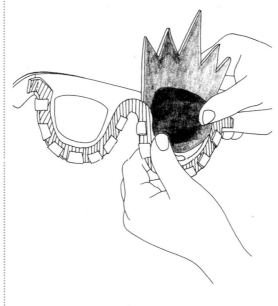

"Help! Call the fashion police!"

29

Messy Curtain (An Outdoor Project)

How easy is it?

What You Will Need:

- an adult
- newspaper
- old sheet
- masking tape
- disposable pie plates and lasagna pans
- fabric paint (must be NONTOXIC!)
- bare feet and hands
- big paintbrushes
- sponges (for splatters and stamps)
- scissors
- buckets or cans of water (for rinsing feet, hands, and brushes)
- needle and thread
- curtain rod

Have you ever done a finger painting? Well, here's a chance to top it. This **OUTDOOR** project allows you to dip your hands *and* feet (and your paintbrushes, too) into buckets of colorful paint—and have splattery fun while making something terrific at the same time.

This one-of-a-kind curtain is wonderful to look at and easy to make. You can change the look of your whole bedroom by hanging it in your window or in place of a closet door. And while we're thinking of it . . . why not make a "messy" bedspread or wall hanging? Just use this technique and your imagination to create a truly "messy" room!

1 Check with an adult before you begin. Gather all your supplies and have them nearby. Be sure to wear old, crummy clothes: You will definitely get messy!

· · · · · · ·

2 Lay out newspapers on the ground in a shape that's larger than your sheet. Lay your sheet on the newspapers. Smooth it flat and tape the corners securely to the papers.

· · · · · · ·

3 Use pie plates to mix the paint you plan to use for handprints; the colors you plan to use for footprints should be mixed in lasagna pans. Keep the paint level shallow.

· · · · · · ·

4 Make a mess! Remember to rinse feet, hands, brushes, and sponges between colors or the colors will turn muddy.

● **To make footprints,** carefully step into a paint pan (take off your shoes and socks first!), then gently step flat-footedly onto the sheet. You might need a friend to hold on to for balance. Try not to smudge the paint when you pick up your foot. Repeat with your other foot, using a different color.

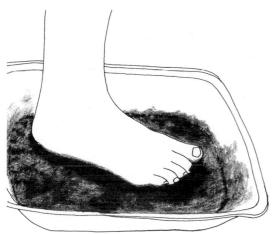

● **To make handprints,** stick your hands in a paint pan and place them flat on the sheet, just like footprints.

● **To make splatters,** fill a brush with paint. Hold the brush about a foot above the sheet, then flick your wrist and let the paint fly.

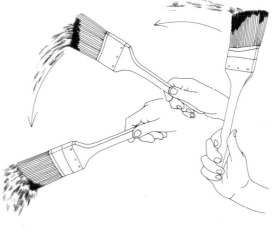

"I love getting messy, too. . . . But don't forget to wear your crummiest clothes!"

31

• **To make shaped stamps** (like Kermit's feet), draw shapes onto kitchen sponges and cut out with scissors. Dip the sponges in paint and gently press them into the cloth. Be sure to keep your colors clean. (See pages 82 and 83 for more instructions on stamping.)

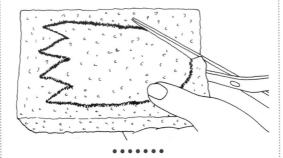

•••••••

5 Take a break and let the paint dry before adding layers. For instance, you might do a layer of footprints and handprints, let them dry, then add sponge splotches and brush sprinkles. Don't glob the paint on too thickly, or it will crack and fall off later.

•••••••

6 Don't move your sheet until it is totally dry! If your fabric paint has directions for setting your design to keep the paint from flaking or fading, have an adult help you follow them. Remove the tape and newspaper.

•••••••

7 If you're using your painted sheet as a curtain, fold the top edge of the curtain down 3 inches toward the back and use your needle and thread to hem it. Push the curtain rod through the hem and hang.

THE RAINBOW CONNECTION

Light from the sun and from lightbulbs looks white, but it's actually made up of seven different colors: red, orange, yellow, green, blue, indigo, and violet. (The name "Roy G. Biv" can help you remember these colors: Each letter stands for one of them!) A prism is an object that separates white light into its seven different colors; when white light shines in one side at a certain angle, a "rainbow" shines out the other. When the sun shines through lots of raindrops at once, a rainbow appears in the sky. That's because each tiny drop of water acts as a prism that separates the sun's white light. Clear plastic and glass pieces can also act as prisms, breaking sunlight into rainbows.

Cutting, Folding, and Gluing

Paper is an inexpensive and readily available craft material that comes in scads of designs, colors, weights, and textures. It's also versatile, with zillions of possible uses: You can draw on it, paint on it, print on it, cut it, fold it, and glue it. You can create paper sculptures by snipping and creasing it, or by making it into a goopy, gloppy, mushy material like papier-mâché.

We use paper of all colors and textures at the Muppet Workshop to create sets and props for Muppet photographs, television shows, and movies. Paper is also used to create special lighting effects for Muppet productions. Many of us make it a habit to collect interesting or unusual papers: shiny metallic paper could be made into a mirror for Miss Piggy; clear plastic "paper" could be used to make a false window in a Muppet movie set; colored tissue paper might create a particular lighting effect in a photograph. But plain paper works fine as well: A simple newspaper can be turned into a fancy hat, a basket, or a sculpted prop.

SIMPLE STARS

The starry night in this "Peter Pan" photo setup employs a simple trick that you can easily use for your own scenes. It's just a piece of navy blue–colored paper with holes poked in it. Shine a light through from behind, and presto! Twinkling stars!

Try experimenting with different kinds of paper—flimsy, glossy, stiff, textured, Day-Glo, gold-flecked, wet, or dry. You'll soon discover that paper is a flexible and useful material for everything from bookbinding to sculpting to . . . some things you'll have to see to believe!

Accordion Photo Album

How easy is it?

What You Will Need:

- Bear Essentials
- thin black cardboard or poster board
- black masking tape
- photographs
- double-sided clear tape
- ribbons, rickrack, stickers, old magazine photos, glitter, and other decorations
- gold pen (optional)

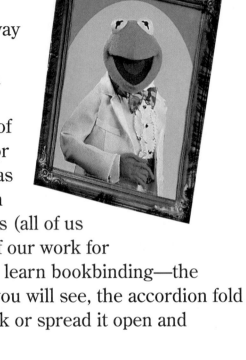

This photo album is a great way to show off your latest and greatest pictures. Fill it with photos of your best friends or your family, or make a photo album full of pictures of you to give to a parent or grandparent. You could also use it as a professional portfolio by gluing in photographs of your other creations (all of us at the Workshop keep a portfolio of our work for reference). With this project, you'll learn bookbinding—the simple accordion-fold method. As you will see, the accordion fold lets you either flip through the book or spread it open and display it.

PROJECT MADE BY VICTORIA ELLIS

1 Decide how many album pages you'll need and how big they should be. Plan to leave good-size margins of black cardboard around the edges of each photo (at least 1 or 2 inches).

· · · · · · · ·

2 Cut the desired number of thin cardboard pieces ("pages") to your page size. Place two pages side by side, leaving about ⅛ inch between pages, and tape the pages together with black masking tape, as shown. Continue laying pages and taping together until your album is as long as you want it to be.

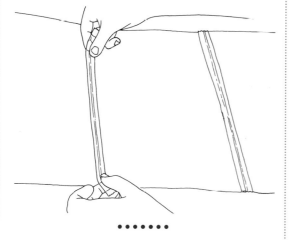

· · · · · · · ·

3 Fold the pages back and forth at the taped joints to form an accordion shape.

· · · · · · · ·

4 Unfold the pages and place your photos in place on the pages. Put double-sided tape on the back and stick them in place.

· · · · · · · ·

5 Add some special touches:

● Use ribbons or other trims to make frames around your photos.

● Use a gold pen to write stories, captions, and messages.

● Add stickers to the page for captions or decoration.

● Cut out pictures from magazines and paste them around the margins.

● Draw a swirly pattern or write your name with white glue on the cover and sprinkle glitter on top. Let dry and brush off the extra glitter.

One at a time Beaker!

A VERY BRIEF HISTORY OF PAPER

Historians believe that the first wood-based paper was invented in China more than two thousand years ago. Here's how it was probably made: First, linen plants or tree bark were pounded until they became a liquidy material called pulp. The pulp was poured into a big vat, then a flat tray with a bamboo screen was lowered into the mixture. When the screen was lifted out of the vat, some of the pulp remained behind on the screen in a thin layer. This pulp layer was then smoothed so that it was evenly distributed across the screen. Next, the water was pressed out of the pulp layer, and the pulp was lifted from the screen in a sheet and laid out to dry. When it was dry, it was a sheet of paper! Paper is often still handmade this way today, using plants, bark, or linen rags and fibers.

Monster Collage Lamp

How easy is it?

PROJECT MADE BY ANN HOLDGRUEN

What You Will Need:

- an adult
- Bear Essentials
- tissue paper in different colors
- paintbrush
- plain small white lampshade (make sure it fits your bulb)
- white glue
- small dish (for glue mixture)
- water
- black felt (for eyes, optional)
- hole puncher (optional)
- large plastic ketchup bottle (empty and clean, of course!)
- utility knife or similar tool (for adult to poke hole in bottle)
- bottle adapter lighting fixture (found in most hardware stores)
- lightbulb to fit socket
- small pebbles (optional)

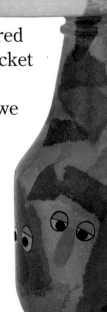

Here's a special way to light up your workshop. This lamp looks great sitting on your desk, and when you turn it on, it casts a colorful glow.

The lamp and lampshade are covered with tissue paper in a *collage*. Collage is the art of pasting various materials onto a clean flat or shaped surface. You can create a collage simply by cutting out personal photographs or pictures from a magazine and pasting them down side by side on a surface. Or you can create a three-dimensional collage using objects you've gathered during a special trip or vacation (ticket stubs, maps, shells, or other souvenirs). For this lamp collage, we chose Muppet monsters as our subject and brightly colored tissue paper as our material. For your lamp, you can copy our design or make up one of your own!

1 Tear or cut tissue paper into monster-head shapes and eye, eyelid, and nose shapes. Tissue paper is delicate, so tear gently.

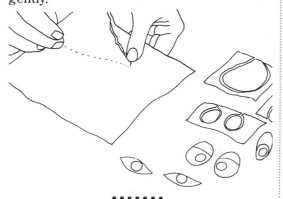

2 Glue on the nose, eyes, and eyelids for each monster. (You will add the pupils of the eyes later.)

3 Paint a small area of your lampshade with a thin layer of glue and carefully lay down a tissue-paper monster. Continue adding monster shapes, slightly overlapping, until the shade is completely covered.

4 In a small dish, mix 1 teaspoon water with 2 teaspoons white glue. Using a paintbrush, cover the lampshade surface with the mixture for a nice, smooth finish. Let dry overnight.

5 When the shade is completely dry, cut out pupil shapes from black felt (use a hole puncher if you have one) and glue onto the monsters' eyes. Outline their eyes and eyelids with permanent black marker.

6 Have an adult poke a small hole in the side of the ketchup bottle, near the bottom. This will be for the lamp's cord.

7 Cover the bottle with monsters, following the directions in steps 1, 2, and 3. Do not cover the hole that was punched in the bottle. When finished, coat the bottle with the glue and water mixture as you did in step 4. Allow it to dry overnight, then follow step 5 to attach pupils to the monster's eyes.

8 Ask an adult to put the adapter lighting fixture and lightbulb in place. If you want the lamp base to be heavier so that it doesn't tip, fill the base with pebbles. Attach the lampshade.

Plug in the lamp and fill your room with monster light!

"Hmmm . . . what a bright idea!"

TISSUE TIDBITS

● When gluing small pieces of tissue paper, small pinpricks of glue will do.

● When gluing tissue paper, it is easier to glue from one corner to the other, smoothing wrinkles as you go.

● When tissue paper is wet, be gentle. If you press too hard on it with a brush or fingers, it will tear.

● Tissue paper colors may run together—test colors with a bit of water to see how they will react.

Spider Piñata and Ghoulish Goodies

How easy is it?

Make the Spider Piñata for your next party.

What You Will Need:

- Bear Essentials
- colored construction paper (including blue and black)
- wrapped candy
- clear tape
- rubber spiders, plastic spider rings, and other prizes
- 12" and 6" round balloons
- large bowl
- papier-mâché glue (see page 6 for recipe)
- newspaper strips about 1" wide
- straight pin
- pliers
- 2 large paper clips
- black masking tape
- black paint and paintbrush
- heavy string or very thin clothesline
- tissue paper (4 sheets black, 1 sheet each of blue, yellow, orange, and green)
- assorted Styrofoam balls and pom-poms (for eyes and nose)

This traditional Latin American party item can be the centerpiece of any birthday or Halloween celebration. Our spider-shaped piñata is a big papier-mâché sculpture made with all kinds of scrunched and folded paper. Inside, candies dressed up in fancy paper outfits form an army of baby spiders. Whack your piñata with a broom handle and hear everyone shriek "Eek!" when they see a mountain of baby spider toys and candies pour out.

PROJECT MADE BY KIP RATHKE

1 Cut construction paper into 5 × 1-inch strips, fold them in half, and cut four slits into both of the short edges, creating "legs," as shown. Fold each leg at the "knee" and "foot." Cut out eyeballs from construction paper. Draw pupils on the eyeballs with a black marker. Place the eyes on top of the candy, with the legs underneath. Wrap a piece of clear tape all around to attach, as shown. Set the decorated candy aside along with any other items to go into the piñata later, such as rubber spiders and plastic spider rings.

• • • • • • •

2 Blow up and knot a 12-inch balloon for the spider's body and a 6-inch balloon for the head.

• • • • • • •

3 In the large bowl, prepare the papier-mâché glue (see page 6).

• • • • • • •

4 Wrap both balloons in one complete layer of papier-mâché glue and newspaper strips and let them dry for

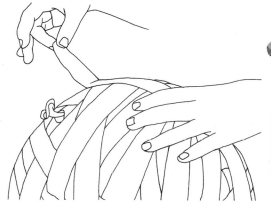

about two hours. Then, wrap a second layer of newspaper around the balloons. Let them dry overnight.

• • • • • • •

5 Stick the straight pin into the body and head to pop the balloons. Cut a round hole about 4 inches across in the body. This hole is where the spider's head will attach.

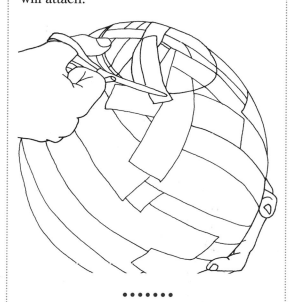

• • • • • • •

6 Fill the body three-quarters full with the candy and prizes you set aside.

PIÑATAS

Brightly colored papier-mâché piñatas (pronounced pin-YAH-tuhs) are traditionally made for festive occasions in both Mexico and Central America. Piñatas are usually designed to look like animals, such as donkeys or llamas. They are then filled with candy and other special treats and decorated with fancy paper. During Christmas festivities and birthday parties, piñatas are suspended from the ceiling. Children are blindfolded, then given long sticks to break open the candy-filled piñatas.

7 Use scissors to cut two ½-inch slits 5 inches apart on the spider's back (the top side of the body). Using pliers, bend large paper clips, as shown. Poke them through the slits inside the body and tape them in place. Your spider will hang from these clips.

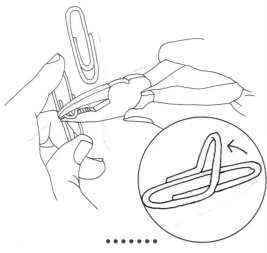

•••••••

8 Put the remaining candy and prizes into the body, then squirt glue around the outside rim of the hole in the body. Put the head in place and tape it on securely with black masking tape.

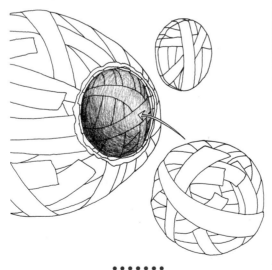

•••••••

9 Paint the head and body with black paint. Thread a 10-inch length of string between the paper clips and knot at

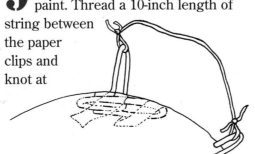

each end. Cut off extra string and hang the body from the string to dry.

•••••••

10 Next, make eight legs:

- First, study the illustrations to see how to create an accordion fold.

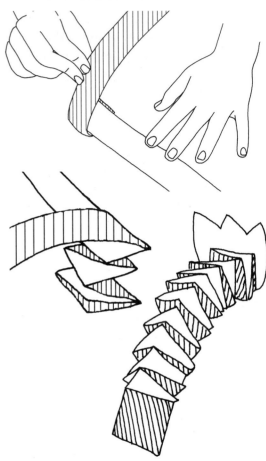

- For 10-inch-long legs (like the ones we made), you will need to fold together two or three accordions for each leg. Keep in mind that as you finish each accordion, you must glue the ends together so they don't unfold.

- Cut strips of blue and black construction paper that are 1 inch wide.

- Begin by taking a black strip and a blue strip and form a perfect corner with them (one strip overlapping the other); glue together. Then begin to fold one strip on top of the other, always keeping the strips in the corner formation until the strip is fully folded.

- Make eight accordions (or more if you prefer). You can also glue finished accordions end to end to form extra-long legs.

- Trace eight construction-paper feet from the pattern on page 296. Cut them out and glue them to the ends of the legs.

11 Attach the legs to the body, four on each side, using the glue and black masking tape to hold them in place.

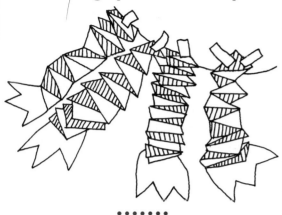

12 Cut the tissue paper into 2-inch squares. (We used four sheets of black paper and one each of green and blue paper for stripes.) Take one square of tissue paper at a time and press it around the end of a thick pencil. Then dip the end in white glue and apply the tissue-paper "fur" to cover the spider's body and head. Do the stripes first, then fill in the spaces between with black.

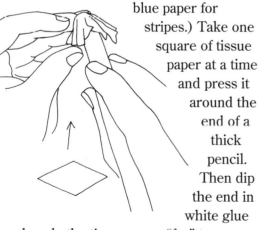

Cover the head with black tissue-paper fur. Leave room for the eyes and nose.

13 Make the eyes and nose with a few different-size Styrofoam balls. Cut them in half. Smear white glue all over the eyeballs and wrap in yellow and orange tissue. Glue the flat sides of the eyeballs onto each side of the head. Make construction-paper pupils and glue them on.

14 Glue on a small Styrofoam ball for a nose. Transfer our pattern for red lips and white teeth (see page 297) onto construction paper and cut out. Glue the lip in the mouth area and glue teeth to the underside of the lip.

15 Hang up your piñata.

You can also decorate the ceiling around the spider with a big crepe-paper web. Invite your friends over and have fun swatting at the spider with broom or mop handles!

"Boo!"

Pop-up Chomper

How easy is it?

Everybody loves to get greeting cards. But can you imagine receiving a greeting card with a big, pop-up mouth that goes chomp, chomp, chomp as you open and close it? Wow! Make one as a special birthday card to surprise a friend. This chomping card shows you the basics of paper engineering (the craft used to make pop-up books). You can make any kind of face you like. Just fold away!

MORE IDEAS!

Play around with other characters: Cut different angles and shapes and see the results. You can invent your own personalities (a version of yourself? a portrait of the birthday boy or girl?), or copy the Muppet characters in the photograph.

1 Fold a piece of drawing paper in half and crease it sharply. Open and lay it flat.

2 Trace the "Robin the Frog" pattern (see page 9 for tracing instructions and page 297 for pattern) onto the creased drawing paper, making sure that exactly one-half of Robin is on each side of the crease. Color it in with your markers.

3 Fold the sheet in half so Robin is on the outside and cut a half-smile along his smile line, as shown. Leaving the page folded in half, fold over the upper and lower mouth along the fold lines, as shown. Crease well and turn over the folded sheet to repeat folding and creasing on the other side.

PROJECT MADE BY KIP RATHKE

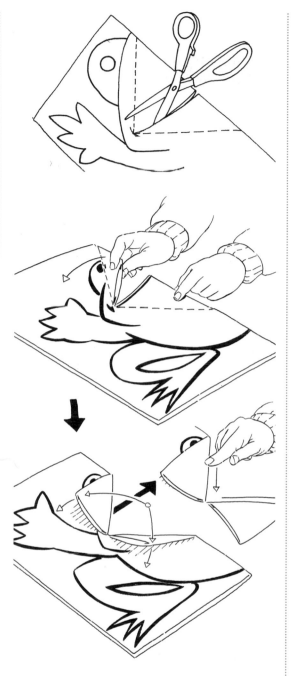

Fold the card so that Robin is on the inside, making sure that the mouth folds flat. Crease well.

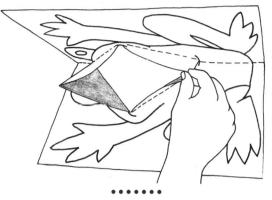

·······

5 To turn your chomper into a card, lay Robin flat again and place him over a sheet of construction paper. Trim the construction paper so that it is about ¼ inch bigger than the Robin sheet on all

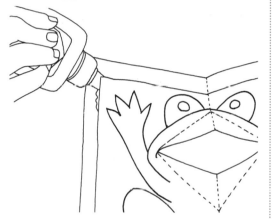

sides. Fold the construction paper in half and crease. Fold the Robin sheet in half again (with Robin inside) and apply glue to the back of the sheet, avoiding all mouth parts. *Make sure you don't put any glue on any of the moving parts or your chomper won't chew!* Glue the Robin sheet to the construction paper and fold in half again (with Robin inside) and press it flat to dry.

Open it up, but watch your fingers!—CHOMP!

"I do not endorse chomping of any kind. It is un-American!"

·······

4 Open the sheet and pull the center of the upper lip up and out. Pull the lower lip down and out.

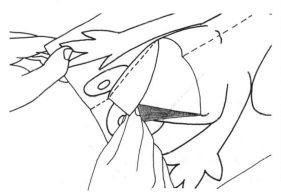

FOLDING FACTS

It is important to have very clean, sharp folds in paper engineering. Here are a few helpful hints about folding:

● For thinner paper, draw folding lines with a pencil and fold along the line. Crease the fold well with your fingernail, or run the rounded side of a marker or pencil along the fold.

● For heavier paper, put the pointy end of a pen cap on the paper, then guide it along the edge of a ruler to create a fold line to follow.

▼▼▼▼▼▼▼▼▼▼▼▼▼▼▼▼▼▼▼▼▼

House of Cards

How easy is it?

**What You
Will Need:**

- **Bear Essentials**
- **regular deck of
  cards plus as many
  extra cards as you
  can find (for a bigger
  house of cards, use a
  second or third deck)**
- **double-sided clear
  tape**

I n this project, you'll learn how to design, join, and build a
support system to create your own miniature architectural
masterpiece. Think of the possibilities . . . you can build a
turreted castle for your royal card characters (king, queen,
knight, and joker), erect a New York City–style skyscraper, or
design your dream house. Then keep it or take it apart and build
another structure.

*For a windproof
house, add a dab of
glue to each slot as
you stick the cards
together.*

PROJECT BUILT BY PAUL HARTIS

1 Set aside a few face cards (a king, a queen, some jacks, and a joker). These will be the "people" who live in your house of cards.

• • • • • • •

2 Measure in ¼ inch from the top right corner and bottom left corner of one card; mark the spots with a pencil. From your marks, cut a 2-inch slot straight into the card (see illustration of the six of

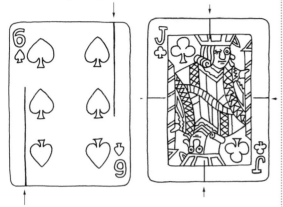

spades). This card will be your guide for the remaining building-block cards.

• • • • • • •

3 Mark another card at the center point on the top, bottom, and each side (see illustration of the jack of clubs).

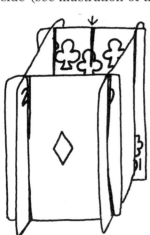

Make a ½-inch cut into the card at each mark. Now the card is slotted on four sides. This card will also act as a guide for other cards.

• • • • • • •

4 Cut the cards as you build your house. Using your guide cards, snip slots into the cards. Attach the cards slot to slot and create little building blocks, experimenting with each of the two types of slotted cards (see illustration).

5 Here are some building tips:

• Place the backs of the cards face out for a consistent look, or have the faces of the cards face out for variety. Or try both!

• The most important part of the house is the base, which is also the largest part. Higher stories can be smaller or the same size (as they would be in a tower) but not bigger or they'll topple.

• Follow our design or create your own house. Try bending several cards into accordions and gluing them together to form a staircase shape or fence for your house, as we did.

• Finally, put double-sided tape on the backs of your royal cards and tape them to their rooms like we did with our Muppet cards.

• Top it all off by adding some handmade flags with your name on them.

"Pick a wall, any wall."

Top Secret Sketchbook

How easy is it?

PROJECT MADE BY CHERYL HENSON

What You Will Need:

- Bear Essentials
- wrapping paper or fabric
- 2 identical rectangles of cardboard—any size you want (shirt cardboard is good)
- hole puncher
- drawing paper
- cloth ribbon
- string or twine
- colored markers

Anyone can learn to draw, but only *you* can come up with your own special ideas. Whenever someone at the Workshop has a great idea, it gets recorded in his or her sketchbook. Here's a sketchbook you can make for yourself. When you're finished, you'll have a useful tool and you'll have learned a new kind of bookbinding. You can use your sketchbook for doodling, copying pictures of things that interest you, and writing down thoughts about ways to make things—just the way artists do. Or use it as a journal or a place to write stories or poems.

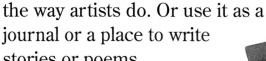

1 Cut two sheets of wrapping paper or fabric that are 1 to 2 inches larger than your cardboard rectangles on all sides.

. . . .

2 To make the sketchbook covers, coat one side of each of the cardboard rectangles with a thin layer of glue and place glue-side down on the "wrong" side of the paper or fabric, making sure that the cardboard is straight and centered. Carefully fold over the top and bottom edges of the paper or fabric and glue them to the cardboard. For the side pieces,

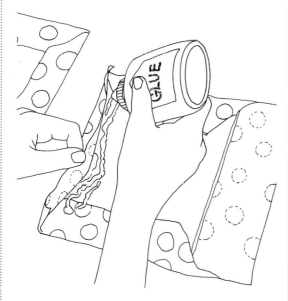

angle the corners in (as though you were wrapping a gift), fold over, and glue the edges to the cardboard.

. . . .

3 Cut two pieces of wrapping paper or fabric to the exact size of, or a little smaller than, the cardboard sheets. Glue each piece to the "inside" of your cardboard covers to hide the rough edges of paper or fabric.

. . . .

4 Decide which edge will be the binding side of your covers (it has to be the same side on both covers). Mark three dots ¼ inch in from the edge of the binding side of each cover. The dots must be spaced evenly from top to bottom and be spaced exactly the same on both

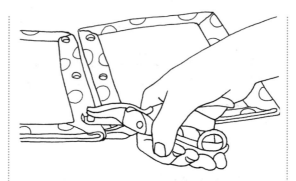

covers. Using your hole puncher, punch holes in the covers where the dots are.

. . . .

5 Cut drawing paper to make pages that fit inside your book. Using one cover as a guide, hold up your pages to the cover and punch holes in the same positions through each sheet of paper.

. . . .

6 Place the covers with the punched edges touching side by side and measure a length of ribbon that is twice as long as the combined width of the covers. Lay the ribbon flat across both covers so that it is covering the center hole in each. Mark dots on the ribbon where the covers' center holes are, then punch out the dots with your hole puncher. Center the ribbon on the covers, lining up the holes in

DEAR DIARY

If you'd like to, you can write something on the front of your journal with a marker. You may title it "My Sketchbook" or "Top Secret: Hands Off!" or put the name of a friend or family member on the cover and give the book as a gift. Maybe you'd like to decorate the cover of your sketchbook by gluing on a favorite photograph or a picture you've cut out from a magazine.

the ribbon with the holes in the covers, and place glue on the back side of the ribbon. Glue the ribbon to the covers and let dry. (The covers are now gently connected.)

• • • • • • •

7 Sandwich the paper between the covers, and thread string through the middle holes in the front cover, the paper, and the back cover.

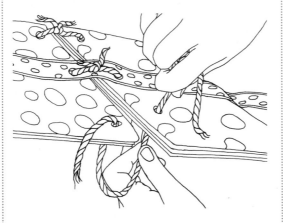

Tie the ends of the string together in a tight knot and slide it around to the back cover to hide it. Trim off any excess string. Repeat for the top and bottom holes.

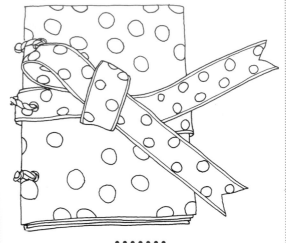

• • • • • • •

8 Tie the ends of the ribbon around your sketchbook in a big bow.

CHRISTMAS SURPRISES

This Jim Henson Company Christmas card was created from doodles Jim Henson made in the early 1960s. All the drawn-on doors use paper engineering to open and reveal many Muppety surprises.

CHAPTER 4 / MOLDING AND MODELING

Squishy, Squashy, Squoosh!

At the Muppet Workshop, we use many different molding and modeling techniques to create characters and props. We're in good company: People have been using these techniques for thousands and thousands of years—turning lumps of clay into marvelous creations—and you're most likely among them. You've probably modeled clay in school, creating sculptures of animals, people, or places. Or maybe you've been to one of those do-it-yourself pottery centers, where you've modeled useful objects like mugs, plates, or bowls.

The main difference between molding and modeling is that when you're molding, you're creating something from scratch; when you're modeling, you're copying something that exists. If you want to create an *identical* copy of something, you can create a mold, which is a hollow space in clay or sand that is shaped by hand or by the imprint of a molded sculpture. Once a mold is finished, it is filled with a liquid that hardens as it dries or cools. When it has dried, the material is removed from the mold and voilà! It's a freestanding sculpture. This process is called "casting."

In this chapter, we'll teach you how to use your molding, casting, and modeling skills to create some very special—and sometimes unusual—things.

FEET OF CLAY

This statue is a spoof of a famous sculpture by Edgar Degas. The Miss Piggy version is extravagantly titled *The La Danseur*. It was molded out of clay and then sprayed to look like the cast bronze of the original.

MAKING MAQUETTES

Sometimes artists try out ideas for creatures, props, and sets by sculpting miniature clay models called maquettes (*mah-KETS*). Clay maquettes are easy to work with; they allow artists to be playful and inventive, while saving the the labor and expense of creating full-size creatures.

Some of the characters in Jim Henson's film *The Dark Crystal* were first built as maquettes. First, clay models of individual characters were built to work out the best possible "look" for each. Then, when Jim and the designer were happy with the look of a small-scale character, the maquette was used as a model to build the full-size creature. Finished, full-size characters are usually not made of clay; they're mostly made of foam, wood, metal, or cloth. These are the full-size creatures you see on film and television.

Most important, you'll learn that a wide variety of substances can be used for molding or modeling—everything from bread dough, mashed potatoes, and juice to newspaper, wax, and wire. And when you're finished, you'll have monster necklaces, treasure candles, silly snacks, a funny bowl, and some neat decorations for your room or for holidays. They all make great gifts, too!

Bread Dough Monsters

How easy is it?

Bread dough is a soft, easy-to-make, and easy-to-model material. It can be molded into large things like monster paperweights, or little things like holiday ornaments and pendants for necklaces. Once baked, it becomes hard and can last a long time, which makes it a great material to use to make long-lasting, memorable presents for any occasion. Just don't let anyone try to eat your bread dough masterpieces while they're drying!

What You Will Need:

- an adult
- measuring cup and spoons and mixing bowl
- bread dough (see recipe on page 52)
- rolling pin
- toothpicks, fork, and large paper clips
- greased cookie sheet
- oven mitts
- tempera paints and paintbrushes
- Mod Podge*, acrylic varnish, or clear nail polish (optional)
- thin satin ribbon (for necklace; optional)
- glue or heavy tape (for pin; optional)
- safety pin (for pin; optional)

*Available at craft stores

"Me want to make monsterpiece, too!"

MAKING DOUGH

1 cup white flour
1/2 cup salt
1/4 cup water
1 tablespoon oil

Mix the flour and salt together in a large mixing bowl. Add the water and oil and knead. Add more flour if the dough is too sticky. If the dough is too dry, add a little water a few drops at a time until it is soft and smooth but not sticky. (This dough can be stored in the refrigerator in a closed container for a few days.)

1 Ask a grown-up to preheat the oven to 350°F.

•••••••

2 Make the dough.

•••••••

3 Pinch off sections of bread dough and roll into separate balls for the head, body, arms, and legs. Shape body parts, horns, and claws. Add tiny flattened balls for the eyes and a big ball for the nose.

•••••••

4 Moisten spots where the body parts will fit together with a tiny bit of water. Gently squeeze the pieces together.

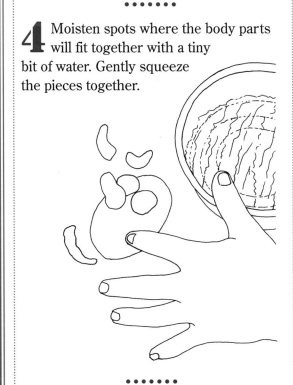

•••••••

5 Use a toothpick to make the mouth opening and to make the pupils in the eyeballs.

Score the dough with a fork to make it look like fur.

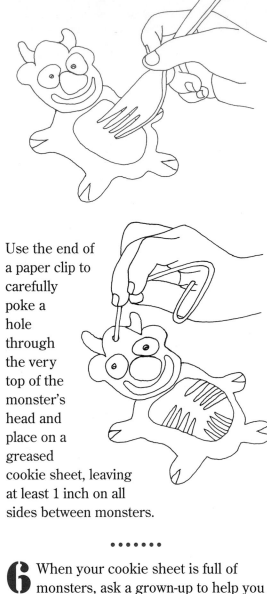

Use the end of a paper clip to carefully poke a hole through the very top of the monster's head and place on a greased cookie sheet, leaving at least 1 inch on all sides between monsters.

•••••••

6 When your cookie sheet is full of monsters, ask a grown-up to help you bake them for five to ten minutes. When the monsters BEGIN to turn brown, have your grown-up take them out of the oven and let them cool. Keep in mind that thicker monsters and monster parts take longer to cook than thinner ones do.

•••••••

7 When your monsters are COMPLETELY cool, paint them any way you like. Let the paint dry. You can then varnish your monsters with acrylic paint or Mod Podge to make them shiny. This also helps them last a long time.

8 Other options:

- To make monster ornaments, open up a large paper clip to make a hook. Put one end through the hole in the top of the monster's head. Carefully squeeze the paper clip ends together to hold the hook in place.

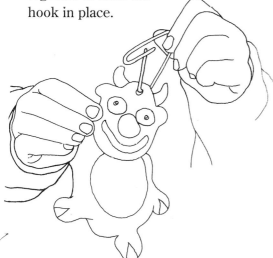

- To make a necklace, slip a ribbon through the hole in your monster's head and tie a double knot to hold it in place. If a ribbon won't fit, use a paper clip (see above) and put the ribbon through that.

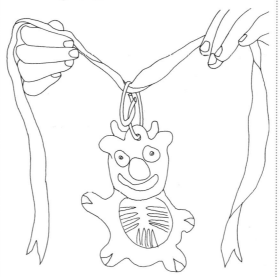

- To make a pin, glue or tape a safety pin to the back of a monster.

Wear or share your creations!

"Burp."

ADDITION AND SUBTRACTION

There are two basic kinds of sculpture: additive and subtractive. The difference is simple: Additive sculpture involves building a project by *adding* material to an object, while in subtractive sculpture, material is *taken away* from the object. Carving a statue out of a piece of marble uses a subtractive technique, and making a papier-mâché bust uses an additive technique. Bread Dough Monsters are additive sculptures.

Mashed Potato Head

How easy is it?

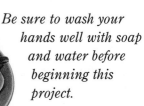

What You Will Need:

- an adult
- paring knife (ask a grown-up to help)
- carrots
- black olives
- red bell peppers
- mushrooms
- cucumber
- alfalfa sprouts
- string beans
- assorted tasty vegetables you like (optional)
- mashed potatoes—the instant or the "real" kind
- baking dish or plate(s)

Here's a fun mealtime project that uses a very simple kind of sculpture to mold food into faces. Using food as your material is an easy and delicious way to get started as a sculptor. You just cook up a creamy batch of mashed potatoes (or pumpkin squash) and you're on your way. Take a close look at the other vegetables when you cut them up, too. Which ones would be great for eyes? For ears? For noses? Then go ahead and play with your food. And don't forget to eat up once you've finished making your funny vegetable faces!

Be sure to wash your hands well with soap and water before beginning this project.

PROJECT MADE BY DAVID ROBERTS

1 Wash all your vegetables and let an adult help you slice them:

- Slice the carrots into thin rounds and trim to make tooth shapes.

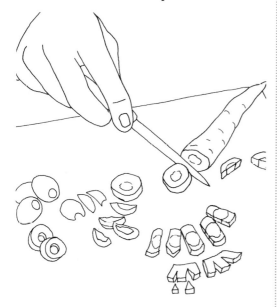

- Slice the olives lengthwise into long, thin pieces for eyelashes. Save one olive to slice in circles for the pupils in the eyeballs.

- Cut the red peppers into big thick slices and gently carve into lip shapes.

- For ears or a nose, cut slices of mushrooms or slice a round of cucumber and cut in half.

- Use alfalfa sprouts or string beans for hair.

2 Ask an adult to help you make a big batch of mashed potatoes from scratch or by following the instructions on the instant potato box. (You can also make pumpkin squash, mashed sweet potatoes, or any mushy side dish you like.)

· · · · · · ·

3 Put a nice big pile of mashed potatoes in a baking dish, on a plate, or on many plates. Mold the potatoes into a blobby round shape. Then quickly add hair, eyes, nose, lips, teeth, ears, and anything else you want.

Now, eat your dinner before it gets cold!

"Pick me!"

"Pick me!"

"Pick me!"

Sandy Turtle

How easy is it?

What You Will Need:

- damp sand in sandbox or deep container
- spoon (for digging)
- shells or pebbles (for decoration; optional)
- plaster of Paris mixture (you will need to buy a box and follow the directions)
- water
- acrylics or poster paint and paintbrush
- varnish (optional)

This project uses a simple method of molding that helps you sculpt inside out and backward! First, you'll do sand casting, turning ordinary sand into a mold. Then, after you've sculpted your mold in the sand, you'll fill the mold with soft, gloppy plaster of Paris. By the next day, the plaster will have dried, forming a strong, solid material that can be painted and decorated. As you will see, this project uses both additive and subtractive sculpture techniques: You take away, or *subtract*, sand to create a mold, and you *add* plaster to the mold to create your sculpture.

You can do this project in sand anywhere, at the beach, at the park, even in your house. You just need a large enough container for your turtle to "lie" in.

PROJECT MADE BY MARY BREHMER

1 Pack the damp sand tightly, flattening it with your hand and compressing it.

. . . .

2 Imagine a turtle lying upside down on its back. That's how you have to "draw" the turtle in the sand! With a spoon and your fingers, begin to dig a large oval hole until it looks like a turtle shell lying upside down. 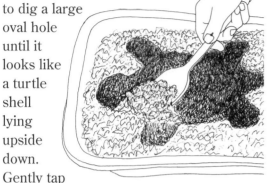 Gently tap the sand so that it is smooth and won't crumble. Dig smaller, more shallow oval shapes for the turtle's head, legs, and tail. Gently tap down the sand in the holes. (Make as many turtles as you like— maybe a whole family!)

. . . .

3 Use your spoon or finger to carefully dig "bumps" on the turtle's shell, leaving spaces in between them. If you want to, press shells or pebbles into the sand (pretty-side  down) to make decorations on the turtle's back.

. . . .

4 Mix the plaster with water according to the package directions, and slowly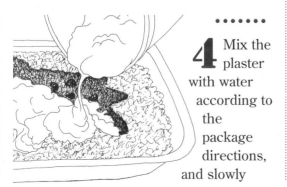

pour it into your sand mold. Let it dry overnight.

. . . .

5 When the plaster is hard, pull it out of the sand. Gently brush away as much of the sand as possible (there's usually a light coating left).

. . . .

6 Use acrylics or poster paint to paint a colorful shell for your turtle. Let it dry. For a shiny finish, apply a coat of varnish.

SCULPTED SET

The set for the television production of *Fraggle Rock* was a large cave with many chambers. The ceiling, walls, and floors of the cave were made from modeling clay with chicken-wire frames underneath. The sets were made in pieces that could be moved about, interchanged, and used in any position.

After *Fraggle Rock* was over, the sets were saved and reused from time to time. Take a look at the ceiling behind the Fraggles. Now look at the opening of the cave behind Gonzo and Kermit in this Muppet Babies parody of *Treasure Island.* Look familiar? It should. . . . It's the same set!

Popsicle Hands

How easy is it?

What You Will Need:

- rubber gloves (rinse them out so they are clean)
- long skewer
- big pot deep enough to hold the gloves upright in the freezer
- duct tape
- mixing bowls
- red, green, or yellow fruit punch (powdered mixes or pre-made)
- platter (optional)
- fruit salad (optional)
- scissors
- punch bowl (optional)
- funnel or turkey baster (optional)

This edible ice sculpture is made by freezing fruit punch inside rubber glove molds! Make these "handy" Popsicles to add to a big bowl of fruit salad, or try putting one in the punch bowl at your next Halloween party!

1 Turn the rubber gloves inside out and wash them well with warm soapy water. Rinse well and let dry completely. Turn the gloves right-side out.

2 Turn down the cuff of each glove for extra support (see illustration). Poke the skewer through the top edge of each glove, and rest the skewer across the pot. Be sure that you poke holes at least ½ inch from the edge of the glove.

3 Tape the skewer to the edge of the pot.

4 If necessary, mix up the desired colors of fruit punch according to the package directions. Fill the gloves with punch to about 1 inch from the top.

Put the pot in the freezer and leave overnight. *(For multicolored fingers, use a funnel or turkey baster to fill each finger of the glove with a different-colored mix. Freeze each color overnight, then add the next color.)*

5 The next day, fill a platter or a punch bowl with fruit salad or fill a punch bowl with punch, leaving room for the Popsicle hands.

6 Remove the pot from the freezer. Hold each glove under warm running water for a few seconds. Use scissors to snip an opening all the way up the glove. Peel the glove away from the hands.

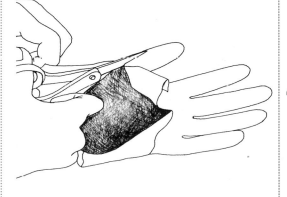

7 Place the hands on the fruit salad platter or in the filled punch bowl, and present your work of art at a party.

"I find this project shocking. Putting hands in punch bowls is unsanitary!"

Treasure Candles

How easy is it?

What You Will Need:

- an adult
- Bear Essentials
- masking tape
- candle wicks*
- quart-size paper milk cartons or small, round wax-paper ice-cream containers (Be sure to wash containers thoroughly before beginning and let them dry. Do NOT use plastic containers—they'll melt!)
- candle wax*
- boil-in bags*
- saucepan
- water
- glitter, confetti, small glass or metal treasures (charms, mini-jewels, other nonflammable objects)
- chipped ice

Available from a craft store

S ince wax is one of the few materials that can be either liquid, solid, or in between, artists like to use it to create sculptures, both large and small. Its versatile nature makes it ideal for additive or subtractive sculpting as well as modeling and casting. At the Muppet Workshop we sometimes use wax to sculpt the heads and bodies of new characters for films and television.

Because candle making is one of the best uses for wax, we'll teach you wax casting in this project and take the wax through all three stages (liquid, solid, and in between) to form an extra-special candle. Why is it extra-special? Because tiny treasures have been added to the liquid wax before it hardens. When you melt the candle, the treasures will appear! Treasure candles make terrific presents.

1 Tape one end of the wick to the inside bottom of the clean, dry milk carton. Tie the top end of the wick around a pencil and balance it across the top of the milk carton.

. . . .

2 Have an adult put the candle wax in a boil-in bag in a large saucepan full of water. Heat the whole thing on the stove over low heat until the water boils and all of the wax is melted. Then have your adult carefully remove the bag of wax from the pot with pot holders and be ready to pour.

Note: *If you want to make a more colorful candle, you'll need to melt different-colored layers of wax in separate bags. When pouring, you'll alternate layers of colored wax, separating each color with a layer of chipped ice.*

. . . .

3 Sprinkle glitter, confetti, or small glass or metal treasures onto the bottom of the milk carton. Then fill the carton with about 2 inches of chipped ice.

Have your adult pour just enough wax to cover the ice.

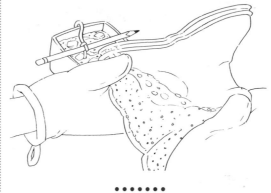

. . . .

4 Repeat this process, adding more glitter, confetti, or treasures, then ice and wax. Keep adding layers until the candle is the desired height.

. . . .

5 Let the wax harden completely (it takes a few hours), then carefully tear the carton away from the candle. Trim the wick so that it is about ¼ inch long.

. . . .

6 If you wish, decorate the outside of your candle by dabbing on glue (in designs or all over), then rolling the candle in more confetti or glitter.

Bring your "Treasure Candles" to the dinner table and share a candlelit meal with your family, even if it's *not* a special occasion.

"You'll need a grown-up to help you heat and pour the wax. And remember, never, ever heat your wax in a pot over an open flame. You need a pot full of water and a boil-in bag for that!"

Hungry Bowl

How easy is it?

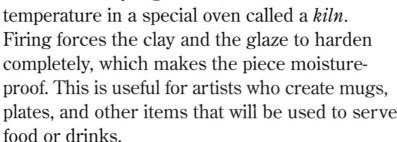

This hungry-looking bowl is constructed of clay that is coiled, modeled, and shaped. Usually, when an artist completes a clay sculpture, it is glazed, then baked or "fired" at a very high temperature in a special oven called a *kiln*. Firing forces the clay and the glaze to harden completely, which makes the piece moisture-proof. This is useful for artists who create mugs, plates, and other items that will be used to serve food or drinks.

You won't be able to put food or water in this "Hungry Bowl" because it's made of a self-hardening clay that you don't have to fire. But it will be a good place to keep special stuff.

What You Will Need:

- self-hardening clay
- carving tools: paper clip, pencil, Popsicle stick, plastic fork, knife, spoon
- rolling pin
- acrylic paints and paintbrushes

HEY!

Read the **CLAY TIPS** on the opposite page before you begin.

1 Roll out a snake of clay about ⅝ inch thick and 1 foot long; score one edge. Coil in a spiral pattern, as shown. The first coiled layer will become the bottom of your bowl.

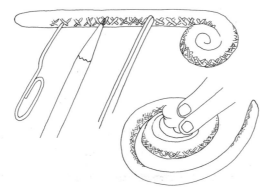

2 Use your fingers to rub *only the inside* coils together to make a solid, smooth surface. (The coil pattern will be the design on the outside of the bowl.)

3 Roll out another snake, score it, and attach it where you left off, rubbing the inside joint smooth. Continue scoring and coiling. When the base of your bowl is about 6 inches across, begin to build the coil on top of the base, along the outside edge, spiraling upward and outward to form the sides of the bowl. As the sides of the bowl are built, support

PROJECT MADE BY ELENA PELLICCIARO

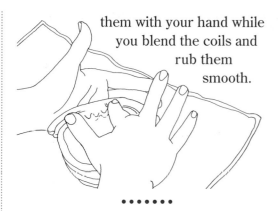

them with your hand while you blend the coils and rub them smooth.

4 When your bowl is the shape of a half globe, spiral the coil inward so that the bowl's opening gets smaller. Roll out the coil "lips" for your pot, mold them into upper and lower lip shapes, and attach them to your pot by scoring and smoothing.

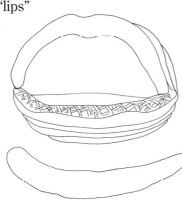

5 For the tongue, use a rolling pin to flatten a thick snaky coil. Score underneath the tongue and score the mouth, then attach the two. With clay, roll out a dangly uvula to hang from the back of the mouth and attach by scoring and smoothing.

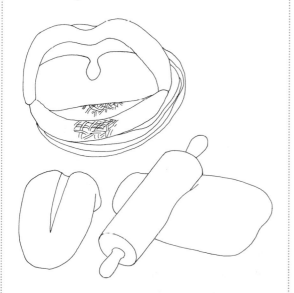

6 Shape feet for your pot, then score the top part of the feet and the bottom of the bowl and gently roll the bowl onto the feet until it is well balanced. Smooth slightly along the joint.

7 Leave your bowl in a cool place until completely dry (it should take a day or two). Then have fun painting it any way you'd like.

"Here are a few pointers!"

CLAY TIPS

● To keep clay from drying out, wrap your project with damp paper towels and put it in a tightly sealed plastic bag whenever you walk away from your project before it's done. Keep any clay you're not using wrapped in a closed plastic bag with a few damp paper towels so it stays soft.

● To attach pieces of clay to one another, you need to "score" them where the two pieces will meet and then join them and smooth the seam or joint. Scoring is done by making crosshatch marks (X's) with a pencil, Popsicle stick, or straightened paper clip. Smooth the joint with your finger, a spoon, or a Popsicle stick. The scoring helps give the clay joints more surface so they can grab on to one another. The smoothing reinforces the joint.

● This is a messy project, so be sure to cover your work space before you begin. A plastic covering is always best, but newspaper will do. Also, keep some water and a damp rag nearby to keep your clay damp and soft as you work on it.

Giant Bird

How easy is it?

What You Will Need:

- an adult
- needle-nose pliers
- 2½ rolls of ¼" armature wire* (about 15') or 30 thick wire hangers
- duct tape or masking tape
- 2 rolls of ³⁄₁₆" armature wire* (about 10') or 20 wire hangers
- wire cutter (for adult use only)
- newspaper
- large Styrofoam ball (for the head)*
- Styrofoam cone (for the beak)*
- papier-mâché glue (see page 6 for recipe)
- tempera paint and paintbrushes
- varnish
- miscellaneous feathers and other decorations

(continued on facing page)

Papier-mâché is usually built on a kind of skeleton called an armature (*AR-muh-chur*). Armatures are most commonly made from wire and wood, but you can also make armatures out of cardboard tubes or even balloons. Because you can use a number of different, often flexible, materials to create them, you can build armatures of just about any shape or size. In this project, you'll use armature wire to build a terrific bird for your room.

PROJECT MADE BY ROLLIE KREWSON

1 Ask an adult to help you cut any wire. Using pliers, you will twist the ¼-inch armature wire (or wire from cut-up wire hangers) to create a "skeleton" for your bird. Cut a 7-foot length of ¼-inch armature wire and bend in half in the middle. At the midpoint, bend the wire to create a foot with three toes pointing forward and one pointing backward. Leave extra "leg" wire sticking straight up, as shown. Repeat to create the other foot. (Both feet should be fairly large—about 6 inches across—because they will have to help support and balance the bird sculpture.)

Note: *If you are using wire hangers, an adult should untwist them with pliers and attach them to each other by twisting end to end.*

• • • • • • •

2 Attach the two legs together by crossing them in a loose X about 18 inches up from the feet, bending as shown. Then wrap duct tape all the way up the lower legs and around the cross of the X. (The legs will carry the weight of this creature, so they need to be strong.)

3 To make the body of the bird, twine the excess wire (above where the legs cross) together to create the bird's neck. Twist 3 feet of the ³⁄₁₆-inch armature wire to make one large horizontal hoop and attach to the X of the legs with duct tape. Then have an adult cut three pieces of wire—2 feet, 1 foot, and 6 inches—and bend into three more hoops, twisting and taping the ends to secure them. Tape each hoop vertically onto the horizontal hoop, as shown. (The smallest hoop should be at the tail end, the largest hoop by the neck.)

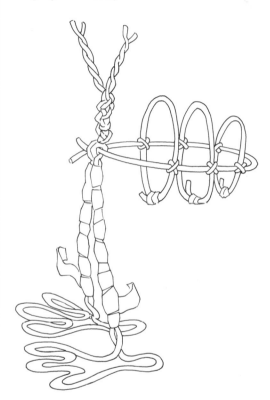

Optional Items:

- old feather dusters and boas
- 2 small Styrofoam balls or Ping-Pong balls (for the eyes)
- glue
- felt
- rubber cement
- old colorful socks (make sure no one wants them anymore)
- rags for stuffing the socks
- needle and thread
- yarn (you can use any kind of yarn or try FloraCraft*, Loopy*, and Junior Loopy*)
- feathers
- Mod Podge, nontoxic acrylic varnish (optional)

You can buy these things at a craft store or improvise with stuff you find around the house.

MOOSING AROUND

Jim Henson bought this papier-mâché moose from an artist as a gift for a friend, but he liked it so much he ended up keeping it instead. It hung over the beautiful fireplace in Jim's office.

4 Scrunch up big wads of newspaper and fill in the wire body frame until newspaper is bulging from the wires. Use duct tape to condense the paper together, and continue to add more paper, finally wrapping the body loosely in tape to hold it all together.

Note: *If you'd like to attach feather-duster wings later on, slip a 24-inch length of wire through the center of the body, as shown above, wrapping around the leg wires. This wire will create the skeleton to support the wings. You can also attach a loop of wire to the end of the body for tail feathers.*

ADDING ON: IT'S UP TO YOU!

You can add all sorts of things to your bird—fancy feathers, big eyes, goofy toes, wildly wrapped legs, silly tails, or wacky shapes popping out of the top of your bird's head:

● For feather-duster wings, use heavy tape to adhere them to the wing armature built in step 4.

● For wacky legs, tails, and necks, wrap wire with FloraCraft, Loopy, or yarn.

● Add a felt tongue.

● Glue on real feathers.

● Eyes can be made of papier-mâché and painted, but small Styrofoam balls or Ping-Pong balls work nicely, too. Glue on felt circles for pupils, and secure the whole eyeball to the bird's head with rubber cement.

● For goofy, colorful toes, cover each of the bird's toes with a different-colored sock. Stuff each sock with rags above the wire only—stuffing at the bottom will unbalance the bird. Sew the socks together to form solid feet.

5 Wrap the neck tightly in duct tape, leaving 3 inches of wire exposed at the top. Stick the Styrofoam ball on the tips of the neck wire to create the bird's head.

• • • • • • •

6 Take two small, thinner pieces of wire and stick them into the ball where you want the beak to be. Have an adult cut the Styrofoam cone in half, then trim one of the halves by cutting 2 inches off the base. Wedge the halves on the wires (the longer cone half on top, the shorter one on the bottom) to form an open beak.

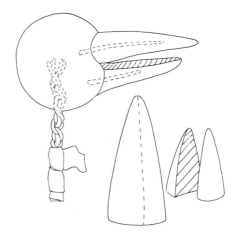

• • • • • • •

7 Mix a batch of papier-mâché glue (see page 6) and tear up some newspaper strips. Cover the whole bird (including legs, neck, and head) in three layers of papier-mâché. Let each layer dry for at least an hour before adding the next layer. The more layers you add, the smoother you can make the surface.

• • • • • • •

8 When the papier-mâché is completely dry (this may take a few days), paint your bird. You may want to use more than one coat of paint to get a nice rich color and cover all the newsprint. Let the paint dry between coats. When the paint is totally dry, you can add a coat of varnish to make the surface shiny and to help protect your work.

CHAPTER 5 / CARVING

Snipping and Chipping

Most people picture a carver as someone with a hammer and chisel, chipping away at stone; or they imagine a person with a knife whittling away at a small piece of wood. But carving, a form of subtractive sculpture, is much more varied than that. A carver can work with many different kinds of materials: sponge, foam blocks, plaster, soap, vegetables, Styrofoam, or ice.

Carved sculptures can be flat, where the artist carves into a flat surface and leaves grooves, or relief, where the artist carves away at a flat surface, leaving raised bumps or shapes. These kinds of carvings are called two-dimensional, because they can be seen from only two sides: the front and

"Artistes like moi always create images that have special meaning for them."

CARVING TIPS

● Whenever you use something sharp to carve with, make sure an adult helps you.

● Always cut away from yourself and keep your fingers out of the way.

● Carving tools are available in art and hobby stores, or you can use kitchen knives, scissors, plastic forks and knives, toothpicks, skewers, and other household carving tools.

● Experiment with different implements and put together your own set of personal carving tools.

67

the side. But carved sculptures can also be three-dimensional, or seen from all sides (front, side, and back). The sculptures you will create in this chapter are all three-dimensional.

At the Muppet Workshop, we often use three-dimensional carving techniques to create Muppet characters. Many Muppets begin life as a square block of foam. The artists begin by drawing the character on a block of foam. Then, they begin to cut away excess foam, being careful not to snip off too much at once. Snip, snip, snip—and slowly but surely, the character emerges.

In this chapter, you will learn our techniques of creating characters out of foam and how to carve and chisel in soap and soft rock. To make our "Gargoyle" bookends, you'll concoct a special sculpting material that starts out soft enough to carve, but later hardens into a rocklike substance. You'll be amazed at how easy carving is, and how professional your results will be.

MOCK MOUNTAINS

The mountains in the background of this shot were carved right out of big Styrofoam blocks and then sprayed with fake snow.

Sea Creature Sponge Mobile

How easy is it?

hink of the many kinds of creatures that live under the sea. Whatever you can imagine, you can create to hang on your sea creature mobile. The creatures for this mobile are carved from foam sponges with a pair of sharp scissors. Sponge is a good material on which to learn carving skills, since it is soft and easily sculpted. Snip your sponges into the shapes you want, then put together several carved pieces to create sea creatures or characters like the ones here. Add decorations or felt eyes, then hang the creatures from pieces of bent hanger wire to create a mobile!

It's fun to hang mobiles over your bed, near a window, or even next to a sink . . . after all, a sink is a sponge's usual hangout!

"Get ready, get set . . . get snippy!"

What You Will Need:

- an adult
- colored markers
- extra-large foam sponges in many different colors
- scissors
- rubber cement
- pipe cleaners
- felt (for eyes, lips, etc.; optional)
- googly eyes and glitter (optional)
- wire cutters (for adult use only)
- 3 wire hangers
- blue and green tempera paint and paintbrushes
- nylon thread
- needle
- clear beads (for bubbles)

PROJECT MADE BY DOUG JAMES

SCRUB-A-DUB BUDDY

If you want to make a sea creature sponge that you can take into the tub, just carve a big sponge into a fun shape. Draw on eyes, mouth, nose, and scales with permanent markers, then scrub-a-dub-dub!

1 Only work on one creature at a time so that you don't get mixed up! Draw rough outlines of your creature on the top and sides of the sponge. (You can trace and transfer our mermaid, fish, and octopus patterns from page 298, or make up your own creatures. See page 9 for tracing instructions.) These lines will guide your snipping. You can use different-colored sponges for each part of your creature; for example, use a green sponge to make your mermaid's tail and a pink or peach-colored sponge for her upper body.

2 Snip away excess foam, following the outlines drawn on the sponge (sharp, pointy scissors are best for details).

. . . .

3 To attach creature pieces, make a small snip into the foam on each piece, where you will attach them. Rubber cement the pieces at those snipped spots, then press the pieces together, holding them firmly in place to set.

. . . .

4 To decorate your characters:

- Stick pipe cleaners into sponges for your mermaid's hair (bend the pipe cleaners into a wavy pattern to make it look as if she's underwater).

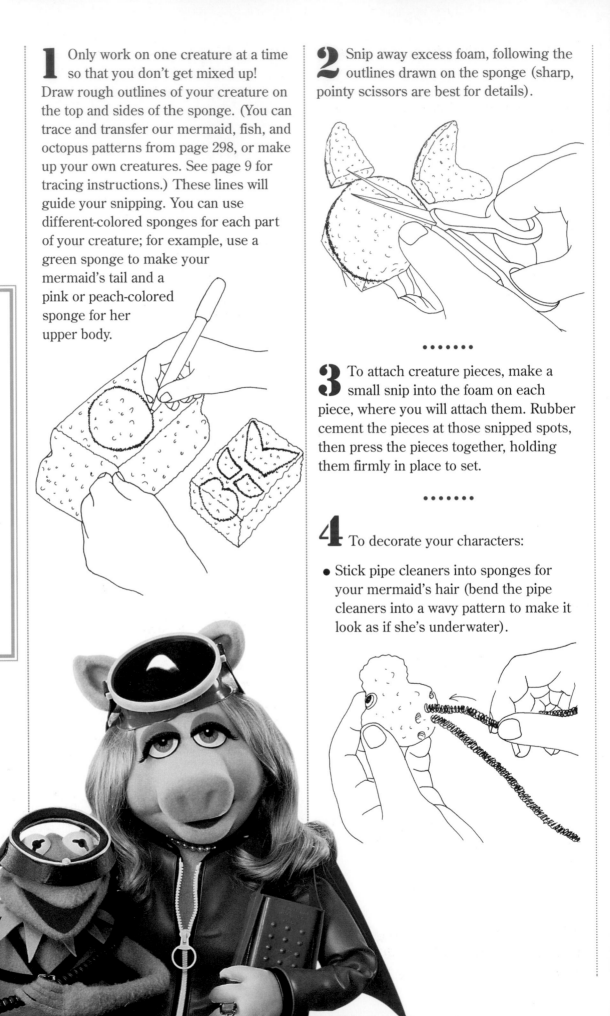

Do the same thing for your octopus's tentacles.

- Cut out tiny felt circles for eyes, or use googly eyes.

- For mouths and other details, use cutout felt pieces or draw directly on your sponge with your colored markers.

- Add tiny drops of rubber cement and sprinkle glitter onto creatures for a glistening, underwater effect.

• • • • • • •

5 Have an adult use wire cutters to cut each hanger into several pieces. Bend these pieces into wavy shapes to look like water.

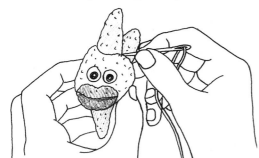

Paint the wire blue and green and let it dry. Once dry, tie a length of nylon thread to the middle of each one.

• • • • • • •

6 Thread the needle with nylon thread (see page 143 for threading information), then poke the needle through the top of each creature and out the other side, making a very small stitch.

Tie the end of the thread in a knot as close to the creature as possible, leaving up to 12 inches of extra thread. (Try leaving different thread lengths, so that your creatures will dangle at different levels later.) String on clear beads for bubbles.

• • • • • • •

7 To make the mobile, make a long wavy wire for your top piece and tie on your characters and shorter wavy wires with their nylon thread. You can also tie the wavy wires to the top wire, then dangle creatures from those, as we did. You will have to move things around to make the mobile balance.

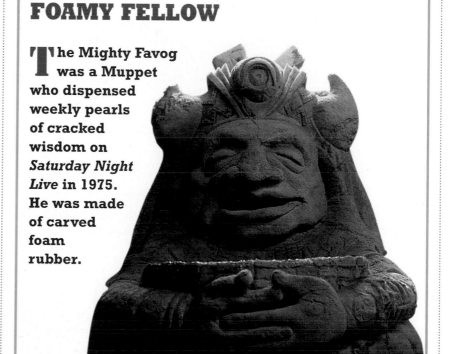

FOAMY FELLOW

The Mighty Favog was a Muppet who dispensed weekly pearls of cracked wisdom on *Saturday Night Live* in 1975. He was made of carved foam rubber.

Bug Soap Gift Set

How easy is it?

What You Will Need:

- an adult
- glycerin soaps in different colors
- sharp pencil
- carving tools or small, dull dinner knives with different types of points
- safety goggles
- water
- pipe cleaners (optional)
- sponge, wrapping paper, ribbon (for gift set; optional)

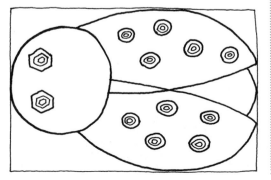

Soap is an excellent carving medium because it is soft, like sponge. This softness makes it easy to draw shapes onto the soap's surface and whittle away the excess soap. In this project you'll be sculpting bugs out of soap. The end result will make bathtime bug you in a whole new way!

1 Select a bar of soap and a pencil. Draw a bug from the top view and side view on each surface of the soap.

2 Ask an adult to help you choose a dull knife, then put on your goggles and shave away long, thin pieces of soap (outside the lines) to form the basic shape of the bug. Use the point of your knife to chip away chunks in tight areas. Look at your bug from all angles each time you chip or shave. Slowly, the shape will emerge.

Note: *Don't carve away too much soap or you'll end up with a tiny soap bug and a lot of wasted soap shavings.*

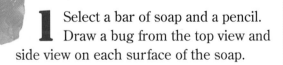

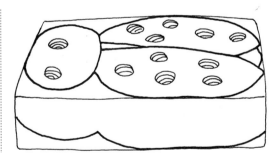

PROJECT MADE BY CHERYL HENSON

3 After the large pieces are carved away, begin carving the details:

● Carefully carve out the head shape you've drawn onto the soap.

● Lightly carve a line down the center of the bug's back as though drawing wing shapes, then gently scrape the soap to shape the wings, as shown.

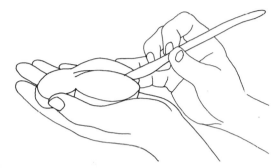

● For eyes and spots of different colors, carve tiny cone-shaped pieces out of different-colored soaps. Dig small pointed holes in the places on the bug where you want to add the eyes and spots. Using a tiny drop of water as

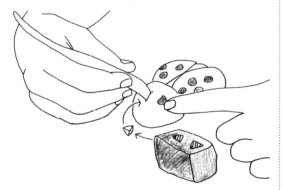

glue, stick each piece into the appropriate hole on the bug. Press down for a few seconds to set in place.

● For antennae, bend a short length of pipe cleaner into a spiral shape and dig one end into the bug's head.

● ● ● ● ● ● ●

5 Once you've finished carving the bug and adding any pieces to it, gently rub any rough spots on the bug with a wet finger. This should smooth things out. Now make a few more bugs so your first one doesn't get lonely!

● ● ● ● ● ● ●

6 To make a nice gift, cut a sponge into a leaf or flower shape and place the soap bugs on it (use the sponge-snipping methods described in the "Sea Creature Sponge Mobile" project on page 69). Wrap the whole set in clear cellophane.

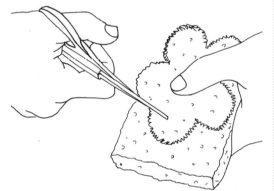

Tie with a bow and it's ready to give!

"Hey, Mom! Who are all the strangers floating in our pond?"

Snake Walking Stick

How easy is it?

PROJECT MADE BY ERIC ENGELHARDT

What You Will Need:

- an adult
- a Perfect Walking Stick
- carving knife (for adult use only, optional)
- sandpaper
- pencil
- colored markers
- acrylic paint and paintbrushes
- file and safety goggles (optional)
- googly eyes, feathers (optional)

This project starts with a walk in the woods to find a Perfect Walking Stick. The key to finding a Perfect Walking Stick is making sure it feels just right. Look around, pick up a stick, and try it out for a while. Does it feel good to hold while you walk? Is it a strong piece of wood? How thick is it? How long is it? Does it have an interesting top to grab on to, like a knob or a crook?

Once you've found a Perfect Walking Stick that fits you, you'll need to make sure your wood is solid, hard, and dry. It's okay if the stick has bark on it; you can peel the bark off and sandpaper the wood, or leave it on and use it as part of your design. When you've found the Perfect Walking Stick, we'll show you how to make it look like a long, winding snake. Then it's time for you to hit the hiking trail with your Extra-Fabulous, Personally Decorated, Clever and Cool, Perfect Walking Stick!

Keep your walking stick by the door so it's always handy when you're ready to hike.

1 Once you've chosen a good solid stick, decide whether you'd like to leave any bark on it. If not, ask an adult to carve away the excess bark, then sandpaper the bare stick yourself until it is completely smooth.

· · · · · · ·

2 Hold the stick out at arm's length and look at it carefully. Try to imagine the shape of a snake slithering its way across that stick. Think about what you'd like to draw or paint into the wood. Maybe you see a rattlesnake's diamond pattern, or perhaps polka dots. Sketch designs onto the surface of your stick with a pencil, and remember that you can make changes as you go.

· · · · · · ·

3 Once you've decided on your design, draw it onto your stick with colored markers or paint it on with paints. You might also try using a file or sandpaper to etch some parts of the design into the wood a little (remember to wear your safety goggles). Or, if you have a very talented adult to help you, ask him or her to carve out the pattern or design, then decorate it yourself.

4 Decorate the top of your stick. We added a googly-eyed owl. You might want to add feathers, fur, or felt to create your own animal, or perhaps a large jewel and a few ribbon streamers. It's up to you.

Have a great hike!

"Always remember to carve away from yourself! See you out on the trail...."

WALK SOFTLY AND CARRY A BIG STICK.

Jim Henson enjoyed woodworking and made walking sticks as a hobby to use on hikes in the woods or to give to friends. Jim carved this crawling snake spiraling its way up to the top of the stick. The snake's eyes are beautiful green gems.

Gargoyles

How easy is it?

PROJECT MADE BY KIP RATHKE

What You Will Need:

- Bear Essentials
- safety goggles
- rubber gloves
- 2 empty half-gallon paper milk cartons, rinsed and dried
- newspaper
- washtub or bucket
- water
- plaster of Paris (available at craft stores)
- wooden spoon
- vermiculite (available at hardware or garden stores)
- paper
- masking tape
- dull dinner knife for carving
- paintbrushes
- sandpaper, coarse and fine

Rock on! These look just like real gargoyles.

Gargoyles are stone carvings of monster-like creatures that perch on high buildings. In the olden days, gargoyles were placed on buildings because people believed gargoyles could frighten away evil spirits. Today, gargoyles are used as decoration.

Carved gargoyles make perfect bookends (they can also hold up your CD collection or your computer disks). This pair is made from homemade "rock," a soft and easy-to-carve sculpting medium. When it hardens, it feels as hard as real rock, and it looks like the real thing, too. Follow our rock-making recipe (see next page), and then carve away.

When you're finished, place the bookends on a table or shelf and see if they frighten away evil book or CD borrowers!

1 Cut the tops off the two milk cartons and place them on newspaper.

· · · · · · ·

2 Put on your rubber gloves and create the rock mixture, following the recipe shown below right.

· · · · · · ·

3 Quickly fill the cartons with the plaster mixture. Carefully thump them down a few times to release air bubbles.

4 After one hour, gently tear off the milk cartons. Leave the "rocks" alone to harden for a few hours; they should still be a little bit soft when you are ready to work on them. Over time they will get very hard.

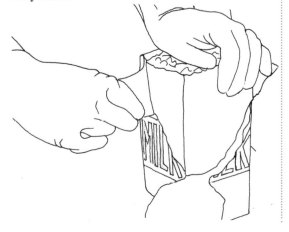

5 Work on one gargoyle at a time. Fold a long piece of paper around one rock, making creases as you turn the corners (you can tape sheets of paper together to make them long enough). The folds will make the four panels for your sketches—the front, back, and side views of your gargoyle.

A TIP:

Always wear safety goggles when you carve.

"Ready to rock? Here's the recipe."

A GALLON OF "ROCK"

This recipe will make about a gallon of "rock," which is enough for two gargoyles.

11 cups water
14 cups plaster of Paris
6 cups vermiculite

Fill a bucket or washtub with the water.
Slowly sprinkle and stir in the plaster with a wooden spoon.
Stir in the vermiculite.

"ROCK" CARVING TIPS

● This is a messy project, so be sure to check with an adult before you begin.

● Work in a place where cleanup will be easy.

● Mix your "rock" in a deep washtub or bucket and wear rubber gloves.

● When you carve this rock, carve it over a bucket or tub for easy cleanup.

● Don't panic if you chip off too much as you carve: Just rethink your creature, or pretend it's a five-hundred-year-old relic.

6 Remove and open the paper and draw a line across it, about 1 inch from the bottom of each panel, as seen on our patterns on pages 299–300. This ledge will keep the gargoyles stable after they're carved. Next, draw the front, side, and back views of your creature (including the ledge), one view on each panel. Or trace, enlarge, and transfer our patterns from

pages 300–301 (see page 9 for tracing instructions). Fold your drawing or pattern around the rock and tape the ends together so it will stay in place.

· · · · · · ·

7 Use a sharp pencil to trace over the lines of your drawing, pressing into the plaster hard enough so that the drawing's outlines show up on the rock. Take off the paper.

· · · · · · ·

8 Imagine the three-dimensional shape you are going to carve into the "rock." Using your kitchen knife, start at the corners and slowly begin to cut away the rock that is *outside* the lines of your drawing. The marks on your rock will be chipped away, but you can refer to your drawing as a guide.

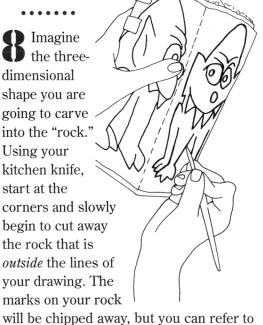

9 Carve the largest areas first, then move on to the detailed areas. Experiment with different tools, like the pointy end of a small paintbrush. Now work on the second gargoyle.

· · · · · · ·

10 When finished carving, use a dry paintbrush to sweep dust out of all the crevices. Smooth your sculptures by rubbing first with coarse sandpaper, then with fine sandpaper.

· · · · · · ·

11 Clean off the dust by brushing lightly with water. Now is the time to make any little changes. Let your sculptures dry completely—for about a week.

· · · · · · ·

12 When the sculptures are completely dry, mix equal amounts of white glue and water to make a glaze. Paint your sculptures with this mixture and let them dry. Add a funny name for your creatures to the ledge area, or add your own initials to personalize your bookends.

First Impressions

Art is usually one-of-a-kind—when you make a painting, you can photograph it, photocopy it, or even scan it into your computer, but there's only one original. Printmaking is different, because although it allows you to create many copies of the same image, each copy is an original. This is because it is reproduced by you, the artist, instead of a machine.

"Impressive!"

A print is an image that is transferred from one surface to another. To make a print, you simply create a picture or design on a "plate" (a flat surface such as wood or stone) using a variety of materials and techniques. For example, plates can be made by carving wood blocks or by gluing household items to rubber tiles. Once it's finished, the plate is coated with ink or paint and pressed onto a piece of paper or fabric to transfer the image. Most of the time, the plate and the paper are placed together and rolled through a printing press to press them really tightly together, but this process can be done by hand as well.

PRINTING TECHNIQUES

Etching:
Etchings are made by drawing onto a coated metal plate. Next, the plate is dipped in acid to remove the coating and then covered with paint or ink. The ink is with of but the grooves trap the substance and transfer it as an image when printed.

Lithography:
Similar to etching, lithography is a printing technique where images are inked onto a plate or stone, then transferred onto paper.

Silk screening:
To make a silk-screen print, a piece of silk is stretched tightly across a wooden frame, then stenciled with an image Ink is squeegeed through the screen onto paper as a print.

Monoprinting:
In monoprinting, a scene or design is painted onto a plastic or glass sheet, then pressed onto another piece of paper or fabric, resulting in a onetime print (*mono* means one).

The result of all of the pressing is a print.

Usually, professional artists make and distribute many copies of each print, and this wide availability makes the prints inexpensive for collectors to buy. But sometimes, these same artists make a limited number, or "run," of their prints, numbering and signing each one. The exclusivity of the small print run increases the value of each print, since only a few people can own them.

In this chapter, you'll learn basic printing techniques, as well as stamping and stenciling.

MUPPETY MASTERPIECE

Sandro Botticelli's famous Renaissance painting is called *The Birth of Venus.* The Muppet version is called *The Birth of You Know Who.*

Printmaking was one of the techniques used by the Workshop in creating this carefully constructed scene. Can you guess where it was used? (Hint: Look at Kermit's cloak, then look at the answer at the bottom of this page.)

Stamps are created in much the same way as plates, but they are generally smaller than plates, and use a quick "punch" technique rather than printing's smooth, rolling, "press" technique to transfer images. Stamps are smaller and easier to use than plates, but the images they leave are as consistent and identical as those of the printing plates.

Stenciling is a technique that is almost the opposite of printmaking, although it has similar results. Stenciling is the art of painting or sponging paint onto a surface through a cutout shape, and like printmaking, it allows you to create consistent and almost identical images.

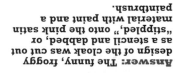

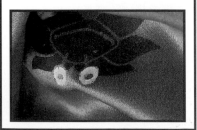

Answer: The funny, froggy design of the cloak was cut out as a stencil and dabbed, or "stippled," onto the pink satin material with paint and a paintbrush.

With homemade stamps and stencils, you can make your own T-shirts, pillowcases, aprons, and initialed stationery. You can also use your printmaking and stamping skills to create tickets to your next puppet show or posters for a play you're putting on in the neighborhood. There are lots of possible uses for the techniques you're about to learn: at the Muppet Workshop, we use printing, stamping, and stenciling to make props, sets, and costumes, and now you'll be able to, too!

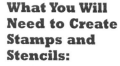
Stupendous Stamps and Stencils

How easy is it?

Stamps are the most basic printmaking tool. Almost anything can be turned into a stamp (even a pear or potato!), and you can stamp onto almost anything that's flat, like paper, fabric, or wood.

Stamping is a great way to print repeating patterns because a stamped image looks nearly identical to every other image created by the same stamp. In fact, many patterned fabrics are still made with wood stamps.

Stenciling is another method of creating a repeating pattern. A simple stencil is a shape or design that is cut out of paper or plastic. The stencil is placed on the printing surface, and when the craftsperson applies paint (with a brush or sponge) through the shaped "holes," a printed image is created on the material beneath. Like stamping, the results are nearly identical, time after time.

This project will teach you the basics of both stamping and stencil making. You can then combine these skills to personalize anything!

What You Will Need to Create Stamps and Stencils:

- Bear Essentials
- woodblock scraps
- cotton string, twine, or thick yarn
- cardboard
- fabrics, lace, ribbon, paper clips, rubber bands, and staples (optional)
- fruits and vegetables, such as potatoes, cucumbers, and apples
- dull dinner knife (for fruits and vegetables)
- safety goggles
- sponge(s)
- cardboard tube (paper towel or toilet paper roll)
- paper or plastic plates

TO MAKE STAMPS

Remember: Any image you create will print in reverse when it is applied. So if you use letters and numbers, they must be carved *in reverse* to appear correctly on the printed surface. If you get mixed up, hold the letter or number up to a mirror to see what it should look like.

Block Stamps

You can make block stamps out of just about anything that is fairly flat and can be glued onto a wooden block. Just coat the block with glue and affix any or all of the following materials:

- a wild, swirly pattern of string

- things you find around the house: textured ribbon, twine, paper clips, rubber bands, staples

What You Will Need to Print on Paper or Poster Board:

- **tempera paints**
- **paper or plastic plates**
- **construction paper, poster board, or blank stationery (cards, envelopes, etc.)**
- **paintbrushes**
- **masking tape**

- cutout cardboard shapes

- fabrics with interesting textures—fake fur, burlap, and lace

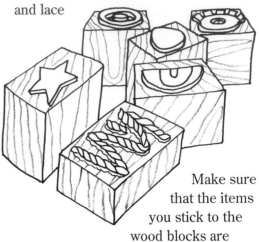

Make sure that the items you stick to the wood blocks are glued on smoothly and firmly, then let the glue dry completely before you start stamping.

Fruit and Veggie Stamps

Cut patterns or designs into fruit or vegetables. Firmer foods like apples and potatoes work especially

well. Cut the food in half to create a flat surface, then carve shapes, pictures, letters, or numbers into them.

Sponge Stamps

Flat kitchen sponges make good stamps, too. Draw your shape directly onto the sponge, then cut it out.

Roller Stamps

Find some cardboard toilet paper or paper towel tubes, then create a very small design out of string or twine on a piece of paper on a flat surface. (To get an idea of

how big the string design should be, cut an extra cardboard tube in half lengthwise, then flatten and measure it. The length and width of the design should be the

same as the length and width of the flattened tube.) Coat the cardboard tube with a thick layer of glue, and roll it evenly and gently from one end of the string design to the other. The string will be picked up by the gluey tube as you roll. Allow it to dry overnight before you use it.

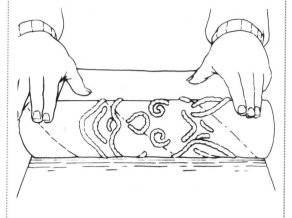

"I've been a stamp collector for a long time!"

STAMPING YOUR STAMPS

● Make sure that the paint is only on the raised part of the stamp. If it gets on the background and the background touches your paper it will ruin the outline of the image.

● Stamp each stamp on scrap paper a few times to get a feel for it before you apply the stamp to something you care about. You'll notice that sponges and fruits and vegetables can hold a lot more paint, while more detailed designs made with string need less.

● Some stamps need to be gently rocked from side to side on the paper so that the entire image gets transferred. However, do not slide the stamps or the images will smear.

What You Will Need to Print on a T-shirt:

- **nontoxic fabric paints**
- **paper or plastic plates**
- **heavy cardboard**
- **clean T-shirt (new or old)**
- **masking tape**

To Print Stamps on Paper or Poster Board:

1 Pour a small, shallow puddle of tempera paint into a disposable plate (use a different plate for each color paint).

2 Lightly dip or roll the stamp in the paint, making sure that the image on the stamp is evenly coated and not drippy.

3 Press the stamp firmly and directly onto the surface of the paper or poster board, and lift it straight up when you're finished.

Or, try another technique:

Using a paintbrush, paint your stamp with tempera paint. The good thing about this technique is it allows you to be precise and to use more than one color on a stamp at once. The bad thing is that you must paint quickly so that the paint on one part of the stamp doesn't dry as you paint on another color.

TO MAKE A STENCIL

Note: *Unlike the images on stamps and printing plates, stencils should not be created in reverse.*

1 With a marker, draw a design onto a paper or plastic plate. The design can be any shape or pattern. You can even cut out letters to form your name or a slogan for your favorite team.

2 Carefully poke through the plate with the point of your scissors and cut out the part(s) of the image that you want to show on your T-shirt or poster.

To Stencil on Paper or Poster Board:

1 Lay out a piece of paper or poster board and place your stencil over the area where you would like the image to appear, then tape the stencil in place or hold it firmly. Dip a paintbrush in paint and gently dab the paint into the cutout area(s), filling them in on the paper or poster board.

2 To sponge your stencils, dip a sponge in a plate of paint and dab it in the cutout part of the stencils. With each dab, lift the sponge straight up from the surface to avoid smudging—do not slide it; this will give your design a unique, textured look.

To Print and Stamp a T-shirt:

1 Be sure to use fabric paints for printing T-shirts and other clothing or fabric. Pour shallow puddles of fabric paint onto paper or plastic plates; each color should have its own plate.

2 Put a piece of thick cardboard inside the T-shirt. (This will keep the paint from leaking through to the other side of the shirt.) Lay out the T-shirt with the printing side up. Make sure it's smooth and flat.

· · · · · · ·

3 Create stamps and stencils of the images you'd like to have on your shirt: letters to spell a slogan or name, images like hearts or flowers, or abstract shapes—anything you wish! (For the T-shirt on page 81, we used a simple, round stencil shape to create the head of our character, and cardboard shapes glued to woodblocks to create stamps for the hair, eyes, nose, and mouth.)

· · · · · · ·

4 Lay your cutout stencil in position on the T-shirt, then tape it in place.

· · · · · · ·

5 Use a paintbrush or sponge to apply paint through the cutout shapes of the stencil (see techniques described above).

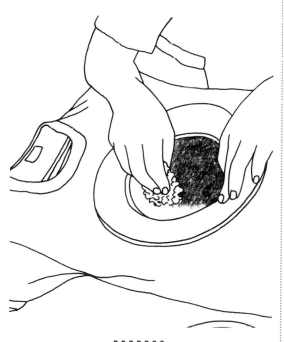

· · · · · · ·

6 When the stenciled image has dried for about a half hour, dip a stamp in the fabric paint, place it in position on your T-shirt, and press down hard.

7 Keep adding stamps until your design is just the way you want it. Let the paint dry completely. Follow the directions on the fabric paint label to set the design permanently.

Now that you've learned the basics of printing and stenciling, you're ready to use these skills to print on paper, posters, and other items. Try making party invitations, a personalized pad of paper, a pillowcase portrait of your dog or cat, or a poster to announce your birthday (or someone else's)!

"You can use anything to make a print— I use my nose!"

NO-SMUDGE STENCILS

● Use strong shapes when you draw your stencils, whether you're creating an abstract design or a representation of something, like a star or fruit.

● Tape stencils firmly in place.

● When applying paint through the stencil, brush from the edges of the cutout image to the center. This will give you a strong outline and prevent the brush from accidentally slipping under the stencil.

● If you are stenciling in layers or placing images very close to one another, be sure to let painted images dry very well before placing a stencil over any part of them; this could smudge existing images.

● If your design is complicated, you might want to use a pencil to lightly trace an outline of the stencil onto the paper or fabric (in case it moves, you can put it back in the correct position).

▼▼▼▼▼▼▼▼▼▼▼▼▼▼▼▼▼▼▼

Monoprint Pillowcases

How easy is it?

What You Will Need:

- nontoxic fabric paints and paintbrushes
- Plexiglas sheet or other flat washable surface (like a flat cookie sheet)
- plain cotton pillowcases
- cardboard (same size as pillowcases)
- sponges (optional)

To Make Posters:

- large sheets of poster board or construction paper
- poster paints

These dreamy pillowcases are made using a traditional monoprinting technique. The first step in the monoprinting process is to paint an image on a hard sheet of plastic or glass. Paper (in this case, a pillowcase) is then gently pressed onto the surface of the paint to make a monoprint. The hard plastic sheet is washed and the process begins all over again to make more one-of-a-kind creations. This process creates a unique, mottled look with unexpected patterns and textures that you can't get from painting directly onto a surface.

A monoprint can be created using a single color or every color of the rainbow. The design can be as complicated or as simple as you like. Maybe you'd like to make a monoprint of Animal or Gonzo on your pillowcase. Or make original pillowcase portraits of your brother, sister, or best friend!

PROJECT MADE BY VICTORIA ELLIS

1 Decide on the design for the pillowcase. Paint it onto the piece of flat plastic.

• • • • • • •

2 Place the cardboard inside the pillowcase so that the paint will not seep through to the back.

• • • • • • •

3 Pull the pillowcase tightly around the cardboard insert, then gently lay it flat on top of the painting. Pat gently all over.

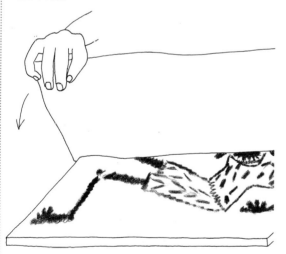

• • • • • • •

4 Carefully peel the printed pillowcase off the flat surface and set aside to dry, leaving the cardboard inside. Add more paint to the plastic surface and repeat the process for a similar print, or wash the plastic and repaint it to make another print.

• • • • • • •

5 For finishing touches:

• Add more texture by dipping a sponge into paint and dabbing the pillowcase as you wish.

• Use a paintbrush to fill in any gaps in the paint if you'd like the color to be more solid.

• Follow the directions on the fabric paint label to set the design permanently.

To make posters or paintings, use the same techniques you have learned in this project—just substitute poster board or construction paper for the pillowcases, and use tempera paint instead of fabric paint. How about making a giant birthday card for your parent or teacher? Or a big sign for your bedroom door? Remember, if you want to write a message on your poster, you have to paint your letters and numbers in reverse!

"Me never sleepy!"

PAINTING TIPS

• If you use thick dabs of paint, the colors will run together when printed.

• If you use a thin application of paint, the colors will be faint when printed and a lot of the background color will show through.

• When printing, DO NOT RUB the paper or fabric or the print will smudge.

Super Apron Stencils

How easy is it?

What You Will Need:

- pencil
- a few thin pieces of cardboard
- scissors
- plain canvas apron
- masking tape
- sponges
- nontoxic fabric paints and paintbrushes (a flat-edged paintbrush is best)

In this project you will use the art of stenciling to make this neat patterned apron to wear during messy projects (like cooking dinner or creating Muppet crafts!). Stenciled aprons make great presents, too.

Note: *See the stenciling tips on pages 84 and 85. See pattern on page 301.*

. . . .

1 Decide how you want your apron to look. Will there be only one picture? Where will it go? Are you going to use a small stencil and repeat the same picture all over the apron? Or do you want a pattern created from more than one stencil?

. . . .

2 Draw the design shapes onto the thin cardboard. Use your scissors to cut away the cardboard in the areas of the design where the paint should come through on the apron.

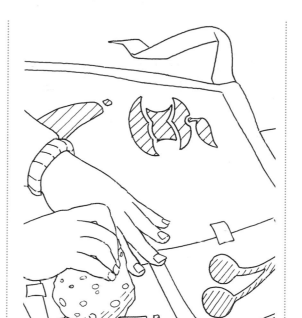

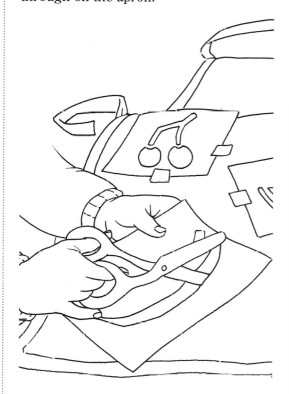

. . . .

3 Place the stencil on the apron and firmly tape it down flat. With the stencil held (and taped) firmly in place, dip a sponge or paintbrush into the paint and paint through the stencil's cutouts onto the apron. Move the stencil and allow the paint to dry for a few minutes. Repeat the process, using the same stencil or new ones.

. . . .

4 Finish the apron by following the instructions on the fabric paint label to set the paint permanently.

Tie on your apron and make a mess!

"Yah Yah! Vöøska dröøksa cöøksy göødy-göødy wit dü spiffy-nifty apröøn!"

Fishy T-shirt

How easy is it?

What You Will Need:

- fresh fish
- newspaper
- thin piece of cardboard
- plain cotton T-shirt
- plain paper
- nontoxic fabric paints and paintbrushes

This T-shirt is decorated with a monoprint just like the pillowcase on page 86. But this monoprint is extra-special because you're working with a three-dimensional subject— a painted fish, to be exact.

1 Wash and dry your fish. Lay down newspaper to keep your surface clean. Put cardboard inside the T-shirt to protect the back from paint that might seep through.

2 Make a couple of practice prints on paper to see what you like best. Try painting one side of the fish all one

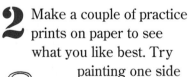

color. Or try painting it all different colors. Maybe paint each scale a different color, or paint the fins and the body each a different color.

3 Carefully place the fish, paint-side down, onto the paper. Firmly press down on all parts of the fish. Do not rub or wiggle it around on the paper or you will smudge the print. Lift the fish straight up and let the print dry. You can wash and dry the fish each time you want to try a new color combination.

4 When you are ready to print your T-shirt, repaint the fish and repeat the printing process in step 3. You can even make a whole school of fish on your shirt.

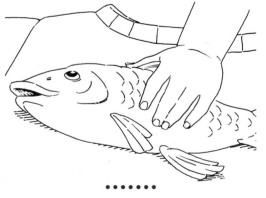

5 After the paint is dry, follow the directions on the fabric paint label to set the design permanently.

PROJECT MADE BY BENJAMIN MUNGO SCHNEIDER

Construction Zone

"**M**ixed media" is a fancy term that means "made from all different kinds of materials." Mixed media creations are made from a little of this and a little of that, all stuck together to create something totally unique and wonderful. In fact, Muppets themselves are mixed media constructions. Throughout the history of the Muppet Workshop, we've tried to find fresh and unusual ways of putting together all kinds of crazy stuff to create wild and funny-looking characters. Take a look at this wacky Muppet sneaker. It's made of things you might find in the back of a drawer or the bottom of a closet!

In this chapter, you'll find out how to make both simple and complex mixed media constructions from a variety of found materials—from a used cardboard box and twigs to furry fabric and beans!

"Frankly, I'm not sure if I'm mixed media or just plain mixed-up!"

VROOM! VROOM!

Almost every material under the sun was used in this shot of Piggy on her motorcycle: metal, plastic, fabric, rubber. And check out those little flippers peeking out from behind Piggy . . . wonder who that is!

And by building your own treasure chest, birdhouse, picture frame, or hungry bank you'll learn that with mixed media projects, anything goes!

Keepsake Treasure Boxes

How easy is it?

PROJECT MADE BY BARBARA DAVIS

What You Will Need:

- Bear Essentials
- standard shoe box with lid

To Make the Frilly Box:

- large sheets of paper or 2 yards of fabric (for lid and box covering)
- wrapping paper (for inside box and lid)
- fringe
- lace trim
- old earrings, buttons
- small silk flowers
- string of fake pearls, small plastic toys, mirror
- photos, postcards, or magazine clippings
- paper or lace doilies
- tassel

Everyone needs a place to keep treasures, so in this project, we'll show you how to transform a shoe box into the perfect place to keep your favorite things. Perhaps you'd like to create a special theme box to hold your seashell or rock collection, or a "vacation box" for souvenirs, maps, and photographs from your latest trip.

Frilly Keepsake Box

You can cover the outside of your box with neat little objects you've been collecting (or objects you find around your house) and make the outside of your box as wonderful as the treasures that go inside! Then, when you're finished, you can use your box to store jewelry, feathers, your key chain collection, or anything that's really special to you.

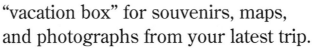

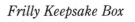

Pirate's Treasure Chest

Note: *If you're making the Treasure Chest Box, you need to do only steps 2, 3, and 6. If you're making the Frilly Box, follow steps 1 through 5.*

• • • • • • •

1 To cover your box's lid with paper or fabric:

• Center the lid on the back side of the paper (you can also use fabric, but we're going to refer to it as paper for the instructions) and measure out a 2-inch border around all the edges of the lid; cut out the paper.

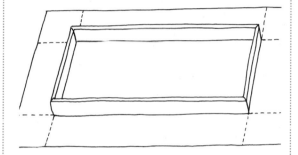

• Next, measure 2-inch square corners into each corner of your rectangle of paper (use the dotted lines in our illustration as your model). Cut out the squares so that the shape of the paper resembles the illustration shown below.

• Keeping your lid in the center of the paper, turn each edge of the paper up, and then fold over and into the rim of the lid. Crease the paper well and glue in place on the lid.

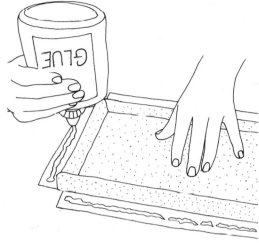

• • • • • • •

2 To make the paper lining for the inside of your shoe box lid:

• Place the top of your lid onto the back side of the paper. Trace the outline of the lid and cut out the rectangle.

• Place the rectangle of paper flat *inside* the top of your lid (if the rectangle is a little too large, trim the edges to fit). When it fits just right, glue in place to cover the inner lid.

To Make the Treasure Chest Box:

• 2 or 3 large maps
• Popsicle sticks or tongue depressors
• 2 different-colored brown Magic Markers
• rubber gloves (optional)
• clasp or belt buckle
• metal nuts, bolts, coins, or rivets
• rickrack (curvy ribbon)
• small objects to use as decorations: tiny toy cars, toy boats, dinosaurs, etc.
• stickers and photos

SPEAKING OF TREASURES . . .

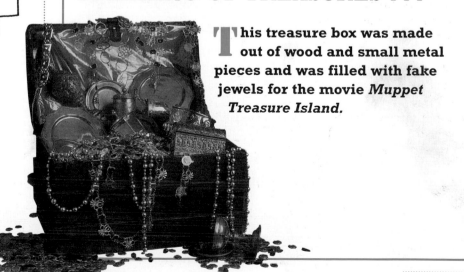

This treasure box was made out of wood and small metal pieces and was filled with fake jewels for the movie *Muppet Treasure Island.*

3 To cover the bottom inside of your box with paper, follow the same method used on your lid in step 2:

- Place your box on the back side of the paper, trace the outline, and cut out the rectangle. Test for size, trim as necessary to fit, then glue to the inside bottom of the box.

·······

4 To wrap the outside of the box itself, follow the same method used for the lid in step 1, but substitute new measurements:

- Place the bottom of the box at the center of the back side of your paper.

- Measure out a 10-inch border on all edges and cut out the rectangle of paper.

- Cut 10-inch corners *into* the rectangle's corners (refer to the illustration in step 1).

- Place your box upright at the center of the paper and fold the edges of the paper up, over, and in, creasing well, as in step 1. Glue the paper to the box.

BE SURE IT WILL CLOSE

When gluing on decorations (see instructions this page), make sure the lid will still fit securely over the box. You should leave about 1 inch of empty space around the top edge of the box.

To make the Frilly Box:

- With glue, attach fringe (or other trim) around the box.

- Glue on earrings or buttons, silk flowers, or fake pearls.

- Glue photos, postcards, or magazine clippings to the center of the lid. Add fancy trim to frame the picture.

- Glue small plastic toys, jewels, or a mirror to the inside of the box or lid.

- Glue on a tassel as a clasp.

To make the Pirate's Treasure Chest Box:

- Line the insides of the box with your maps, following steps 2 and 3.

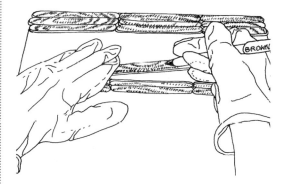

- Draw wood patterns onto Popsicle sticks with brown markers to simulate wood (you may want to wear rubber gloves to keep your hands clean for this part).

- Glue the Popsicle sticks side by side onto the box until the sides and top are completely covered.

- Glue a clasp or old belt buckle to the center front of the box lid for decoration. Glue the decorative metal nuts or bolts around the edges of the front and back

of the box, then across the lid, as shown in the photograph on page 92.

- Glue a "road" of rickrack on the inside of the box, then glue tiny toy cars to your road. Or, use blue rickrack to create a "river," then glue small toy boats to the river.

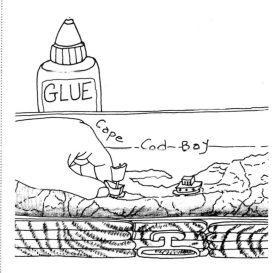

- Glue stickers, coins, photos, rubber animals, "Keep Out" warnings, and other items to the outside of the box.

BEVY OF BOXES

You can make keepsake boxes with any kind of theme. Why not make a:

- **Boat box:** cover with ocean maps; glue on miniature boats. Add a "rope" closure.
- **Candy box:** cover with candy-print giftwrap. Store wrapped candy inside.
- **Friendship box:** cover with a collage of photos. Enclose mementos and keepsakes.
- **Celebrity box:** cover with a collage of photos and articles about your favorite celebrity.

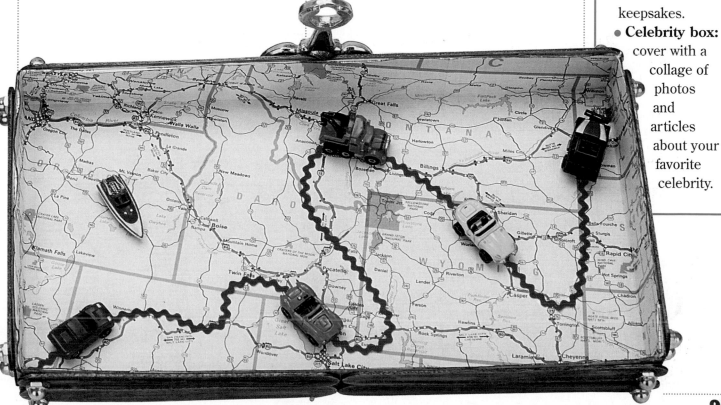

Wild and Wacky Pen and Pencil Set

How easy is it?

What You Will Need:

- **Bear Essentials**
- **tracing paper (optional)**
- **different-colored felt**
- **white chalk**
- **aluminum foil**
- **a few pencils and pens**
- **small googly eyes**
- **fun trim and feathers**

"BOINGGGG . . ."

"BOING . . ."

Just by snipping, pasting, and using a little imagination, you can turn your ordinary pens and pencils into kooky Muppet characters. You can make them flat or three-dimensional, then mix and combine all kinds of funky materials to make tiny props for your characters to carry or wear. When you're finished, you can write with them, draw with them, or put them in starring roles in your latest puppet show. Why not create extras for your friends? For a really special present, make mini portraits of your friends or relatives in felt, and add them to the pencil and pen tops.

By the way, pencil toppers with feathers are excellent for tickling, so *watch out!*

PROJECT MADE BY JANE HOWELL

1 Think up your own wacky creatures or trace our patterns on page 302 onto tracing paper and cut them out (see page 9 for tracing instructions).

· · · · · · ·

2 Each head has two separate sides that are identical, so fold your felt piece in half and draw or trace a head shape onto it with chalk. Carefully holding the folded felt in place, cut out both heads at the same time through both layers of felt.

· · · · · · ·

3 Wrap a small amount of aluminum foil around the top of a pen or pencil.

· · · · · · ·

4 Cover the insides of your felt head pieces with glue and place them together over the foil. Let the glue dry thoroughly.

5 Make arms out of felt—design them yourself, or trace our patterns on page 302 (see page 9 for tracing instructions). Cut out and attach to the pencil body with glue.

· · · · · · ·

6 Decorate your wacky character with googly eyes, feathers, and any other trim you can think of.

It's show time (or tickle time)!

"BOING . . ."

"BOING . . ."

"BOINGG!!!! . . ."

MUPPETS BIG BOOK OF CRAFTS

Funky Fur Frame

How easy is it?

What You Will Need:

- an adult, briefly
- Bear Essentials
- precut cardboard "mat" frame (6" × 8")
- fur fabric of any color (about ¼ to ½ yard)
- sheet of clear acetate (for "glass")
- masking tape
- googly eyes (store-bought) or Styrofoam balls or Ping-Pong balls or white buttons (for homemade eyes)
- black felt (optional)
- colored markers
- large paper clip (for hanging)

A shortcut! You can also buy a pre-made plain picture frame and just decorate it as we've decorated these.

Fake fur is a very useful and versatile crafts material. It comes in many different colors, textures, and in several different lengths, like fluffy fake shearling or close-cropped "pelt." You might have gussed that fake fur is one of our favorite materials here at the Workshop. We've probably used *acres* of it over the years to bring many of the Muppets to life.

In this project, we have used long, luxurious Muppet-style fur and googly eyes to make picture frames that look as if they might come to life at any moment! You can try making frames of different sizes, either tiny or humongous, but our directions make a frame that holds a standard 4 × 6-inch photograph. If you decide to make a larger or smaller frame, remember to buy more (or less) fake fur!

98

1 Place the precut mat frame onto the back side of your fur fabric. With the marker, trace around the outside edge of the frame and the inside edge of the "window" directly onto the fabric.

• • • • • • •

2 Use the scissors to cut the whole outer rectangle out of the fur. Next, poke a hole at one corner of the inner rectangle where the fur frame's window will be. Carefully cut out the center, using the outline as your guide.

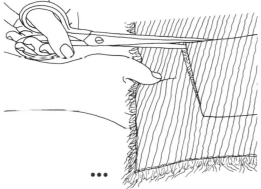

• • •

3 To make the "glass" for your frame:

• Place your precut frame on the acetate sheet and trace the outline of the whole frame with your marker (you don't need to trace the window outline onto the acetate).

• Cut out the acetate rectangle about ½ inch *inside* your outline, so that the acetate is slightly smaller than your frame. Set aside.

• • • • • • •

4 Cover the front of your mat frame with white glue and place the cutout fur onto the mat, carefully lining up the edges and the window. Let dry.

• • • • • • •

5 Turn over the fur frame and tape the acetate in place onto the back side of the frame to fill the frame's window.

• • • • • • •

6 Arrange the googly eye shapes around the fur frame. When you're

happy with the arrangement, glue the eyes in place and let dry.

To make your own googly eyes:

• Ask an adult to slice a Styrofoam ball (or a Ping-Pong ball) in half. Cut out black felt pupils and glue on, or use a black marker to draw them on. (For the green frame, we painted the Ping-Pong balls black and glued on googly eyes.)

• Use white buttons of any size and shape. Glue on black felt pupils.

• Draw on eyelids with different colored markers.

• For eyelashes, cut a piece of black felt in a sawtooth pattern on one edge to fit the eyeball. Glue to the top of the eye or to the eyelid.

• You can add eyebrows using black paper or a different-colored piece of fur. Just cut a small, eyebrow-shaped piece of fabric to fit over each eye. Changing the eyebrow position can change the expression a lot. Experiment!

• • • • • •

7 Align a special photograph in the frame's window and tape it in place. Tape a large paper clip vertically near the top center edge of the back side of your frame. Hang from a nail or pushpin.

FRAMING FUN

You can make other funky frames by gluing on all kinds of stuff. Try some of these materials:

• colorful old buttons of different shapes and sizes (check your sewing box!)
• small plastic animals
• tiny cars and trucks
• seashells
• colorful yarns and ribbon in wild patterns

"My cousins were framed! Grrr!"

Twiggy House

How easy is it?

What You Will Need:

- an adult, briefly
- scissors
- clean empty milk carton or round plastic bottle
- string or wire (for hanging the house)
- lots of thin, dry twigs
- white glue
- nutshells, googly eyes, bottle caps, film containers, or plastic cups
- waterproof varnish (optional)

Here's a plan for building a house of twigs that little birds can live in (or even little fairies, when you're not looking!). Although these instructions tell you how to build a house of twigs, you can use any materials to cover your house; just start with a good foundation (a clean plastic bottle or milk carton) and build from there. And be sure to make it cozy inside for your own special creature, real or imaginary.

PROJECT MADE BY PATRICIA FARR

Note: *This project is a lot easier and faster to do if you use a hot glue gun instead of regular white glue. However, you must have an adult with you at all times if you are using a hot glue gun.*

....

1 Cut into one side of the milk carton, making a hole about 1 inch up from the bottom and about 1½ inches high; this will be the mouth or doorway. Ask an adult to carefully poke a hole through the top of your carton with the scissors, then slip a length of string through the hole (for hanging the house later).

....

2 To cover the house, break the twigs into pieces that will fit vertically (top to bottom) onto the house. Keep some very short sticks to fill in under and around the mouth. Cover one surface of the carton with glue and place the sticks onto the surface, side by side. Fill the spaces between the sticks with smaller twigs so that the entire side of the milk carton is covered. Let each side dry before you work on the next side.

3 To cover the roof, break twig pieces to size and glue in place, radiating sticks outward from the center of the top.

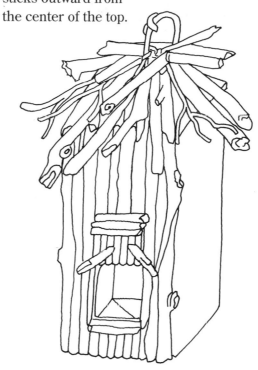

....

4 Once everything is dry, check for any bare spots and fill in with skinny twigs.

"Hey, did you see those groovy new twig houses going up down the street?"

"Yeah, that's my kind of nest."

5 To give your house a personality:

• Use twigs or nutshells to make a nose, eyes, and eyebrows.

• Stick on googly eyes or make your own

eyes from camera film container caps, bottle caps, or anything else you might have around (we made these eyes by cutting up white plastic cups).

· · · · · · ·

6 To make a perch for a bird, break about ten sticks into 6 to 10-inch pieces. These will stick out from the bottom of the carton. Cover the bottom of the carton with glue and attach the sticks so that the ends stick out in front of the carton.

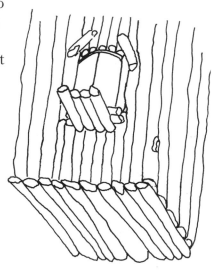

· · · · · · ·

7 To weatherproof your house so that you can put it outside for birds to use, ask an adult to help you paint it with several coats of waterproof varnish. When the varnish is completely dry, nestle your house in a tree branch or hang it from an outside fence. You might want to leave a little birdseed inside to encourage your feathered friends to move in!

YUM!

The witch's house built for this Muppet retelling of "Hansel and Gretel" looks good enough to eat, but it sure would taste gross. It was made with real cookies and candy, which were attached (very carefully!) onto a wooden base, using a glue gun and glue sticks.

Furry Monster Bank

How easy is it?

Made of an empty oatmeal container, some fur, felt, and a couple of Ping-Pong balls, this fuzzy-faced monster bank devours loose change through a secret opening under its tongue. Even better, its scary features (long, grabby arms and big teeth) warn off potential thieves.

PROJECT MADE BY BRYAN CROCKETT

What You Will Need:

- an adult, briefly
- Bear Essentials
- cardboard oatmeal container
- cardboard
- white chalk
- black, white, and red felt (one 8½" × 11" piece each)
- fake fur of any color (about ½ yard)
- masking tape
- string
- 2 Ping-Pong balls

1 Glue the lid of the oatmeal container in place on the base. Let dry.

• • • • • • •

2 Mark a slanted cutting line all the way around your oatmeal container, as shown below. Cut the container all the way around until it's in two pieces. The large bottom part of the container will be the monster's "body" and the smaller top part will be its "head." Set aside the head for a minute.

• • • • • • •

3 Trace the open oval end of the body onto cardboard, then use white chalk to trace it twice onto the black felt. Cut out all three ovals, then cut a slit measuring 1 inch long and ¼ inch wide in the exact same place in the center of each oval. Set aside all three ovals.

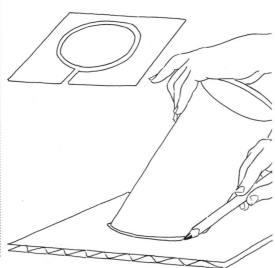

4 To cover the bank with fur:

• Cover the outside of the body with a thin layer of glue and lay it on the back side of the fur. Wrap the fur smoothly around the sides of the container until the ends meet up. Trim off excess fur all around the edges.

• Cover the sides of the monster's head in the same way.

• To cover the top and bottom of your monster, trace the flat top of the head onto the back side of the fur twice. Cut out two circles of fur, and glue one to the top of the head and the second to the bottom of the body.

• • • • • • •

5 Set the head back on the body, and use a few pieces of tape to create a sturdy hinge, as we did.

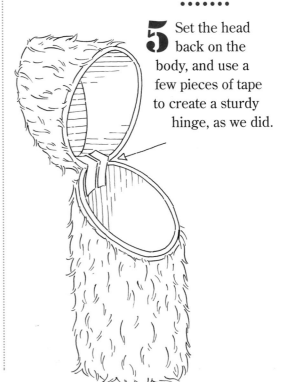

6 Tilt the head back, and tape the cardboard oval to the head and body, as shown.

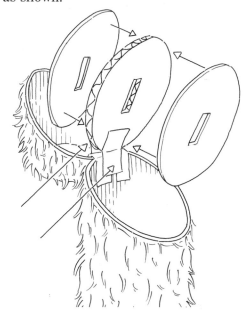

• • • • • • •

7 Cover both sides of the cardboard oval with glue and stick onc black felt oval on each side, making sure to line up the slits in each circle.

• • • • • • •

8 To make the arms:

• Ask an adult to use scissors to punch a hole through the fur and cardboard in the middle of either side of the body.

• Thread a string in one hole, then out the other hole so that string hangs out on each side of the body.

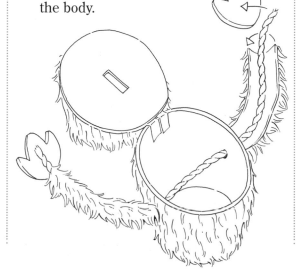

• Cut out two strips of fur (each piece about 1 inch wide and as long as each arm). Glue the fur *around* the hanging string on either side of the bank. Trim any leftover string. Cut out two felt monster paws (any color), and glue to the end of each arm.

• • • • • • •

9 Add a few details:

• Draw black pupils on Ping-Pong balls to make eyes (or cut round pupils out of black felt and glue on). Glue the eyes on top of the lid. (If you point the eyes slightly inward, the monster will seem to be looking at you.)

• Cut out a red felt lip and glue to the front, lower rim of the mouth.

• Cut out a few jagged white felt triangles and glue them to the upper rim of the mouth so that they point down.

• Cut a long tongue shape out of the red felt and glue just the back end of the tongue to the black felt on top of the cardboard oval (make sure that the tongue covers the slit in the oval, but do not glue it onto the slit).

Find a good place to keep your monster, then make sure to feed it coins three times a day.

"Can it, oatmeal breath!"

Bean and Pinecone Baskets

How easy is it?

PROJECT MADE BY BARBARA DAVIS

Traditional baskets are woven with reeds, paper, wire, and other flexible materials, but we've made our baskets from simple cardboard boxes and some natural things we found in our backyard and kitchen. Here, patterns are "woven" together using pinecones or beans, glue, and a little imagination. We've used a zigzag, or "herringbone," pattern on our baskets, but you can try anything: swirls, squares, circles, whatever! You can create beautiful basket patterns in any size with all kinds of ordinary things you might find around your house.

What You Will Need to Make the White Bean Basket:

- an adult, briefly
- Bear Essentials
- small corrugated cardboard box with flaps
- 1 yard of "wired" white ribbon
- lightweight cardboard (enough to line the box)
- ½ to 1 yard of fabric (for liner)
- white or cream-colored beans (examples: pinto, baby lima, black-eyed peas, white kidney beans)
- white berries

Note: *These projects are a lot easier and faster to do if you use a hot glue gun instead of regular white glue. However, you must have an adult with you at all times if you are using a hot glue gun.*

To make the White Bean Basket:

1 Turn down the four top flaps of the box, cutting the corner off each flap and rounding the edges with your scissors.

• • • • • • • •

2 To make the basket handle:

• Ask an adult to punch two holes with scissors near the top at the center of both long sides.

• Thread the ribbon through both holes from the inside to the outside to create a handle. You can help the ribbon through with your scissors, as shown.

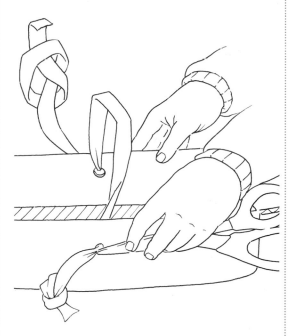

• When the handle is the length you want it, make two large knots with your ribbon to hold the handle in place.

3 To line your basket with fabric:

• Measure the width and height of each of the five *inside* panels of your box, as shown.

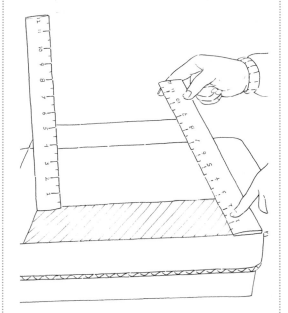

• Measure and cut out five lightweight cardboard panels to fit inside the box. If the panels are too large, trim the edges to fit snugly. These panels will be covered with fabric to line the inner box.

• Lay your fabric out flat. One at a time, place each panel of cardboard on the back side of your fabric. Cut 1 inch of extra fabric all the way around each cardboard panel.

• Squeeze glue onto all four edges of the panel. Turn the fabric edges over onto the back of the cardboard, folding and gluing the edges flat. Set aside to dry.

"A basket is a tres chic place to put one's valuables."

- **Bear Essentials**
- **small corrugated cardboard box with flaps**
- **lightweight cardboard (for lining)**
- **½ to 1 yard of fabric (for liner)**
- **small pinecones**
- **ribbon (optional)**
- **googly eyes, white berries, red cotton pom-poms (for decoration; optional)**

4 To put your fabric-lined panels in place, insert the bottom panel first until it is flush with the bottom. Place each panel in the correct position until all panels are flush with the box edges.

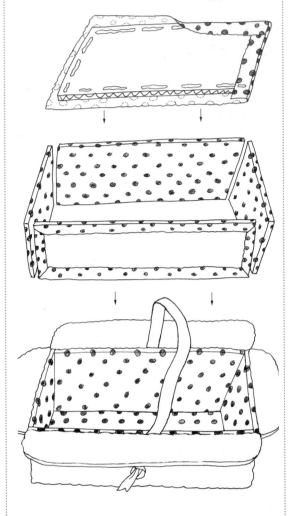

•••••••

5 Glue beans to one side of the box at a time, starting at the bottom edge and working upward. You can glue the beans on randomly, or in a pattern. The weight of the beans will help make the flaps stick out.

•••••••

6 Make two bows for the sides of the handles, then glue down and add a few berries to each bow.

To make the Pinecone Basket:

1 Remove the flaps from the box with scissors.

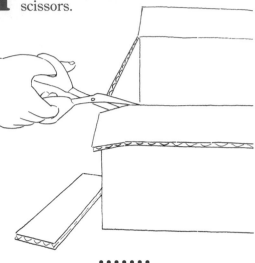

•••••••

2 If you'd like to line your basket with fabric, follow step 3 of the "White Bean Basket" project on page 107. Fit the fabric-covered liner panels inside the box (insert the bottom panel first) as described in step 4 of the "White Bean Basket" project.

•••••••

3 Glue pinecones to all four sides of the box in a zigzag pattern or in a pattern of your choice. Let dry.

•••••••

4 Glue on a bow and googly eyes to one corner. Add any other details you like; we used white berries and red ribbon for a festive touch.

Now that you've made these beautiful baskets, decide what's worthy of being inside them. (Hint: Try dried, scented flowers or use the baskets to hold special holiday ornaments or gifts.)

▲▲▲▲▲▲▲▲▲▲▲▲▲▲▲▲▲▲▲▲▲▲▲▲▲▲▲▲▲▲▲▲

CHAPTER 8 / WOOD SHOP

Building Blocks

t the Muppet Workshop, we use wood to make sets, props, and puppets. Sometimes wood forms just part of a structure; other times it is the only material used.

We have our own wood shop full of special woodworking tools, like saws, drills, lathes, and more. But you won't need all that equipment; the projects in this chapter require only a few simple hand tools. As for wood, much of the time you will be working with wood scraps. You can buy big bags of shaped wood pieces, dowels, knobs, and beads at most craft stores. And don't forget to look for wood close to its source— trees, that is! Fallen branches and twigs or pieces of old tree trunks can make terrific project material.

When you work with wood, make sure to notice

"Don't break any branches off living trees."

"Besides harming the environment . . ."

"The wood will be too soft to use."

WOODWORK WISDOM

ake these steps to make woodworking safe:

● Always have an adult help you use drills, saws, vises, or machines.

● Always wear safety goggles when sawing, cutting, or drilling wood.

● Examine your materials carefully before beginning to

work; discard split, rotten, moldy, or bug-infested pieces of wood. Do not use wood that contains any metal objects like old nails or screws.

● When looking through wood scraps, wear work gloves to protect your hands from splinters.

● Smooth wood's rough edges with sandpaper.

the patterns and colors in the grain of the wood; sometimes a piece of wood will have a unique natural design that makes it perfect for a particular project. Pay attention to the texture and durability of various woods; some woods are very strong and hard, while others are soft. For carving, choose soft wood like balsa that's easy to cut. For building, use harder wood like pine that's sturdy and strong.

Wacky Wooden Statuettes

How easy is it?

PROJECT MADE BY JANE HOWELL

What You Will Need:

- an adult (optional; needed only if you're using a handsaw)
- wood scraps—all different shapes and sizes
- thin dowels, wood strips, twigs
- handsaw (optional; not needed if wood pieces are precut)
- sandpaper
- wood glue
- scissors
- felt (for joints)
- paint and paintbrush
- buttons, beads, fur, feathers, yarn, silky string, fabric (for decoration)

These statuettes can be played with, or they can be displayed in your home (perhaps with a spotlight shining on them?). In either case, you'll first need to gather a selection of wood scraps to create your statuette. While looking for scraps, keep in mind the different parts of the body you'll create. Once you've collected a good batch of wood, you can get started on building your own characters.

Note: *This project is a lot easier and faster to do if you use a hot glue gun instead of regular wood glue. However, you must have an adult with you at all times if you are using a hot glue gun.*

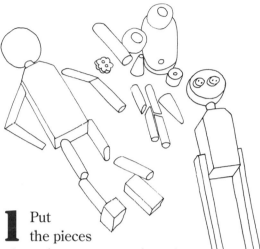

1 Put the pieces of wood onto your work surface and begin to lay out the form of your statuette. If you'd like to cut pieces to different sizes, have an adult help you cut them with a handsaw. Use sandpaper to smooth any rough edges.

• • • • • • •

2 Build in stages, letting the glue set after each attachment.

• Glue the head and neck pieces together first. Let the glue set.

• To make movable, jointed arms, choose an upper-arm piece and a lower-arm piece. Cut out a tiny rectangle of felt, then glue half of it to the front bottom of the upper arm and the other half to the front top of the lower arm. Glue an identical felt rectangle to the back side of the same

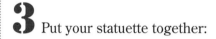

arm across the joint you've created. Let the glue dry. Repeat the steps to make a second arm.

• To make legs:

  • For jointed legs, follow the jointed arm instructions above.

  • For "shapely" legs, take a short length of thin dowel "calf" and a slightly longer and thicker dowel "thigh," and glue end to end.

  • For very basic legs, take two equal-length twigs or slats and glue to either side of the torso.

• Glue on clunky wooden feet (like Animal) or none at all (like Janice).

• • • • • • •

3 Put your statuette together:

• Glue the head and neck to the torso.

• Glue the arms and legs to the torso, if you haven't already. Allow the glue to dry thoroughly.

"Animal look good in wood!"

DRESS UP AND DECORATE YOUR CHARACTER

Here are a few suggestions:

• Paint it.

• Glue on facial features: buttons, beads, or felt.

• Glue on fur, feathers, yarn, or silky string for hair.

• For hands, cut out two identical mitten-shaped pieces of felt and glue one to each wrist.

• Glue on fancy fabric clothes of any style and color, or just paint clothes directly onto the wood.

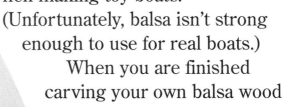

Balsa Wood Boat

How easy is it?

What You Will Need:

- an adult
- Bear Essentials
- balsa wood block (approximately 3" × 6" × 2")
- safety goggles
- carving knife or small handsaw (for adult use only)
- fine sandpaper
- acrylic paint and paintbrush
- white paper
- toothpicks or very thin dowel (for mast)
- wood glue
- small bead

Balsa wood is a light, soft wood that is easy to carve into simple or complicated shapes. Because this wood has a lot of air trapped inside, it floats really well on water. For both of these reasons, balsa wood is the best material to use when making toy boats. (Unfortunately, balsa isn't strong enough to use for real boats.)

When you are finished carving your own balsa wood boats, dress them up with paint and sails and have a sailboat race. If there are no lakes or ponds nearby, try your bathtub! Land ho!

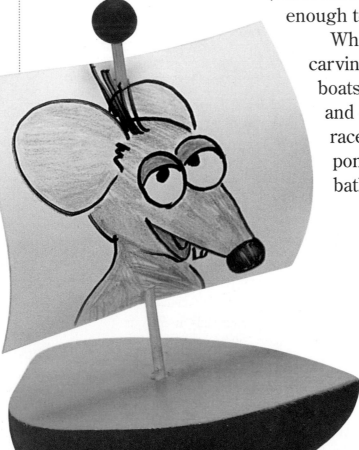

PROJECT MADE BY JANE HOWELL

1 Sketch your boat shape onto the balsa wood block. Design it so that one end of your boat is more pointed than the other. Leave the top side of the boat flat, but make the bottom curved.

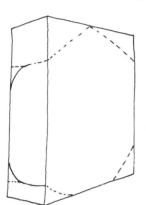

2 Have an adult help you carve out the shape with a knife or small handsaw.

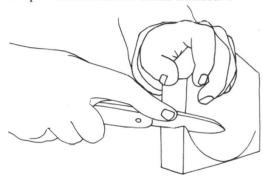

3 Use sandpaper to help smooth out the shape of

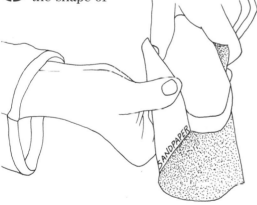

4 Wipeoffallthewooddust carefully and paint your boat with acryli paint.

5 Ask an adult to use the point of the knife to make a tiny hole in the center of the deck of the boat.

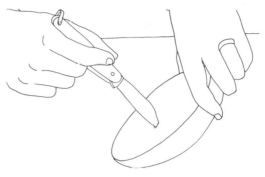

6 Cut sail shapes out of white paper for sails. Make sure they're a little shorter than the toothpick mast. Decorate your sail with a sticker or your name, or paint a picture on it. Then poke holes in each sail and thread onto the mast. Gluc a small bead on the end of the mast to seal in place.

7 Dab a little glue in the hole on the boat and insert the mast.

Set your sails, man your tillers, and away you go!

"What do sea monsters eat?

Give up?

Fish and ships!

Wocka wocka!"

GOGGLES ON!

When carving or sawing, always wear goggles and keep your hands out of the path of the blade.

Surprise Cupboard

How easy is it?

What You Will Need:

- an adult
- handsaw
- safety goggles
- various pieces of wood (see "Take This List to the Lumber-yard," opposite)
- sandpaper
- hammer and small nails
- eye screw
- finishing nails
- wood glue
- 2 cardboard jewelry boxes approximately 2¾" × 2¾" and 1½" tall (discard lids)

continued on page 116

Surprise is a wonderful element in any project; unexpected features make a project memorable. From the outside, this sweet and funny-looking cupboard doesn't reveal its secrets. But when you open it up, watch out! It's full of tricks, motion, visual jokes, and treasures.

This project uses a series of complicated wood joining and hinging maneuvers that require some patience to achieve. But your patience will be well rewarded with a piece that will make you truly proud.

"SURPRISE!"

Closed

Open

114

PROJECT MADE BY MARK ZESZOTEK

1 With the help of an adult, cut and label the ten main wood pieces and the four latches to size (described in "Take This List to the Lumberyard"). Smooth rough edges with sandpaper.

. . . .

2 Take the ten pieces of the "main structure" of the box and place them on their sides in their correct positions, as shown.

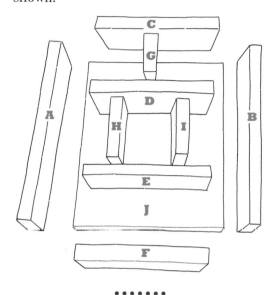

. . . .

3 Nail together the inner unit first:

• Nail both H and I to E (each piece should be 1¼ inches in from either end of E). **(Nail through E and into H and I.)**

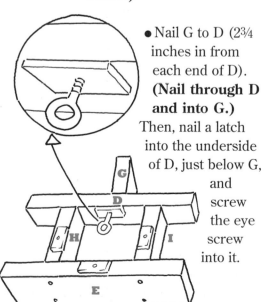

• Nail G to D (2¾ inches in from each end of D). **(Nail through D and into G.)** Then, nail a latch into the underside of D, just below G, and screw the eye screw into it.

• Nail H and I to D, making sure that D is lined up with E. **(Nail through D and into H and I.)**

• Take three "latch" wood pieces and hammer into position in the center front of panels E, H, and I, as shown (use small nails). Do not hammer the nails all the way in—keep the latches movable. Test and adjust.

"Keep this list handy."

TAKE THIS LIST TO THE LUMBERYARD

For the main structure:

When complete, this pine and plywood box is 8¾" (high) × 7¼" (wide) × 2¾"(deep). The main structure of the box is made up of 9 main pieces of wood, plus 1 piece of backing. Here are the sizes you'll need (we suggest you label each piece in pencil with a letter, listed below in bold type):

• 2 pieces **(A, B)**: 8¾" long × 2¾" wide (pine, ⅝" thick)

• 4 pieces **(C, D, E, F,)**: 6" long × 2¾" wide (pine, ⅝" thick)

• 1 piece **(G)**: 1½" long × 2¾" wide (plywood, ¼" thick)

• 2 pieces **(H, I)**: 2½" long × 2¾" wide (plywood, ¼" thick)

• 1 piece backing **(J)**: 8¾" long × 7¼" wide (plywood, ¼" thick)

For the drawer and door fronts:

Cut ¼" thick plywood to the following sizes (again, label each piece in pencil with its name listed in bold type):

• 2 pieces **(Top)**: (top drawer fronts) 2¾" × 1¾"

• 2 pieces **(Side)**: (middle-row side doors) 1⅛" × 2⅜"

• 1 piece **(Center)**: (center door) 2⅜" × 2⅜"

• 1 piece **(Bottom)**: (bottom door) 6" × 2¼"

For the door latches:

*Cut ¼"-thick plywood to the following size (label each piece **Latch** in pencil):*

• 4 pieces: ½" × 1"

What You Will Need (continued):

- beads, sticks, or nuts (for drawer pulls and doorknobs)
- 4 small wooden scraps (for doorstops; similar in dimensions to latches)
- scissors
- felt (for hinges)
- paint (as many colors as you'd like) and paintbrushes
- 2 Ping-Pong balls (for eyes)
- black construction paper
- 5" length of 1" diameter spring (or use pipe cleaners)
- 2 old, dangly earrings
- 4" length of string
- large, round wooden bead
- 8½" × 11" sheet of thin cardboard (the kind on the back of a pad of paper)
- cellophane tape (such as Scotch tape)
- pink sponge or foam

- Next, place the four "outer box" pieces on their sides in the correct places (A, B, C, and F) and make sure the inner unit you just built fits snugly into the center of the outer box. If so, nail A and C together to form a corner, then B and F to form another corner; then nail A to F and C to B to form the outer box.

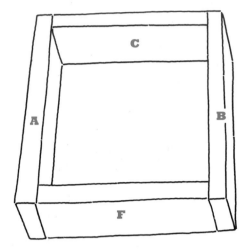

- Place the inner unit into the outer box and nail into place:

  - Nail piece A to D and E;

  - then C to G;

  - and last: B to D and E.

• • • • • • •

4 Check the measurements of piece J, the wooden backing you've cut out, and nail it to the back of the box.

• • • • • • •

5 To create drawers:

- Glue one of the cutout plywood drawer fronts (one of the two pieces you've labeled **top**) onto the side of each cardboard jewelry box.

- Place the drawers into the cupboard to test for fit. Modify as necessary.

- Glue a drawer pull onto each plywood drawer front (use beads, nuts, or twigs as pulls).

• • • • • • •

6 To create doorstops, glue one of the small doorstop scraps about ¼ inch inside each of the four remaining compartments so the doors don't fall back into them.

- Glue one to the "floor" of each side compartment.

- Glue one to the "roof" of the bottom compartment.

- Glue one to the "roof" of the center compartment.

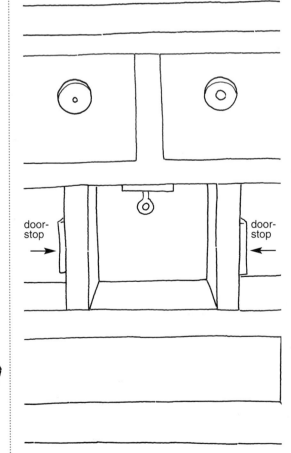

7 To create door hinges, cut out nine small felt rectangles, each measuring ½ inch × ¼ inch. Glue the felt pieces to the front of the doors, as shown below. Then glue or nail doorknobs onto each door front. Let all glue dry.

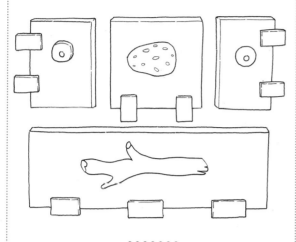

• • • • • • • •

8 To attach the doors to the box, glue the felt hinges to the front of the box. Let dry.

• • • • • • • •

9 Paint the whole cabinet inside and out in any colors you'd like. Refer to the photos on page 114 to make yours look like ours.

• • • • • • • •

10 For the eyes:

• Paint one Ping-Pong ball yellow and one green. Let dry, then paint on black pupils.

• To make eyelashes, cut out two 2 × ½-inch strips of black construction paper and cut a sawtooth pattern along one long edge of each strip. Glue the opposite edge of each around the middle of each of the balls.

• Have an adult poke a hole in the bottom of each ball. Put glue on one end of the spring and feed that end at least 1 inch into the hole in the ball. Let dry.

• Glue the opposite ends of the springs to the insides of the drawers so that the eyes pop up when you open the drawers.

• • • • • • •

11 For the earrings:

• Glue the earrings to earlobes painted inside each side door so that the earrings flop out when you open the door

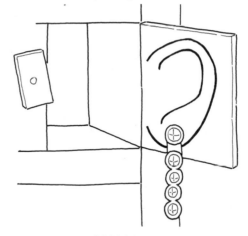

• • • • • • •

12 For the nose:

• Knot one end of the 4-inch length of string and thread it through the large wooden bead.

• Hang it by knotting the loose end of the string around the eye screw in the roof of the center compartment.

"I hate surprises!"

13 For the tongue:

- First, you need to make a "false backing" to bring the tongue forward in the compartment. Cut a piece of thin cardboard to about 4¾ inches × 2¼ inches, then cut a 1-inch horizontal slit in the middle, near the bottom, as shown below. Paint the strip with a mouth design (refer to illustrations and project photograph), then cut another piece of cardboard, about 3 inches × 2¼ inches. Bend this second piece of cardboard into a three-sided square, with a tab folding in from each direction on the fourth side. Tape to the back of the first piece, as shown opposite.

"We're just full of surprises!"

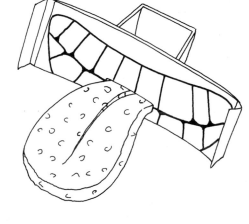

- Cut pink sponge into a tongue shape (about 3 inches × 1 inch). Feed the back of the tongue through the slit in the cardboard mouth, then tape the mouth piece just inside the bottom compartment. Fold the tongue inside and latch the door.

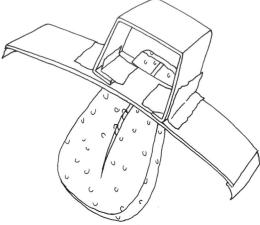

Fill door spaces with feathers, toy spiders, gumballs, and other yummy or icky treats, and watch as your cupboard goes boing!

Rolling Thingamajig

How easy is it?

This rolling thingamajig, with its slappy, happy feet, is a kooky, quirky, wheely toy that wobbles as it walks. Once you understand the wheel-turning mechanism and all the movable wooden parts, you can build a variety of rolling characters with dancing feet.

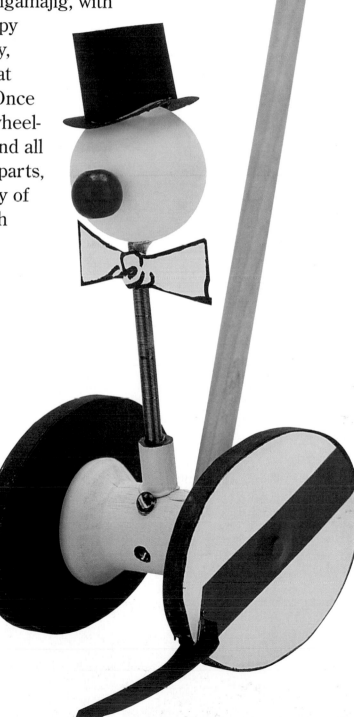

What You Will Need:

- an adult
- wooden spool (approximately 2" tall)
- clamp or vise grip to hold wood while drilling
- safety goggles
- hand drill and assorted drill bits (for adult use only)
- acrylic paints and paintbrushes
- 36" length of ³⁄₈" diameter dowel (for handle)
- scissors
- 4" × 8" sheet of ¹⁄₄"-thick balsa wood (for wheels)
- pencil and tracing paper
- handsaw (for adult use only)
- sandpaper
- 2¹⁄₂" length of ¹⁄₄" diameter dowel (for axle)
- wood glue
- ³⁄₄" long screw, ¹⁄₈" wide (with nut)
- ¹⁄₂" length of ³⁄₈" diameter dowel (for lower neck)
- 3" length of ³⁄₁₆" diameter spring (for upper neck)
- Ping-Pong ball (for head)
- colored bead (for nose)
- black marker
- black and white construction paper (1 small sheet of each)

1 Place the spool in a vise, hole side up. Have an adult enlarge the spool's hole by drilling straight through the hole with a ⅜-inch drill bit.

Note: *The hole must be large enough for the ¼-inch dowel to fit through loosely, with room to spare; there's no need to drill if your spool's hole is already big enough.*

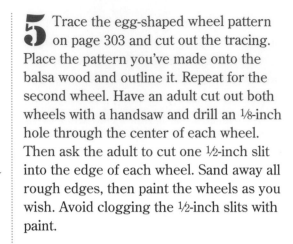

· · · · · · ·

2 Turn the spool on its side and clamp back into the vise. Have your adult drill another ¼-inch hole into the body of your spool just above and perpendicular to the existing spool hole, as shown at right.

· · · · · · ·

3 Paint the spool as you wish (ours is painted white).

· · · · · · ·

4 Place your handle dowel into the vise and ask your adult to drill an ⅛-inch hole through the dowel at a slight angle, as shown at right.

5 Trace the egg-shaped wheel pattern on page 303 and cut out the tracing. Place the pattern you've made onto the balsa wood and outline it. Repeat for the second wheel. Have an adult cut out both wheels with a handsaw and drill an ⅛-inch hole through the center of each wheel. Then ask the adult to cut one ½-inch slit into the edge of each wheel. Sand away all rough edges, then paint the wheels as you wish. Avoid clogging the ½-inch slits with paint.

· · · · · · ·

6 Slip the 2½-inch axle dowel through the spool. Glue one wheel to each end of the axle. Let dry.

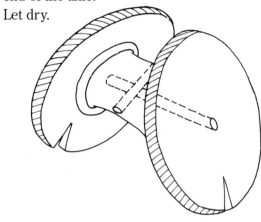

· · · · · · ·

7 Slip the screw through the spool (perpendicular to the axle), then through the handle dowel's hole. Screw on the nut at the back of the handle dowel to hold the unit together.

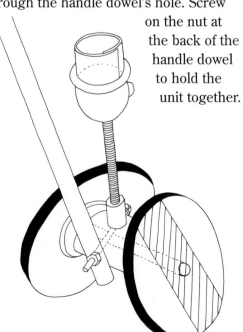

Clamp the ½-inch length of lower-neck dowel in the vise, end-side up, and have an adult drill a shallow 3/16-inch diameter hole into the center of that end. Remove from the vise and glue the opposite end to the center of the top side of the spool, as shown below left. Glue the upper-neck spring into the lower-neck dowel's shallow hole. Then glue the Ping-Pong ball to the top of the spring and the bead nose to the ball. Let all glue dry for at least two hours.

• • • • • • • •

8 Use construction paper to make a top hat and a bow tie:

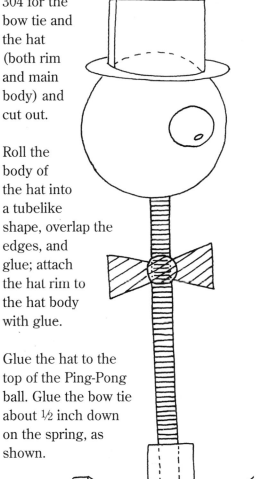

• Trace and transfer our patterns on page 304 for the bow tie and the hat (both rim and main body) and cut out.

• Roll the body of the hat into a tubelike shape, overlap the edges, and glue; attach the hat rim to the hat body with glue.

• Glue the hat to the top of the Ping-Pong ball. Glue the bow tie about ½ inch down on the spring, as shown.

9 To make the floppy feet, cut out two strips of black construction paper ¼ inch × 3 inches. Put glue on one end of each strip and slide those ends into the wheel slits. Fold the feet toward the back of each wheel, and let dry.

Roll out the red carpet, and roll your slaphappy thingamajig away!

WOODEN IT BE NICE

Talk about tough! Almost all the Swedish Chef's food is made of wood: the turkey, the fish, the cheese, even the butter curls on the left.

Animal Step Stool

How easy is it?

What You Will Need:

- plain or unpainted stool
- damp cloth
- yellow and brown latex paint, black acrylic paint, and paintbrushes
- wooden scraps: cylinders, large beads, spools, and odds and ends (you'll need pieces with holes in them for tail)
- wood glue
- string or twine (16")

Note: This project is a lot easier and faster to do if you use a hot glue gun instead of regular wood glue. However, you must have an adult with you at all times if you are using a hot glue gun.

Nearly any object can have hidden personality that just needs to be brought out. Would you have guessed that a wooden stool would have a wonderful creature lurking beneath its surface? As you can see, you can bring an ordinary object to life just by adding a few touches like beads and paint.

Our project tells you how to make a giraffe stool, but with different materials, you could make a dinosaur or an ostrich or something fantastic from your own imagination. Maybe you'd like to make a whole stool set of the kinds of animals you might see on a safari. You could make one for every member of your family! Or just make a set for your room. Then make an animal print curtain and bedspread (see page 30) and suddenly, you'll be living in a jungle!

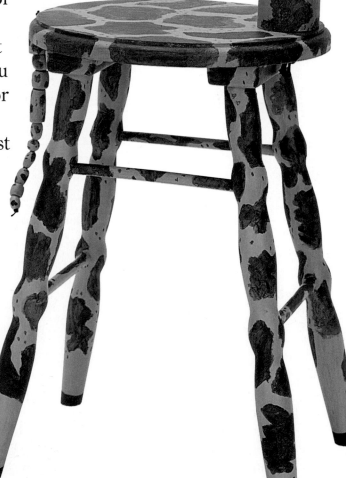

1 Wipe the unpainted stool with a damp cloth. Paint the stool all over with yellow paint and let it dry. Paint brown giraffe spots all over the stool. Paint brown strips at the very bottom of the stool legs to look like hooves.

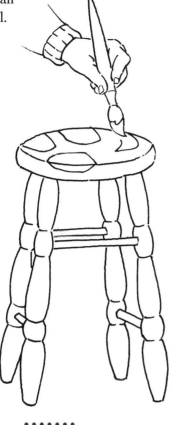

· · · · · · ·

2 Lay out the collection of spools and cylinders in position to make the neck, head, and tail:

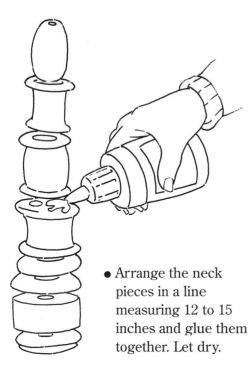

- Arrange the neck pieces in a line measuring 12 to 15 inches and glue them together. Let dry.

- For the head, choose a head-shaped wood scrap (if you don't have a head-shaped bead, glue together a few spools or beads to form a head). Glue on two small spools as horns.

- For a 12-inch tail, string beads onto your string. Fray the string's ends to make the end of the tail bushy.

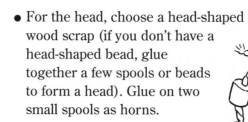

· · · · · · · ·

3 Paint the neck, head, and tail to match the body: first yellow, then with brown spots. When the paint is dry, glue the neck, head, and tail onto your step stool, as shown in the photograph. Paint the eyes, nostrils, and mouth onto the head with black paint.

WOODEN IT BE EVEN NICER

This is what a master woodworker can do with the right tools and a load of experience. The reception desk at The Jim Henson Company's New York office uses about fifty different kinds of wood carefully cut into Muppety shapes and inlaid side by side.

Toy Twig Chair

How easy is it?

What You Will Need:

- large collection of twigs broken by hand to correct lengths (see checklist, opposite)
- wood glue
- coarse sandpaper
- masking tape (optional; to hold twigs in place while glue dries)
- peppercorns and acorns (optional)

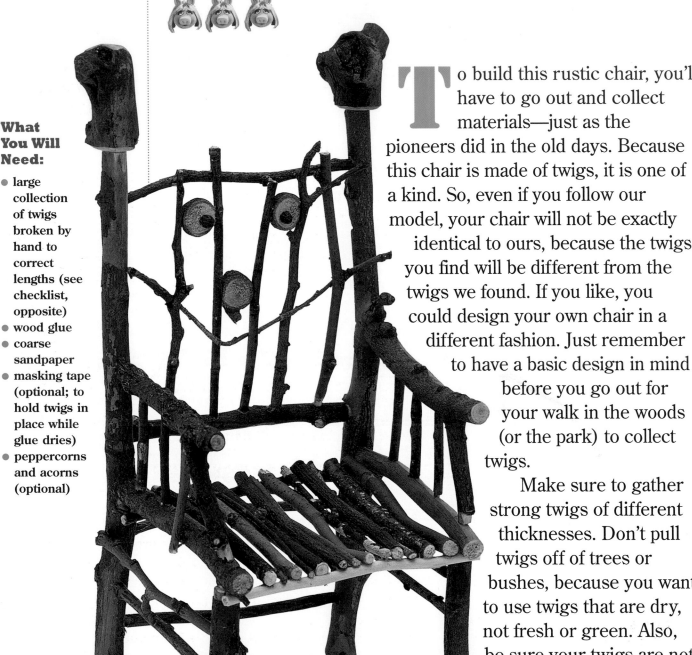

This is the perfect little seat for a teddy bear, doll, or your favorite little monster.

To build this rustic chair, you'll have to go out and collect materials—just as the pioneers did in the old days. Because this chair is made of twigs, it is one of a kind. So, even if you follow our model, your chair will not be exactly identical to ours, because the twigs you find will be different from the twigs we found. If you like, you could design your own chair in a different fashion. Just remember to have a basic design in mind before you go out for your walk in the woods (or the park) to collect twigs.

Make sure to gather strong twigs of different thicknesses. Don't pull twigs off of trees or bushes, because you want to use twigs that are dry, not fresh or green. Also, be sure your twigs are not rotting or buggy. As for bark, you can leave it on or peel it off.

PROJECT MADE BY PETER MACKENNAN

Note: *This project is a lot easier and faster to do if you use a hot glue gun instead of regular wood glue. However, you must have an adult with you at all times if you are using a hot glue gun.*

1 Draw a design for your chair or copy our design in the directions that follow.

2 Lay out the precut twigs in a flattened version of your chair shape, as shown below. Sand any ragged ends, if needed.

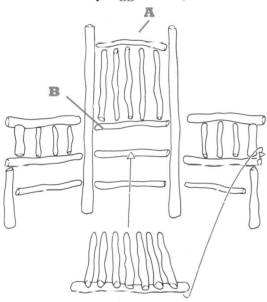

3 Make each of the two sides of the chair with three twigs. Be sure both sides are even and symmetrical, then glue the twigs together. If you like, use masking tape to hold pieces in place while the glue dries.

4 After the glue has dried on the chair sides, glue arms and armrest support pieces to them, as shown. Leave to dry.

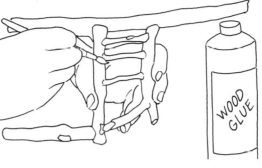

5 Assemble pieces for the chair back as follows:

- The top strut is labeled **A** and the bottom strut is labeled **B**. Glue the struts each about 4½ inches apart across the back of the main back supports.

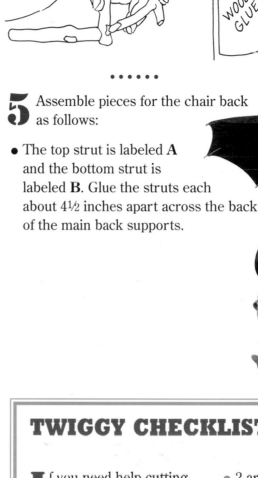

"Search for twigs after a storm."

TWIGGY CHECKLIST

If you need help cutting the twigs to the correct lengths, have an adult cut the twigs with garden shears or a small handsaw. You'll need:

- 2 main back-leg supports (thicker than the rest of the twigs and approximately 12½" long)
- 2 front legs (same thickness as the back-leg supports and approximately 6½" long)
- 2 armrests (approximately 6" long)
- 6 to 8 armrest supports (approximately 3" long)
- 4 seat supports (approximately 6½" long)
- 7 seat centers (approximately 6½" long)
- 4 leg struts (approximately 6½" long)
- 2 backrest struts (approximately 6½" long)
- 5 back supports (approximately 5" long)

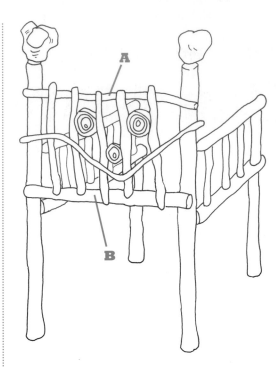

A

B

6 To make the seat:

- As shown, glue each of the 4 leg struts and the front and back seat supports in place. Let the whole thing dry before you go on to the next step.

- Take the seven seat centers and glue them pointing from front to back on top of the seat struts. Let dry completely.

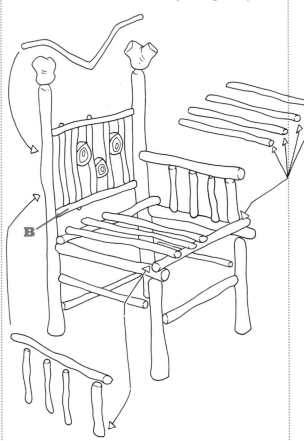

B

Dolls and animals, please be seated!

- Glue the five twig uprights to **A** and **B** as shown.

- Decorate your chair back with eyes, a nose, and a twig mouth. We used small slices of twigs for the eyes and nose and glued on peppercorns as pupils. You can also use acorns or other hard nuts or knots of wood as "finials" on the top of the main back supports. (Finials are decorative knobs or ornaments added to the tops of poles or sticks or pillars.) Leave the back section to dry.

" I like to direct all my projects from a good chair."

126

Tin Can Alley

Y ou might think of metal as a heavy and hard material that's difficult to work with. After all, metal is used to build tall buildings and long bridges. And welders employ complicated and dangerous machinery to create those buildings and bridges.

But metal is actually a flexible and versatile material that can be easy to manipulate. For instance, at the Muppet Workshop, we often use metal to build "skeletons" for puppets. These skeletons give our characters structure and support and are often electronically animated to create convincing body movements. We also use metal to make large sets and props for movies and television shows. And while we do have welders and other metal experts on staff for the big stuff, we've also figured out many tricks, techniques, and shortcuts to use when working with smaller metal projects.

If you've ever wrapped a sandwich in silver foil, bent a wire hanger, or opened a can of vegetable soup . . . well . . . you were working with metal!

"If you can't catch 'em, build 'em!"

MAKE YOUR MATE

I f Miss Piggy can't get her frog in the usual way, she'll try anything—like making a frog robot of her very own.

Tin Can Lanterns

How easy is it?

This project uses a metal-puncturing technique to create decorative lanterns. In many Spanish-speaking countries and in parts of the Middle East, this method of decoration is used to jazz up metal crafts from picture frames to jewelry to toys and games. Along with puncturing, craftspeople often use a similar technique known as embossing, in which they firmly press or hammer the back side of soft metals (like tin or aluminum) to create a raised pattern on the reverse side (check out the "Fabulous Foil Pin-Ups and Pin-Ons" project on page 136 to learn how to emboss). Metalworkers often use these methods to create beautiful and elaborate lanterns, like the ones in this project. When lit from inside, tin can lanterns project a pattern of tiny dots of light that looks really special. Why don't you make a few and use them at a cookout on a starry night?

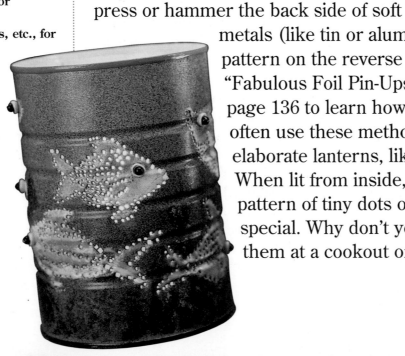

PROJECT MADE BY ED CHRISTIE

128

Note: *This project requires you to freeze water in a can overnight.*

. . . .

1 Draw your lantern design all around the outside of the can with the indelible marker. This design will be the guide for the holes you punch later, so think about whether your holes will form a picture or a pattern or both.

. . . .

2 Fill the tin can almost to the top with water and place it in the freezer overnight (this trick will make the puncturing process easier).

. . . .

3 The next day, put on your safety goggles, then place the frozen can on its side on a folded towel to keep it from slipping.

. . . .

4 Take the hammer and nail, and place the sharp end of the nail in a spot where you want a hole. Tap the nail head gently with the hammer until you puncture the can, then

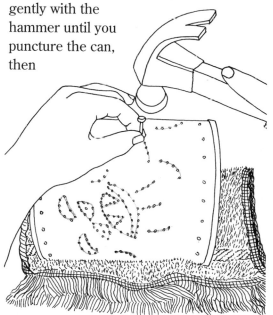

remove the nail. Repeat this step, making sure to leave a little space between each hole (about ⅛ inch). Try different-size nails for a variety of hole sizes.

5 When all the holes of the design are in place, dump out the ice. If you have difficulty removing the ice, pour warm water over the can until the ice melts away from the edges.

. . . .

6 Dry the can with the towel and paint the outside of your lantern.

. . . .

7 If you want a handle to hang your lantern, have a grown-up punch two holes in opposite sides of the top of the can, either with a church key can opener or a hammer and nail; thread 10 inches of wire through the holes as a handle, and twist securely.

. . . .

8 Stand a small flashlight on end inside your lantern or ask an adult to light a votive candle and place it inside. For a flashier or spookier version, put a glowstick in your can and watch the eerie light shine out.

MINDING METAL

Metal can have sharp edges, particularly once it has been cut—so be careful. You should especially watch out for the insides of cans that have been opened with a can opener of any kind, and for the sharp points on the back side of any piece of metal that has had holes punched through it. If you need to smooth these edges and sharp points, cover them with duct tape or electrical tape, project permitting.

● Check with an adult before you start any metalwork project.

● Never use metal that has jagged edges.

● Always wear goggles when working with metal.

● Wear heavy work gloves when handling and collecting metal recyclables.

● Never use metal that is rusty or corroded in any way.

Canned Robot

How easy is it?

Here's a great way to turn recycling into an art form: Build your very own robot out of used cans! In this project, we'll show you how to design and build a large supported metal structure using simple metal-joining and joint-making techniques. The best part is that you can do all of this with just cans, tape, a can opener, and some thin-gauge wire.

PROJECT MADE BY ERIC ENGLEHARDT

WARNING: *Can edges that have been cut are very sharp, so check with an adult before handling them, then be very careful and make sure to wear heavy work gloves when possible.*

. . . .

1 Remove the labels from your cans, then wash and dry the cans thoroughly.

. . . .

2 To make the spine, tape five small soup cans together to form a column. See page 132 for taping tips.

. . . .

3 To make the torso, stack two large coffee cans on top of each other and tape together. Repeat with two more large cans, then set aside both stacks. The top of each stack should be a closed end of a can.

. . . .

4 To make the rocket boosters, tape three medium-sized cans in a stack to form a column. Repeat to form the other booster. The top of each booster should be a closed end of a can. Set aside both boosters.

. . . .

5 To put the torso unit together:

• Stand the two torso stacks side by side, and tape them together from top to bottom in the back and front.

• Stand the spine column in front of them, where they join (but not between them).

• Tape all three stacks together at the side seams on the right and left of the spine column (where the spine column touches the two torso columns) from top to bottom, as shown above, right.

• Tape the three stacks together again by wrapping tape around the tops, middles, and bottoms of the cans, as shown.

Side View

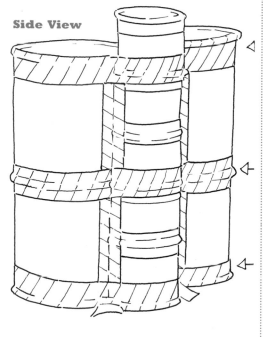

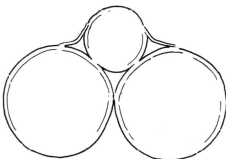

Top View

"This robot is uncanny! Wocka-wocka!"

CAN DO!

For all used cans, one end will have already been opened, but the other end will remain closed.

• 5 small soup cans (3" × 4"; for spine)
• 4 extra-large coffee cans (6" × 7"; for torso)
• 6 medium soup cans (2½" × 4"; for the rocket boosters)
• 4 regular-size coffee cans (4" × 7"; for legs)
• 7 large juice cans (4" × 4"; 6 for arms, 1 for head)

6 To add the rocket boosters to the back of the torso:

● Stand the torso unit up, and prop a rocket booster up on a small box or stool, to the left of the torso's middle seam; the booster should peek over the robot's "shoulder" about 1 or 2 inches and should have a closed end on the top. Tape along the left and right seams

on each stack, from top to bottom. Wrap tape horizontally around torso and boosters at the top and middle of the torso.

● Repeat with the other booster, this time to the right of the torso's middle seam.

. . . .

7 To make the legs:

● Stack and tape two columns of two regular-sized coffee cans each. Make sure the bottom cans are closed-end down.

● Stand the legs next to each other. Set the torso upon the legs and check for balance (if the torso doesn't rest evenly on the legs, move the legs around until it does, or stick a wad of paper towels between the leg and torso). When the balance is right, wrap a length of tape around the top edge of each of the leg cans so that half of the tape is on the leg can and half is flattened against the bottom of the torso can, as shown here.

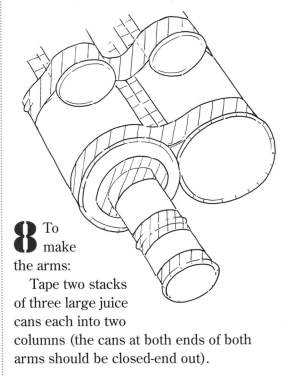

8 To make the arms: Tape two stacks of three large juice cans each into two columns (the cans at both ends of both arms should be closed-end out).

TAPING CANS

● Only join two cans at a time.

● When joining two cans, make sure the cans are the same size and that the ends are lined up together evenly (the directions will tell you when the top or bottom of a column needs to be the "closed" end of a can).

● To attach the tin cans to each other, you will tape

together **only the edges** of the cans with duct tape or electrical tape, as shown below.

● Start the tape at one point on the edges, making sure that half of it is stuck to one can, and half to the other, with no space in between the cans.

● Wrap the seam carefully and evenly, circling it at least three times.

9 To attach the arms by creating joints:

● Have an adult poke two holes with the church key can opener in the side of the can at the top of one arm. The two holes should be side by side, near the edge, as shown below. This will be the inside upper arm. Repeat with the other arm.

● At one of the torso's outer shoulders, have an adult poke two holes into the top of the can and another just below it on the side of the can, as shown below (you'll probably need to peel the tape back a bit to expose the metal underneath). Repeat on the outside of the other shoulder.

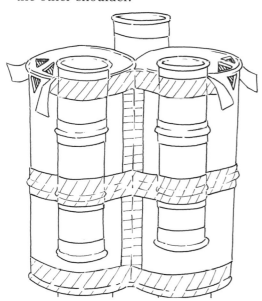

● To attach an arm to a shoulder, loop a 10-inch length of wire in one arm hole and out the other, with an even amount of wire sticking out of each hole. Take both ends and stick them into the side hole in the shoulder. Pull one wire end up through one hole on top of the shoulder, and one wire end up through the other hole on top of the shoulder. Tie the two ends in a knot on top of the shoulder. Repeat on the other arm.

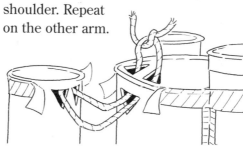

· · · · · · ·

10 To make the head:

● Choose a large juice can and place it over the neck, closed-end up.

● Use colorful wire for hair. We strung ours through an old funnel, but see what scraps you have around *your* workshop. Glued-on steel wool or old springs might be just right. Pipe cleaners could be fun, too.

● Use refrigerator magnets for the robot's face, or glue on buttons, bottle caps, washers, nuts—whatever!

· · · · · · ·

11 If necessary, add more electrical tape to seal off edges and to make sure everything is tightly attached.

Now, see if you can program your robot to do stuff for you (let us know if you can!).

MUPPET ROBOTS? (Ribb-bot)

Some of the Muppets are electronically animated; this means Muppeteers control the movements of the creatures with remote controls. **The character's voice is pretaped or added later.**

Metal Wind Chimes

How easy is it?

What You Will Need:

- an adult
- safety goggles
- pliers
- hammer
- metal soup skimmer or slotted spoon with a hole in the tip of the handle
- fishing line or thick nylon thread
- scissors
- upright metal cheese grater with handle top
- stuff to dangle (aluminum utensils, keys, metal nuts; make sure no one wants to use them again!)
- metal napkin rings
- screws and screwdriver

Wind chimes make wonderful tinkling sounds as the wind blows through them. This wind chime is also special because it doubles as a kind of "kinetic" kitchen sculpture. (Kinetic sculpture is sculpture that involves some kind of movement— like mobiles and chimes.)

You can build this handsome metal creature using an assortment of old kitchen tools and utensils, then hang it from a hook outside your window or door and listen as it dances in the breeze.

1 Put on those safety goggles.

. . . .

2 Bend or hammer the handle of the skimmer or slotted spoon into an arc. The chimes will hang directly below the "head" of the spoon.

. . . .

3 To hang the cheese grater from the skimmer, tie two equal lengths of fishing line to the grater's handle, then tie them to the center of the skimmer's head. Make sure the grater hangs evenly, and be careful not to touch the inside sharp edges of the grater.

. . . .

4 To make the jingly-jangly legs, use pliers to bend single loops into the handles of unwanted aluminum forks and spoons. Tie them to the head of the skimmer on long threads so that they hang down *through* the middle of the grater. Tie old metal nuts and keys, and any other "loopable" metal objects to the skimmer with fishing line. For all objects, be sure the thread is long enough for the legs to dangle below the bottom of the grater.

. . . .

5 To make the arms, use pliers to bend the tips of the handles of two forks

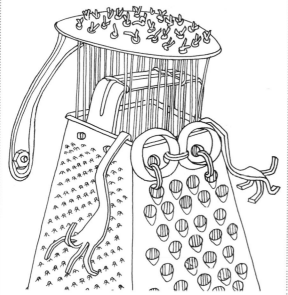

into tight hooks, then bend the little prongs to resemble fingers and hang them on the sides of the cheese grater.

. . . .

6 To make the eyes, tie the metal napkin rings onto one side of the grater near the top, as shown below, left, or tie them to the top of the grater handle, as we did in the photograph on page 134. Add any other details you'd like.

. . . .

7 If you haven't already hung your wind chimes in their final location, ask an adult to screw the skimmer handle onto a suitable outdoor wall as shown in the illustration below, left.

Now enjoy the heavy metal music!

"Don't mind me. I'm just hanging around!"

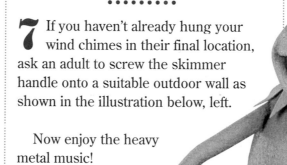

HANG IT!

It's easiest to make this project while it is hanging. Ask a grown-up to help you bend or hammer the skimmer's handle forward or backward into an arc, as shown below, and screw it to the wall or window where it will remain (it will look sort of like a showerhead). Or, bend the handle into an arc, then close the handle in a heavy drawer that will remain firmly shut while you work on your project (try a heavy wooden dresser, or a full file cabinet).

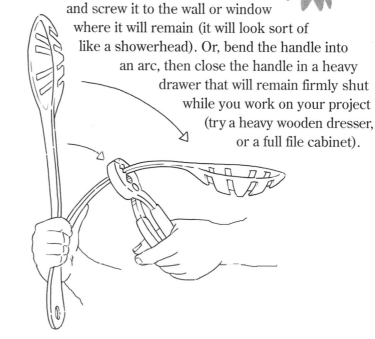

Fabulous Foil Pin-Ups and Pin-Ons

How easy is it?

What You Will Need:

- textured objects (keys, coins, shells, anything with an interesting shape)
- scissors
- 36- to 40-gauge colored craft foil (you can also use regular aluminum foil if you put together several layers to make a thick sheet)
- embossing tools (any kind of stick with smooth edges: spoon handles, tongue depressors, ice cream sticks, etc.)
- heavy cardboard
- white glue
- shoe polish or acrylic paint and paintbrush
- string, tape, ice cream sticks (for frame; optional)
- felt and safety pins (optional)

Want to impress someone? Emboss some aluminum (foil, that is)! Aluminum is a metal that's very easy to cut, bend, and shape; in fact, it can be cut into thin sheets that are easy to mold into things like car bumpers, soda cans, and sandwich wrap, depending on the thickness of the aluminum. Very thin sheets of aluminum are known as foil, and that's the stuff that you wrap around sandwiches and leftovers; but it's a great craft material, too.

If you lay foil over a penny and rub the foil, the image of that penny will appear as a raised design impressed in the foil. This technique is called embossing. You can make foil embossings of all kinds of textured things—tree bark, feathers, shells, coins. You can even cut out cardboard shapes, letters, or numbers to make an embossed sign or sheriff's badge. Do some experimenting. Use different colors and thicknesses of metal foil. When you're finished, you can frame your designs, or glue a piece of felt to the back of a mini-embossing and attach a pin to create a wearable impression!

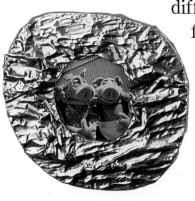

136

1 Place the textured objects on a smooth, flat surface. Arrange them in a pattern you like, with the sides that you want to emboss faceup.

•••••••

2 Cut a piece of foil larger than the objects you want to emboss, and place it over the shapes. With your fingers, press the foil sheet down onto the objects. Once you've got the shapes pretty well covered, use your embossing tool to rub the foil against the objects so that details appear. Rub gently; be careful not to poke through the foil.

3 Remove the foil sheet. Cut the foil into a shape slightly larger than the embossed area. Cut a piece of heavy cardboard into a shape slightly smaller than the embossed cutout. Place glue along the edges of the foil cutout and fold them over the cardboard. Smooth the edges onto the back side of the cardboard, but don't smooth the embossing itself or it will be ruined.

•••••••

4 To enhance the images, rub the embossing *gently* with a little shoe polish or apply acrylic paint with a paintbrush to the raised area.

•••••••

5 Make a plaque by attaching a string with tape to the cardboard backing to create a hanger, or glue on an ice-cream-stick frame. To make pins or badges, cut felt to the size of your embossing. Glue the felt to the back of the embossing and attach a safety pin.

Now wasn't that impressive?

CLANG! CLANG! CLUNK?

The Workshop doesn't usually make props for Muppets out of metal, because the props need to be lightweight enough for puppets to "hold." But when the Workshop was building swords for *Muppet Treasure Island,* they created swords made of lightweight aircraft aluminum. Check out the sword fighting in the movie: It's very realistic!

Teeny Tiny Croquet Set

How easy is it?

Croquet is an old-fashioned lawn game in which a course of arches, known as wickets, is laid out and marked off with stakes. Players try to shoot their ball around the course using a mallet, which is a wooden hammer with a heavy head and a long, upright handle. An official American croquet course uses six wickets and one stake, while a traditional British course uses nine wickets and two stakes.

But what do you do if you don't have enough room on the lawn for a full-sized croquet set? Well, how about a game of teeny tiny croquet? A tiny game of croquet needs tiny arches to set up on the course. You can turn wire hangers into wickets, and stick them into grass, dirt, or sand. Then paint a chopstick to use as a tiny stake to mark the end of your teeny-weeny croquet course, and you're all set. To play, just use your thumb and forefinger instead of a mallet, and use a marble as a teeny tiny ball.

PROJECT MADE BY CINDY FAIN

1 Put on those safety goggles!

· · · · · · ·

2 Have an adult use wire cutters to cut off the hanger's hook just below its twisted wire "neck."

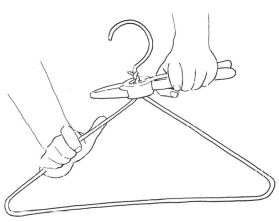

· · · · · · ·

3 Using pliers, start bending the remaining wire into a weird shape near the middle of the hanger, leaving equal amounts of straight hanger on each side, as shown on page 138.

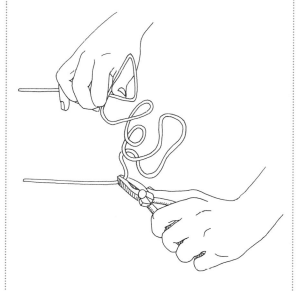

· · · · · · ·

4 Paint your wickets in wild colors (or pattern them with stripes or tiny dots). Let them dry.

· · · · · · ·

5 Decorate the chopsticks with stripes of colored tape or, if you prefer, paint them in rainbow colors.

Anyone for a game? Check out the rules on the next page.

"Where's the next wicket?"

HOW TO PLAY TEENY TINY CROQUET!

To set up your tiny croquet course in the traditional American style, see the illustration below. Six wickets are stuck in the ground as shown, and a stake marks the end of the course.

To play, each player gets a marble as a "ball," then players take turns trying to get their ball through the wickets in the correct order. Only this time, instead of using a mallet, use your thumb and forefinger to shoot the ball along the course. If anyone else's ball gets in the way of your ball, just shoot your ball into theirs and try to knock their ball far off course. The first player to complete the course must then hit the chopstick to win.

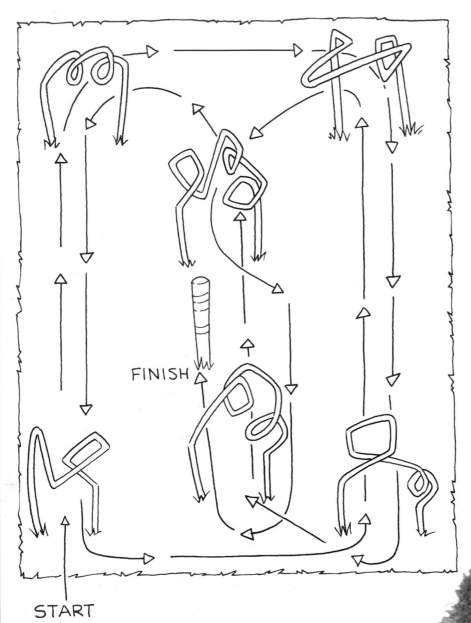

START

FINISH

You can also create your own version of tiny croquet by making as many wacky wickets and chopstick stakes as you like, and then laying them out in your own wild way.

"Be sure you don't have a sticky wicket! Wocka! Wocka!"

CHAPTER 10 / SEWING AND WEAVING BASICS
A Stitch in Time

Fabric is a key component in many of the projects at the Muppet Workshop, and sewing is a very big part of what we do here. Lots of the props and most of the costumes we make are sewn by hand or machine, and sewing is used in Muppet making as well. A part of almost every Muppet has been sewn in some way, whether it's the fur, a soft body, a face, or an outfit. Needless to say, we have some of the busiest needleworkers in the world at the Muppet Workshop.

But there's a lot more to sewing than just Muppet making. Embroidery, beadwork, rug hooking (a kind of stitching, as you'll see), quilting, and appliqué work can produce terrific clothing, quilts, stuffed animals, pillows, rugs, and gifts galore. And these techniques are not only useful for making new things—they can easily be used to spiff up your existing wardrobe or your room. As an added bonus, we're going to teach you how to do some simple weaving so that you can weave place mats out of pretty satin ribbons, or a simple tapestry from wool

"So now you know where all your missing socks are...."

WEE WORK

The tiniest details in Muppet sets are often handmade to fit the tiny scale, like the framed cross-stitch embroidery sampler in this photo of Wee Willie Winkie.

yarn. We'll also show you how to braid a colorful rag rug—the perfect way to use up the scraps in your rag basket.

To get started, you just need fabric, needles, thread, scissors, and pins. Add an iron, ironing board, ruler, tape measure, and pin cushion and your sewing station is complete. All of these projects can be made by hand, or you can use a sewing machine (with the help of an adult) to make the stitches fly!

RIGHT FROM WRONG

Sometimes we refer to the "right," or printed, side of a piece of fabric. This is the side that is clearly and boldly printed, while the "wrong" side is the reverse or back side of the fabric, where the design looks faded.

KEEPING YOU IN STITCHES

There are a few basic stitches you'll have to master before you can make the following projects: the running stitch, the basting stitch, the whipstitch, and the hemming stitch. First, practice threading your needle and knotting your thread. When choosing a thread color, think of the color of the fabric you're sewing, and whether you want the stitches to blend into the background or show up brightly in a contrasting color as a design element. Then try the following stitches on scrap material. Before long, you'll be able to stitch without a hitch.

Running stitch.

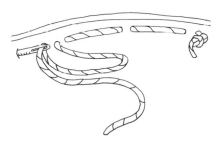

The running stitch is the most basic method of sewing fabric pieces together: Poke the needle up through the back of the fabric and pull through. Poke it back down through the fabric about ¼ inch away from where the needle came up. Now poke it up again, about ³⁄16 inch from where you poked it down. Make sure the spaces between your stitches are even and that each stitch is ¼ inch long. Don't pull the thread too tightly.

Basting stitch.

This stitch is often the first step in constructing anything out of fabric. Usually used as preparation for the final, finer stitching, it simply anchors your fabric pieces together, allowing you to check for proper fit. The stitching method is the same as for the running stitch, but the stitches are about ¾ to 1 inch long.

Whipstitch.

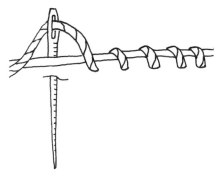

The whipstitch strengthens and finishes the raw edges of your fabric. Poke the needle and thread up through the back side of the fabric about ³⁄16 inch in from the edge. Bring the needle up through the fabric, around the edge of the fabric, and behind again. Continue stitching, keeping the spaces in between your stitches small and even.

Hemming stitch.

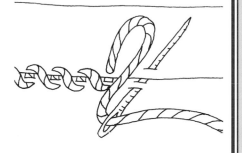

When altering clothing or cleaning up the edges of a project, a hemming stitch helps keep stitches from showing through on the "right" side of the fabric. To hem your projects, fold the raw edge of the fabric under twice (toward the back side of the fabric). The first fold should be ½ inch or so and will hide the raw edge of your fabric; the second fold should be the length you need for your hem, depending on what you're hemming. Stitch down through the folds and pick up a few threads of the *outside* fabric with your threaded needle. Then poke the needle back up through the turned-over edge of your hem and pull through.

Terrific Ties

How easy is it?

What You Will Need:

- Bear Essentials
- old ties
- 2 or 3 sheets of white paper
- chalk
- needle and thread
- beads or buttons of any shape or size
- trim such as rickrack or ribbon

These fabulous ties are covered in beadwork, a very specialized fabric-decorating technique that was invented hundreds of years ago. All over the globe, beadworkers can be found sewing beads onto fabric, often in very complex designs and patterns. Some of the world's most talented beadworkers create one-of-a-kind beaded items like dresses or purses that sell for tens of thousands of dollars and may take years to make. On the other end of the spectrum, our easy-to-make ties will take you very little time to create—even if they don't sell for as much!

We used wooden animal beads, plastic ladybug beads, painted beads, and rickrack to create the wacky ties you see here. It doesn't matter what kind of tie you choose to bead—just be sure nobody wants to wear it as is.

PROJECT MADE BY BARBARA DAVIS

1 To decide on your design, trace a few outlines of the larger end of the tie onto a sheet of paper. Then sketch out different ideas for beadwork designs. Or sketch out your design directly on the tie—very lightly—with pencil or chalk . . . or just do a freehand design, adding beads as you go. If you like our ties, use the photographs as models.

•••••••

2 To sew on each bead, thread the needle and knot the thread at the end. Insert the needle into the underside of the tie and pull it through to the top side. Next, thread a bead onto your needle and push it down the string. Now, poke the needle back down through the tie, in a spot just next to the bead. Pull the thread so that your bead sits on the tie's surface, but don't pull too tightly. To speed the beading process, you may add two or three beads at a time to your thread.

3 Cut and sew on rickrack or ribbon using a running stitch (see page 143 for stitch information) through the center or along both edges of the ribbon (depending on the width of the ribbon).

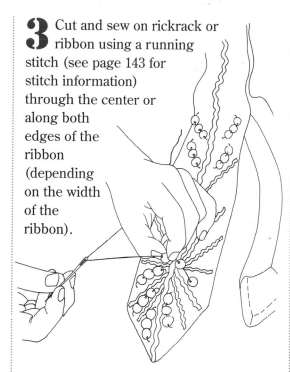

•••••••

4 Repeat steps 2 and 3, following your design until your tie's pattern is completed.

BEAD SMART

Make sure you don't sew beads onto the underside of the tie or the parts of the tie that get knotted or touch the wearer's neck. If you do, your tie will be very hard to tie—and uncomfortable to wear!

BEAD-DAZZLING

At the Muppet Workshop, our expert sewing team is often asked to make complicated beaded accessories as props. Take a look at Miss Piggy's glamorous headpiece in this picture to see what can be done with a lot of beads and a lot of patience.

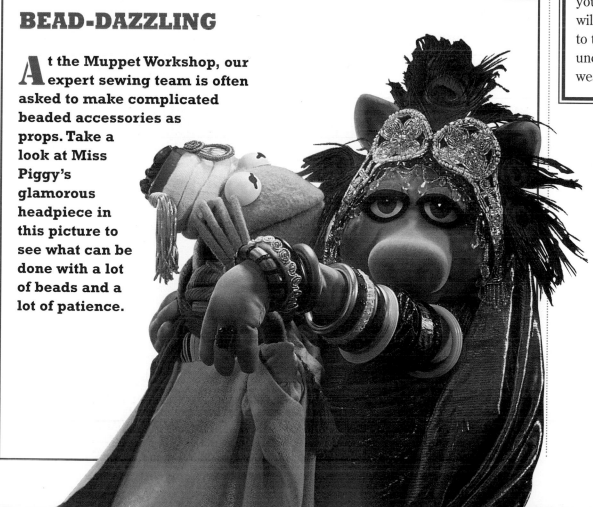

Stuffed Creature

How easy is it?

What You Will Need:

- Bear Essentials
- tracing paper
- straight pins
- old terry cloth towel
- yarn and needle with larger eye for yarn
- needle and thread to match terry cloth
- three buttons (for eyes and nose)
- fiberfill, small pieces of old rags, or small dried beans (for stuffing)

This cute, hand-sewn stuffed creature can be made from an old terry cloth towel, a couple of buttons, and some bright bits of yarn. Once you see how easy it is to make a stuffed creature, you'll want to play around with other designs (how about a cat? a bunny? a hippopotamus?) and fabrics (try green fake fur, soft fleece, or flannel). These little creatures make great stocking stuffers.

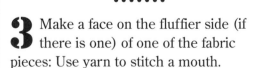

1 Trace our pattern (on page 305) onto tracing paper and cut out along the outline, or make a pattern of your own. You can enlarge our pattern to any size you wish (see pages 8 and 9 for tracing and enlarging instructions).

2 Pin your pattern to the towel and cut the shape out of the towel. Repeat to create a second identical cutout.

3 Make a face on the fluffier side (if there is one) of one of the fabric pieces: Use yarn to stitch a mouth.

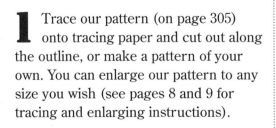

PROJECT MADE BY CHERYL HENSON

Sew on button eyes and nose. Dress your creature up if you want. Give it a bow tie or sew buttons down its front.

· · · · · · · ·

4 Pin the two body shapes together along the edges; the fluffier sides of the fabric (if there are any) should face each other. (The face you sewed on will be facing the inside.) Use a running stitch (see page 143 for stitch information), to sew a seam ¼ inch in from the outside edge around the whole shape, leaving a 3-inch section open on one side of the torso.

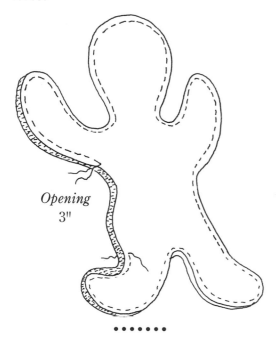

Opening 3"

· · · · · · · ·

5 Turn the creature right-side out by pushing it through the 3-inch opening, and gently push out all the arms and legs with the eraser end of a pencil. Stuff the creature with fiberfill, old rags, or small dried beans.

6 Turn the edges of the 3-inch opening to the inside and pin shut. Use a whipstitch (see page 143 for stitch information) to close up the opening.

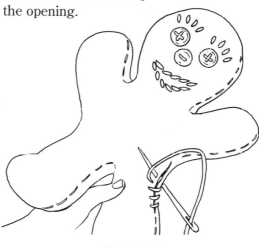

· · · · · · · ·

7 For strands of hair, thread yarn through needle and sew once through the seam at the top of the head. Cut yarn to end

strand and knot it as close to the seam as possible. Repeat until you have as many strands of hair as you like. Stitch thread across the center of the creature's head to make a part.

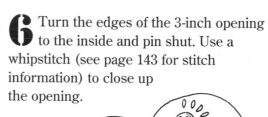

"Hey, who's calling who stuffed??"

Cuddly Quilt

How easy is it?

What You Will Need:

- an adult (to help with the iron and the sewing machine, if you use one)
- Bear Essentials
- piece of cardboard (6" × 6" square)
- fabric (for quilt squares)—2 different colors or designs, 1½ yards × 1 yard of each
- straight pins
- needle and thread (or sewing machine)
- iron
- patterned fabric (for quilt "backing") 1 square yard
- batting (for inside the quilt), 1 square yard
- yarn and needle with larger eye for yarn
- bias trim

Quilting is the art of piecing together scraps of fabric into decorative patterns and sewing the pieces together with a needle and thread (sewing machines can be used to speed up the quilt-making process). For warmth, quilters add layers of padding known as "batting" and stitch all the layers together in plain or fancy patterns.

People all over the world—from Asia to America—have been making quilts for centuries. Oftentimes, quilters form quilting circles and work on large quilts at gatherings known as quilting bees. Quilting bees are a good example of the expression "many hands make light work," since complicated, oversize quilts can be finished quickly with so many people working on them at once. Quilting bees are also a good way for friends to get together.

PROJECT MADE BY STEPHEN ROTONDARO

148

Note: *If you're using a printed fabric with a design that must be featured in the center of each square, you will probably need at least two yards of your chosen fabric to accomplish this. Then, in step 1, you should center your cardboard square over the part of the design that you want to appear in the square's center, and trace the cardboard square accordingly.*

. . . .

1 Place your 6 × 6-inch cardboard square at the corner of one of the yards of fabric. Trace the square twenty-five times to create cut lines for twenty-five squares, then cut them out.

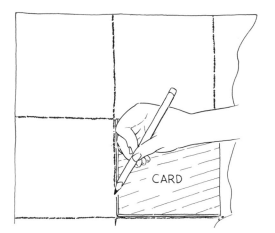

CARD

2 Repeat step 1 for your second kind of fabric, but this time, trace and cut out only twenty-four squares. Now you should have a total of forty-nine 6-inch squares.

. . . .

3 Once all of your pieces are cut, lay them out on the floor or tabletop. To achieve a true patchwork effect, make sure that each color alternates within each row and that alternate colors start each row.

"A quilt is the ultimate recycling project!"

IMPORTANT INFORMATION FOR MAKING THIS QUILT

Making even a simple quilt requires quite a bit of planning, measuring, and cutting. But once you learn the basics, you'll be able to design quilts of your own using more kinds of fabric and all sorts of interesting patterns.

● The overall size of this "starter" patchwork quilt will be 35 inches by 35 inches. You may use it as a wall hanging or as a quilt for a doll or stuffed animal. Each patchwork square will be

6 inches by 6 inches before sewing (your seams will be ½-inch wide, so the squares will appear to be 5 inches by 5 inches once sewn).

● This quilt uses only two different fabrics, and you'll be making rows of squares that alternate colors, just like the rows in our quilt. For instance, you might start a row with a blue square, then add a white square, then a blue, and so on. On the next row, you'd start with white,

then add a blue, then a white, and so on.

● Each row of your quilt will be seven squares long. (So, 7 times 5 inches equals 35 inches—the length of each side of the quilt.) Overall, the quilt will be seven squares by seven squares. If you do some more multiplication, you'll see that that means there will be forty-nine squares in the quilt—twenty-four squares of one fabric, and twenty-five of the other.

STATUS QUILT

This quilt's central design or "motif" has a Kermit face on it. The alternating rows of color boxes are easily made once you learn the basic methods of quilting. When you feel you're ready, try a design like this one, using our photograph as a guide. You can choose to use any picture or design you like for the center square. Or you can appliqué your own picture onto your central square before you start sewing your quilt together.

4 To begin sewing the quilt rows:

● Place the printed sides of two squares (**A** and **B**) together and pin one edge together. Sew a seam on that edge using a running stitch ½ inch in from the edge (see page 143 for stitch information). Open flat.

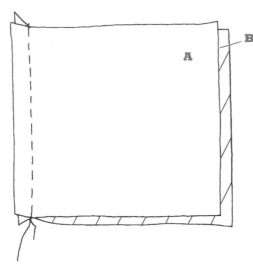

● Next, sew square **C** to the opposite edge of square **B,** then continue to sew on each of the remaining four squares in the same fashion to finish the row.

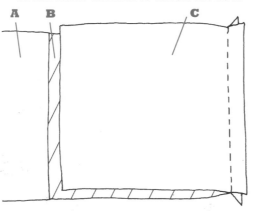

● Repeat these steps until you have completed seven rows with seven squares in each.

● ● ● ● ● ● ●

5 Ask an adult to help you iron open each of your squares' seams. This will help your quilt lie flat.

6 To begin sewing the seven rows together:

● Take two rows and lay one row directly on top of another, printed sides together. Match up the corners and press flat. Pin together along the long edge and sew together as shown, using a running stitch ½ inch in from the edge.

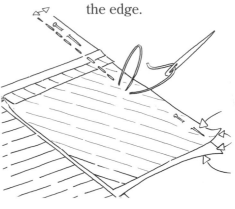

● Open the two attached rows and lay a third row atop one of them, printed sides together. Match up the open edges, pin, and sew together as in the previous step.

● Repeat until all the rows are sewn together to form the 35 × 35-inch quilt front. Ask an adult to help you iron all seams open to help the quilt front to lie flat.

● ● ● ● ● ● ●

7 For the back of your quilt, trim your yard of backing fabric to 35 inches × 35 inches. Then cut out a 36 × 36-inch square of the batting for the in-between layer (slightly larger than the quilt).

● ● ● ● ● ● ●

8 Lay the quilt's backing with the printed side down, then lay the batting flat on top of it. Lay the top of your quilt out flat on top, with the printed side facing up. Sew basting stitches through all three layers (backing, batting,

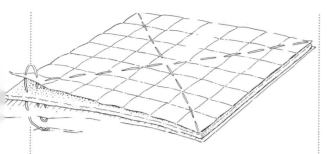

and top) in a giant "X" to hold the layers in place.

. . . .

9 To attach the three layers, use a needle and yarn to sew knots at each corner of each square. Start with the center square and work outward as you go. Tie off each length of yarn in a double knot and trim.

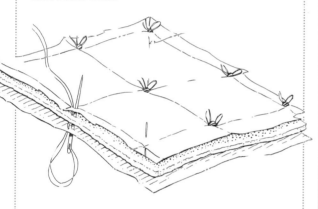

. . . .

10 Trim the excess batting so it's even with the quilt's edges. Finish the quilt by sewing the bias trim down each side (follow the directions on the package).

FRIENDSHIP QUILTS

Throughout history, people have made quilts with special patterns or designs that symbolize events, places, or emotions. Sometimes the folks at the Muppet Workshop make quilts for their own enjoyment, or as gifts for special occasions. The quilt directly below was made to welcome a baby adopted from China by a Henson employee.

The one at the bottom was created as a group effort by the people in the Workshop in memory of Richard Hunt, a Muppet puppeteer. Many of the quilt's squares show the characters he made famous.

Awesome Appliqués

How easy is it?

Appliqués (*ap-lee-KAYs*) are three-dimensional fabric pictures that are made by cutting shapes out of fabric and sewing or gluing them on top of each other. The finished appliqué is then sewn (appliquéd) directly onto an item of clothing, a quilt, a pillow, a tote bag, or anything made of fabric!

In this appliqué project, the Kermit design is made up of simple felt shapes layered on top of each other. Starting from the bottom, each layer is stitched in place until the Kermit face is complete. Then the face is appliquéd onto the vest. You can sew simple appliqués of Kermit's feet onto the front of your vest, too. Or try making your own design. Then look around for things to sew your appliqué to, like the back of a denim jacket, a canvas bag, or a backpack. Go appli-crazy!

APPLIED TO A TIE

If you'd like to make a tie to complete your Kermit-y outfit, find an old tie and sew on an appliqué.

1 Decide where you'd like the appliqué to appear and keep in mind that the design will have to fit in that spot. Trace our appliqué pattern (on page 306) and enlarge it to the desired size (see pages 8 and 9 for tracing and enlarging instructions), or design your own pattern. Cut each pattern piece out of the tracing paper.

· · · · · · · ·

2 Pin each pattern piece onto the appropriately colored felt and cut the pieces of felt out along the edges of each tracing paper pattern piece. Re-pin the foot pattern and cut out as many extra feet as you like.

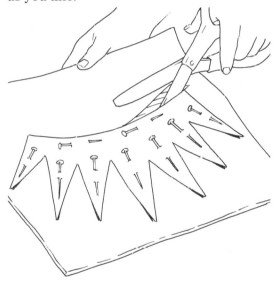

· · · · · · ·

3 On Kermit's face, use black marker to draw in his dimple and chin line. On Kermit's pink tongue, use red or dark pink marker to draw in the line down the middle of his tongue.

· · · · · · ·

4 Build up your design, sewing each layer in place using a running stitch (see page 143 for stitch information) along the edges of each layer. (If you are using iron-on fabric adhesive instead of sewing the appliqué, grab an adult and follow the directions on the package label.)

ADVANCED APPLIQUÉ

Check out this amazing vest showing the fabulous Dr. Teeth dressed to the nines! You can get ideas for your own appliqués by looking at all the details on this one. Notice the fancy feathers added to his hat, the fringe on his jacket, and the furry orange hair, not to mention his gold lamé tooth. He's even wearing beads that spell out his name!

"Appliques are groovy, man!"

· · · · · · ·

5 Take the finished appliqué and the Kermit feet, place in position on your vest, and sew on with a running stitch.

Pets' Holiday Stockings

How easy is it?

What You Will Need:

- pencil
- tracing paper
- scissors (and pinking shears, if you have them)
- straight pins
- white felt (about ¼ yard)
- green felt (about ¼ yard)
- purple and red felt (for salamander; 8½" × 11" sheet of each)
- hole puncher
- needle and different-colored threads
- white glue or iron-on fabric adhesive (optional)
- black felt or marker (for eyes)
- colorful rickrack (for salamander's back)

These colorful stockings are for hanging on the mantelpiece at holiday time or holding presents for your favorite pet on his or her birthday; just stuff them with catnip mice or doggie treats or whatever your pet fancies.

The following instructions are for the "Salamander Stocking," but you can copy the other stocking from our photograph or dream up a design of your very own. Just use the same basic cutting, sewing, and simple appliqué techniques shown here.

PROJECT MADE BY BARBARA DAVIS

1 To make the front of the salamander stocking, trace the stocking pattern on page 307 onto tracing paper and enlarge it if you like (see pages 8 and 9 for tracing and enlarging instructions). Cut out the pattern and pin onto the white felt. Cut out the stocking shape.

· · · · · · · ·

2 To make the back of the stocking, place the pattern for the stocking front onto the green felt. Trace an outline about ¼ inch outside the edge of the pattern piece and cut out carefully (or use pinking shears to create zigzag edges).

· · · · · · · ·

3 To make the purple salamander, trace the salamander pattern on page 308 and enlarge it if you wish. Cut out the pattern and pin on to the purple felt. Cut the salamander shape out of felt.

· · · · · · · ·

4 Use a hole puncher to punch out tiny circles of red felt, then sew or glue them onto the salamander's back. Use scissors to cut out white felt circles and black felt circles for eyeballs and pupils. Sew them in place. (Or just draw the pupils on the white eyeballs with black marker.) Now, sew the rickrack down the salamander's back using a running stitch (see page 143 for stitch information).

· · · · · · · ·

5 Place the decorated salamander at the center of the white stocking front and sew in place, using a running stitch around its outside edge.

6 Lay the white front piece directly on top of the green bottom piece (there should be a green edge showing evenly all the way around) and smooth away wrinkles. Sew the two pieces together using a running stitch.

· · · · · · · ·

7 Cut a piece of white felt 6 inches × 2 inches to be a cloth loop for hanging. If you'd like it to have a backing like ours, cut out a piece of green felt (6½ inches × 3 inches) with pinking shears, and sew the white felt to the green felt with a running stitch along each edge. Fold the loop in half and sew the front edge to the inside front of the stocking and the back edge to the inside back of the stocking.

Now hang the stocking on your mantelpiece—and fill 'er up!

"Pour moi?"

STOCKING SHORTCUT

If you're not in the mood to sew, just use white glue (or ask an adult to iron on the iron-on fabric adhesive) in the same spots where sewing is required!

Rag Rug

How easy is it?

Do you have lots of old cloth scraps you don't use or old clothes you don't wear anymore? Then turn them into a rag rug! Making a rag rug is the ultimate recycling project. If you have basic sewing skills and can make a braid, you can make a rag rug. This project involves cutting up fabric into long, narrow strips, braiding them, and then sewing the extra-long braid into a large spiral. You can use any kind of cloth in any color or pattern, but we used brightly colored polar fleece (another recycled product!) because it is soft and very easy to sew.

You can use this technique to make pot holders, seat covers, place mats, or even a tiny rug for a dollhouse.

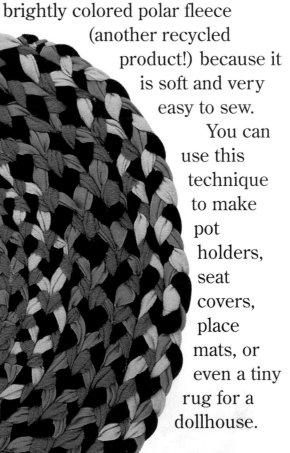

PROJECT MADE BY MARY MAGUIRE

1 Using at least three different-colored fabrics, measure and cut 2-inch-wide strips of each material that are as long as possible. If you want to make the rug more quickly, make the braiding strips even wider.

· · · · · ·

2 Use a running stitch (see page 143 for stitch information) to neatly sew three strips together at one end (as shown to the right) and begin to braid. As the braid grows, tie the sewn end of the braid to a sturdy chair or door-knob so you can braid evenly and firmly.

· · · · · · ·

3 Each time you get to the end of an individual strip, just sew a new fabric strip to the end of the previous strip. Simply fold the new strip around the end of the previous strip and sew two rows of stitching to hold in place. This way, you may continue braiding as long as you like. Trim the rough ends (if necessary) or tuck them into your braid as you go along.

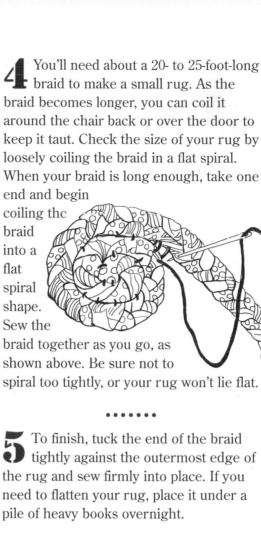

4 You'll need about a 20- to 25-foot-long braid to make a small rug. As the braid becomes longer, you can coil it around the chair back or over the door to keep it taut. Check the size of your rug by loosely coiling the braid in a flat spiral. When your braid is long enough, take one end and begin coiling the braid into a flat spiral shape. Sew the braid together as you go, as shown above. Be sure not to spiral too tightly, or your rug won't lie flat.

· · · · · · ·

5 To finish, tuck the end of the braid tightly against the outermost edge of the rug and sew firmly into place. If you need to flatten your rug, place it under a pile of heavy books overnight.

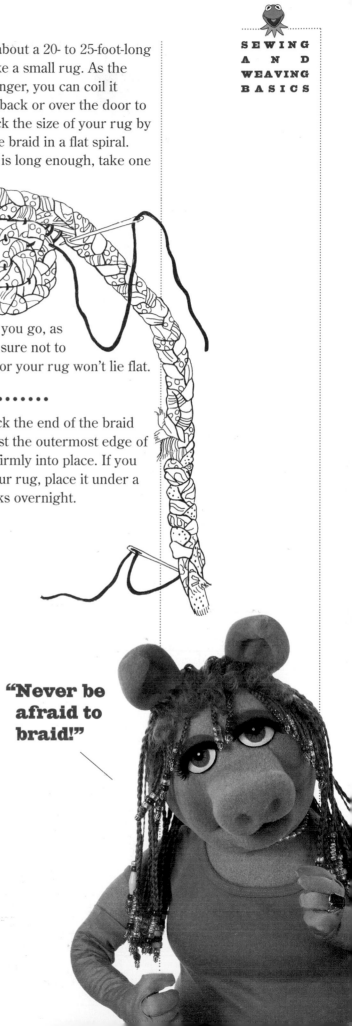

"Never be afraid to braid!"

Loop-de-Loop Hooked Rug Wall Hanging

How easy is it?

- Bear Essentials
- rug-hooking canvas (at least 12" × 12" for this project)
- masking tape
- tracing paper
- colored yarns (precut rug-hooking yarns are best): deep orange, black, white, red, pink, yellow, pea green, baby blue
- rug hook (see opposite)
- heavy-duty thread and needle
- thin wooden dowel, about 16" long
- 2' to 3' ribbon (for hanging; optional)

Rug hooking is a craft technique that has been used for centuries to create rugs and tapestries. The basic procedure is to pull short lengths of yarn through an open-weave canvas using a tool known as a rug hook. Although there are a wide variety of materials and methods that can be used in rug hooking, the technique for this project is a simple one called latch hooking, and the materials are common yarn and a basic rug-hooking canvas.

Once you learn how easy rug hooking is, you can make all sorts of things.

PROJECT MADE BY ED CHRISTIE

1 Cut the canvas to 12 inches × 12 inches. Tape masking tape around the edges to keep your canvas from fraying.

• • • • • • •

2 Trace and enlarge the Scooter pattern on page 309 (see pages 8 and 9 for tracing and enlarging instructions). Center the Scooter pattern under the canvas and trace it onto the canvas with a black marker, leaving a 1½-inch border of plain canvas all around the edge of your picture.

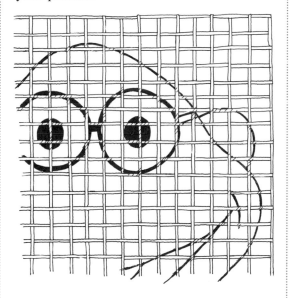

• • • • • • •

3 Cut all yarn into 3-inch pieces if it's not precut. You are now prepared to "latch."

• Choose an area toward the center of the canvas where you would like to begin hooking. (You should always start in the center and work outward, because it's easier to follow the pattern that way.) You will be working with the "right" side of the canvas (the part that you drew your design onto) face up. Pick the color yarn that matches the chosen area (refer to the photograph of our Scooter wall hanging) and begin by folding the yarn evenly in half. Insert the hook through the loop in the yarn so that the yarn is just below the open latch. Hold on to the ends of the yarn with your free hand, pulling them out

and slightly up, as shown below. Weave the hook down through one square of the canvas and back up through the square directly above it.

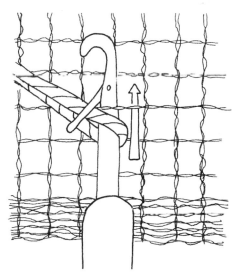

• Pull the yarn ends around to the right side of the hook, catching the yarn on the hook.

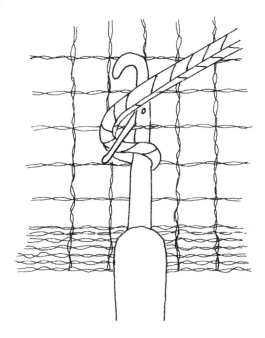

• While tightly holding on to the two yarn ends, slowly pull the hook down toward the bottom edge of the canvas, closing the latch over the yarn. (It helps to keep the handle down low, parallel to the canvas.) Pull the hook back down through the top square and up out of the bottom square, with the "head" of the hook being pulled out

Rug hook

through the loop created by the piece of yarn. Pull the yarn ends back out and up through the yarn loop, too.

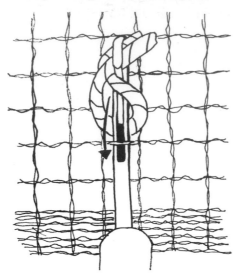

● Remove the hook completely from the canvas to form the knot in the yarn.

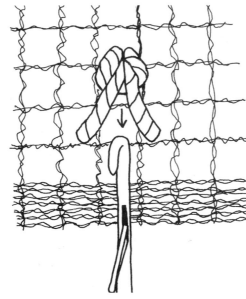

● Give the yarn ends a tug to set.

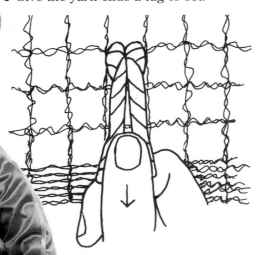

"I'm hooked!"

● Make your stitches side by side to fill in your design. Try not to skip around to different spots, as this will cause ridges and gaps.

· · · · · · ·

4 When you have finished hooking the entire design, remove the tape from the canvas edges and turn the edges under to make a 1½-inch hem all around. Sew the hem to the back side of the canvas with a whipstitch (see page 143 for stitch information). Finish the wall hanging by trimming any wayward yarns on the rug surface to make it even and smooth.

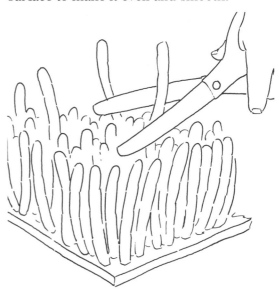

· · · · · · ·

5 To mount as a wall hanging, sew a thin wooden dowel to the top edge of your rug. Take a piece of ribbon or yarn and tie it to each end of the dowel, then hang the rug on the wall.

Now try this with your own design!

Ribbon Place Mat

How easy is it?

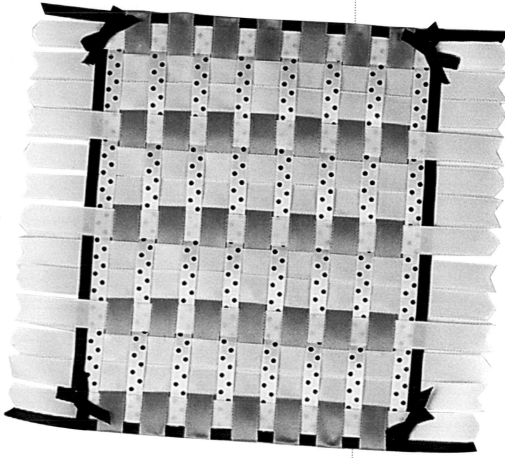

Weaving is a very basic process in which string, yarn, or thread is interlaced to create a sheet of fabric. Some weavings are designed plainly and made from simple materials like cotton. Others may be woven with the finest materials, like silk or cashmere, in intricate patterns that can take years to create.

Weaving is usually done on structures known as looms. In the olden days, people wove fabrics by hand on wooden looms. Today, big factories weave large quantities of fabric on huge, computer-operated looms. Looms have frames that hold a series of vertical strings (known as the warp) stretched in a row, parallel to each other. The weaver (or machine!) then interlaces horizontal strings (known as the weft) across the warp.

This place mat project will teach you the basics of weaving using ribbons and a simple weaving technique. If you don't have ribbons, but do have pretty fabric, you can make your own ribbons by cutting the cloth into long, narrow strips.

PROJECT MADE BY CHRISTINE MOYES

What You Will Need:

- an adult (for iron)
- Bear Essentials
- ribbons or fabric strips
- a piece of cardboard about 12" tall × 18" wide (for a "loom")
- masking tape
- bows, lacy trim, fringe (optional)
- Iron (for adult use only)

WARPED ADVICE

When you choose the ribbons or strips of material for your weaving, choose colorful and fun ones. Try picking ribbons of different widths as well, to make a more interesting pattern. Experiment with colors, widths, and patterns and see how changing them can add spice to your weaving.

Reminder:

Warp

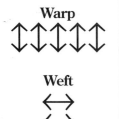

Weft

1 Cut the warp (vertical) ribbons into 14-inch-long strips and lay them side by side on the cardboard; the number of warp ribbons will vary depending on their width, but they should touch each other at the edges and cover the entire piece of cardboard, from left to right. If you have many kinds of

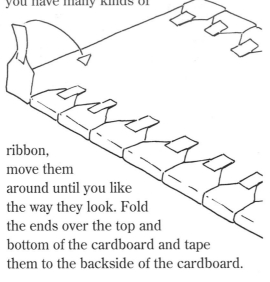

ribbon, move them around until you like the way they look. Fold the ends over the top and bottom of the cardboard and tape them to the backside of the cardboard.

·······

2 Cut your weft (horizontal) ribbons into 20-inch-long strips and clip each ribbon end to a point (pointy ribbons are easier to weave).

3 Starting at the top-left corner, weave your first weft ribbon across the warp ribbons by going *under* one warp ribbon and *over* the next one, under and over, one ribbon at a time, weaving all the way across until you reach the end of the row. Your ribbon ends should stick out about 1 inch on either side of the cardboard.

········

4 Your second weft ribbon will be the second row. Again, begin at the left, just below your first row. Only this time, begin by weaving *over* the first warp ribbon and *under* the next, continuing on until you reach the end of the row. This reversing of the "over" and "under" is what holds your woven place mat together.

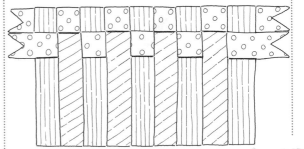

RIBBON ROUND AND ROUND

Ribbon can be used in many ways other than weaving. It can be wound around almost any form to create interesting looks, as it is in this Egyptian headdress made especially for Miss Piggy as Cleopigtra. Check out the other special details in this outfit, like the bracelet and beaded dress collar.

5 Nudge the second weft row snugly up against the first weft row so that the ribbons' edges are touching. Repeat this step as you finish each row. If you find that your ribbons are slipping, glue the weft ribbons onto the warp ribbons using a tiny dot of glue, every few ribbons.

· · · · · · ·

6 When you reach the bottom of the weaving, untape the lengthwise ribbons and trim off stray threads, if necessary. You can also cut V's into the ends of the warp ribbons for a decorative finish. If you prefer a more formal look, you may hem the edges of your weaving by having an adult

press either the warp or the weft ribbons, or both, to the back side with an iron. Then put a tiny dot of glue onto the back of each folded piece of ribbon and press flat. Let dry.

· · · · · · ·

7 At this stage, you can add bows, lacy trim, or fringe by sewing or gluing them into place on the place mat.

If you liked this project, think about making a whole set of place mats—one for everyone in your family—or make a set as a gift for a friend or relative.

EXTRA CREDIT

Some of the Muppet builders like to weave in their spare time, and they've created many useful and beautiful weavings; this table runner is just one of many. To create the slightly more complicated weave shown in our table runner, you'll need a piece of cardboard that's longer than the length of your table by about 2 feet, plus lots of ribbons or fabric strips in varying widths and designs.

● Following the same technique described in the place mat directions, prepare your warp.

● When you begin to weave your weft ribbons, start the first ribbon by going over *two* warp ribbons, then under *two*, then over *two*. On the next row, start by going under *two* warp ribbons, then over *two*, then under *two*, and so on. Or vary the pattern by going over *two*, then under *one*, then over *two*, and so on. Whatever you do, the weaving will look best if you follow the same pattern for at least a few weft rows, varying the width and design of the weft ribbons in a repeating pattern as well.

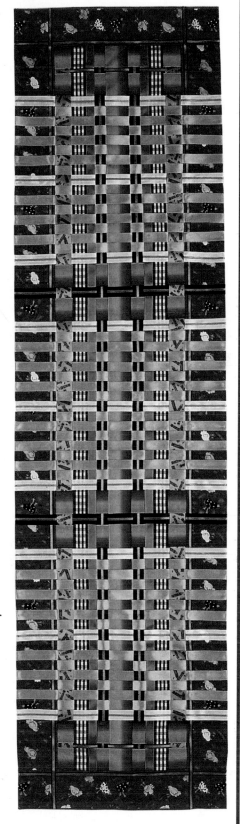

Beaker Tapestry

How easy is it?

- Bear Essentials
- corrugated cardboard (about 14" × 6")
- string (for the warp)
- clear tape
- tapestry needle (which has a nice, large eye for yarn)
- yarn— black, white, light orange, dark orange, peach, green
- two 7" lengths of ³⁄₁₆" dowel

Have you ever seen a woven rug with a picture or pattern in it? That's a kind of tapestry. Tapestries are fancy weavings created on looms with pictures or patterns "drawn" into them using cotton, wool, or silk threads or yarn. (To learn more about weaving, see page 161.) A few of the Muppet builders like to weave tapestries in their spare time, and their creations may occasionally make it onto the set of a Muppet production as props or decoration.

This Beaker tapestry begins with a drawing sketched directly onto a simple handmade loom of corrugated cardboard. Practice with your cardboard loom to get the hang of using it. When you feel comfortable with the way it works, get ready to tackle any project, large or small— make a rug, a wall hanging, whatever you like. Weavings take a while to finish, but they're easy to set aside then pick up whenever you have a little free time.

PROJECT MADE BY ELENA PELLICCIARO

To Make Your Cardboard Loom:

1 Measure and draw a rectangle on your cardboard 12½ inches long × 4¼ inches wide. Then draw another rectangle ½ inch outside the first rectangle (on all sides) and cut out the cardboard along this outside rectangle.

• • • • • • •

2 Trace our Beaker pattern on page 310 onto the cardboard (see page 9 for tracing instructions).

• • • • • • •

3 Using a pencil and a ruler, make a mark every ³⁄₁₆ inch across the top and bottom edges (the shorter sides) of the cardboard, as shown below. At each mark, cut ½-inch slits straight into the

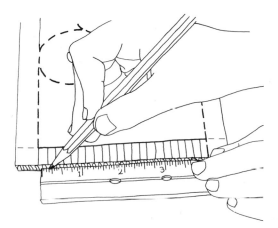

cardboard's edge, as shown below. The slits should just touch the edge of your design. These slits (approximately twenty-two of them) will hold the vertical (up and down) strings, or "warp," that will be the base of your weaving.

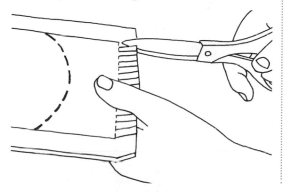

To String Your Loom:

• Take the loose end of the string and insert it into the top left-hand slot from back to front, leaving a string "tail" of about 4 inches in the back. Tape the tail to the back of the loom so it won't slip. Bring the string straight down over your design drawing and slip the string through the first bottom left-hand slot.

• Loop the string behind and around the next "tooth" of the lower edge of the loom, bringing it to the front through the next slit. Run the string back up to the top of the loom, and thread it

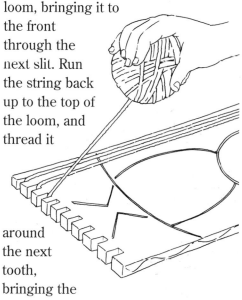

around the next tooth, bringing the string back to the front through the next slit; then run the string back down again. Make sure to pull the string tightly as you go.

WEAVING LINGO

The warp strings are the vertical (up and down) strings, and the weft strings are the horizontal (side to side) strings in a weaving. See page 161 for a complete explanation of weaving.

"Meep-meep-meeeeep!"

● Continue threading until all the slots are filled with string. Cut the string leaving a 4-inch tail. Tape the tail end to the back of the cardboard loom to secure the "warp."

To Practice Your Weaving:

1 Thread a tapestry needle with a strand of yarn about 24 inches long. Beginning at the bottom left of your newly strung loom and leaving a tail of yarn about 4 inches long at the end, insert the needle under the first warp string, then over the second warp string, under the third, over the fourth, etc., until you reach the end of the row.

2 Turn your needle around and go back through the strings in the opposite direction, only this time go over the strings you went under, and under the ones you went over. (These horizontal yarn strands are the "weft.")

3 Weave about five rows to get the hang of it, then remove the strings carefully with your fingers to prepare the loom for the Beaker tapestry.

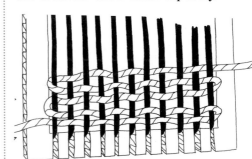

"Here's some wefty advice."

TAPESTRY HINTS

● When starting a new piece of yarn at the left-most or right-most warp string, paper clip the 4-inch tail to the cardboard's edge or tape it to the back of the cardboard to hold it tightly in place and to prevent it from being pulled along with the yarn as you weave.

● Be careful that you don't pull the weft yarn too tightly when you weave, especially when going around the outermost warp strings, or it will pull too tightly on the warp strings and you'll end up with an hourglass-shaped tapestry.

● Whenever you have about 4 inches of yarn left, pull the yarn through to the back of the tapestry, tucking it between the warp strings and the cardboard. Remove the needle and insert a new length of yarn onto the needle. On the back side of the weaving, between the warp and the cardboard, tie the 4-inch tail end of the new piece of yarn to the 4-inch length of the old piece of yarn, as close to the weaving as possible; let the ends dangle for now. Begin weaving again where you left off, continuing across in the same direction.

● It's generally easier to fill in sections in the center of a design, and then weave around them later. For instance, it's easier to start with Beaker's pupils, then weave the whites of his eyes in around the pupils afterward. Otherwise, you have to leave an open space to fill in later, which is difficult.

● As weft rows build up, make sure to push them snugly together to create a tight, dense weaving.

To Weave Beaker:

1 Begin with Beaker's pupils, one at a time. Using a short length of black yarn—about 8 or 10 inches—start at the bottom of the pupil (remember to leave a 4-inch tail at the end of the yarn, tucked between the warp and the cardboard). With your drawing as a guide, weave across the warp strings at the bottom edge of the pupil, keeping in mind the under-and-over technique you learned during the practice weaving session. Because the pupils are tiny, the yarn will only be woven through three or four warp strings at most. Because the pupil is a circle, the middle weft rows may go across more warp strings than the top or bottom weft rows. It is important to begin and end each row as close to your outline as possible. When you finish, leave a 4-inch length of yarn loose on the end, and tuck it between the warp and the cardboard, with the 4-inch tail from the other end of that piece of yarn.

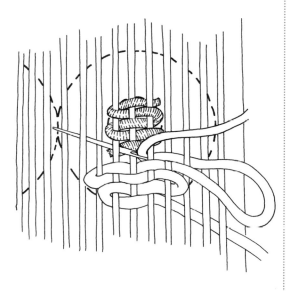

2 For the whites of Beaker's eyes, use white yarn and weave it to fill in around the pupils, following the technique in the previous step. Then use light orange yarn for the nose. Weave using the same technique used for the eyes.

3 Weave the face in peach-colored yarn. The mouth will be embroidered on later.

4 Weave the black tie in the middle of the "shirt," then weave the shirt in two sections (left and right) using the green yarn.

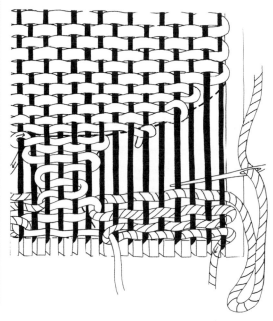

5 Lightly draw the mouth with pencil. Embroider it on with black yarn using the "chain stitch," as shown below.

6 The dark orange hair is done a little differently. Begin the first row of hair by tying the yarn to a warp string at the top left corner leaving a 4-inch tail (this tail is Beaker's first strand of hair). Weave across three or four warp strings and tie a knot into the next warp string. Cut the yarn, leaving another 4-inch tail. Every inch or so, cut the yarn and leave a tail to create strands of hair. Continue across the whole top row. Turn the corner when you get to the edge, and continue weaving and cutting all the way down and around the eye areas. Then weave back again, filling in the empty warp strings to give him a full head of hair.

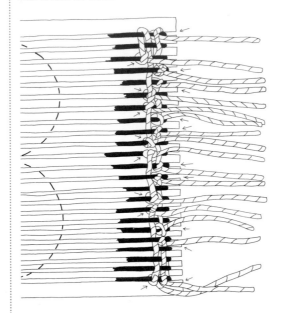

"Meep, meep, meep."

To keep Beaker's hair in the "up" position, just dab a little white glue here and there between layers of the hair. Brush the layers up and let dry.

7 To finish the tapestry, pull any loose ends through to the back (use a needle if necessary). Tuck all loose threads through other woven strands on the back side of the tapestry, as shown on right.

8 Very carefully remove the weaving from the loom by bending the teeth of the loom. Insert the dowels through the loops at the top and bottom of the weaving. To make a hanger, braid a few strands of yarn together and tie to the ends of the top dowel.

CHAPTER 11 / DIPPING AND DYEING

Kooky Colors

Often, the first thing we do at the Muppet Workshop—before we make any of the Muppets, costumes, or props for our TV shows, movies, or photo shoots—is dye our materials. If a character needs fur of a certain brownish-orange color; if Miss Piggy needs the perfect pair of lavender gloves; if a blanket needs to be a particular shade of green in a movie scene, we mix up batches of dye and go to work dipping and dyeing. All of this fabric coloring is done at the Muppet Workshop in a special room that's used just for dipping, dyeing, and drip-drying cloth. The room is full of big sinks, drying racks, and rows and rows of jars of colorful dyes.

Whenever a dyer mixes a dye, a fabric swatch is dipped in it and hung to dry. Because fabric looks much darker when it's wet, the dyer waits until the fabric is dry to see the true color. When the color is just right, the master color recipe is recorded for future use (alongside a snippet of the dyed fabric swatch).

In this section, we'll teach you how to use fabric-dyeing techniques to create tie-dyes, ombré, and batiks. You'll also find out how to use other dipping and dyeing techniques to make mosaics out of eggshells and beautiful, marbleized paper out of plain, ordinary stationery.

There are many different kinds of dyes you can use—some of which you can actually make yourself. Throughout the ages, people have made their own dyes from natural ingredients like fruits, tree bark, seeds,

"These projects are to dye for!"

169

DIPPING, DYEING, AND DRIP-DRYING

● **Always** get an adult's permission to begin a dyeing project.

● **Always** wear rubber gloves so that you don't dye your skin.

● **Always** carry newly dyed wet fabric in a container to keep it from dripping and staining other surfaces.

● Think about how colors mix: If you dye something entirely yellow and then dip it in blue dye, you will have green fabric.

● Think about dyeing fabric in sections: Hang different parts of it in different dye buckets at the same time.

● **Remember this:** You can always dye fabric a darker color, but you can never dye it lighter.

● The longer an item stays in the dye, the darker it will become. A quick dip will give fabric a lighter color; a longer soak will give it a darker color.

● The color of wet, dyed fabric is usually twice as dark as the color of dry, dyed fabric. If you don't like the color while the fabric's wet, wait a while . . . it'll change!

● Cold water helps to "set" the color into the fabric. After you put your

fabric in a warm dye bath, rinse with clear cold water.

● When hanging your dyed fabric to dry, make sure you put an old towel or plastic sheet beneath the dyed item to avoid staining your floor, rug, or bathtub.

"Be sure to wear old clothes and work in an area that will be easy to clean up!"

roots, and spices. If you're interested in creating natural dyes, ask for recipe books at your local library, or search the Internet for information on natural dyes.

The projects in this chapter call for commercial dyes. Food coloring dyes, made from vegetables, are very safe and easy to use, while fabric dyes like Rit and Tintex are also easy to use and produce a wide range of beautiful colors.

Many different types of fabric can be dyed, but natural fabrics like wool, cotton, and silk work best. Synthetic fabrics, such as polyester, don't hold dyes very well and can end up looking splotchy and blotchy. So choose your fabrics carefully and be sure to test them if you have any doubts—just dip a hidden corner of the fabric into a dye mixture to see what happens.

One warning: Be careful. Dyeing is *really* messy—and also pretty permanent. Whenever you are doing a dyeing project, be sure to wear old clothes and work in an area that will be easy to clean up afterward. And wear rubber gloves—or you might end up with dye on your skin that won't wash off for days!

Terrific Tie-Dye

How easy is it?

Tie-dyes are made by twisting and tying fabric, then dipping it into dye "baths." Because the dye can't penetrate the areas that have been tied and twisted, all kinds of wild (and sometimes unexpected) patterns result. Tie-dyeing produces fun and unique results and tying fabric is as easy as tying your shoes!

T-shirts are the classic item to tie-dye, but you can use tie-dyeing techniques to make cool tie-dyed sheets and pillowcases for your room, or leggings, or socks, or . . . well, the possibilities are endless!

What You Will Need:

- an adult
- cotton or silk fabric (T-shirts, scarves, socks, pillowcases, sheets)
- water
- rubber bands, string, twist ties, or strips of fabric for tying
- rubber gloves
- Rit or Tintex fabric dye (in as many colors as you like)
- stainless steel saucepans or soup pots
- large metal spoons (for stirring dyes)
- metal mixing bowls or old plastic bins
- heavy plastic wrap or bags
- old towel or washing machine

171

1 Wash the fabric you are planning to dye in hot soapy water and rinse well.

· · · · · · ·

2 Tie fabric as shown on the next page, or dream up knots and ties of your own.

· · · · · · ·

3 Put on your rubber gloves and ask an adult to help you prepare the dye according to package directions.

· · · · · · ·

4 Place the part of your fabric to be dyed into a dye-bath of your choice, and make sure it is fully soaked. Remember, the longer the cloth stays in the bath, the darker it becomes, so you decide when to take it out—after five minutes or thirty minutes. Squeeze out excess dye solution and rinse the fabric with cold water. Do *not* remove the ties.

5 When you are ready to dye the next part of your fabric with another color, cover the already dyed section with heavy plastic (use wrap or bags) and wrap tightly, securing with tight elastic bands before putting the fabric into another colored dye-bath. Repeat this step until you like the way the fabric looks.

· · · · · · ·

6 When all the dyeing is completed, rinse the fabric in a sink full of cool water. Extract the water by squeezing the fabric in an old towel or putting it *by itself* into the washer spin cycle. Remove the ties and wash the item in cool water and mild detergent.

Remember, tie-dyeing is an imperfect science, so there's no such thing as a mistake. If you don't like the results of one project, just start another! Enjoy!

"Moi Piggy. Vous Kermit!"

Kermit's Tarzan outfit was made using batik, just like the animal-skin project on page 180.

TIED UP IN KNOTS

Different tying methods achieve different tie-dye patterns.

Spirals:

Drape your fabric over a dowel or broomstick. Tie a length of string around the fabric at the top, then wrap the string evenly down the length of the pole at an angle, leaving fabric peeking through. Knot the string when you reach the bottom of the fabric, and slide the stick out.

Doughnuts:

Lay out your fabric and place stones, coins, or marbles on it in whatever pattern you like. Gather the fabric around each object and tie it tightly with rubber bands or string, as shown.

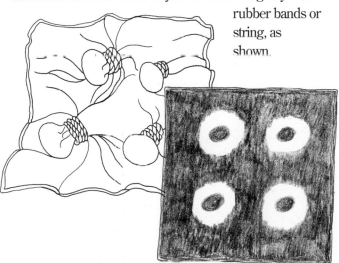

Stripes:

Fold your fabric into narrow pleats. Loop rubber bands around it, as shown.

Concentric circles:

Hold the fabric at a center point, and let it hang naturally. Tie with two or more rubber bands in a row, as shown.

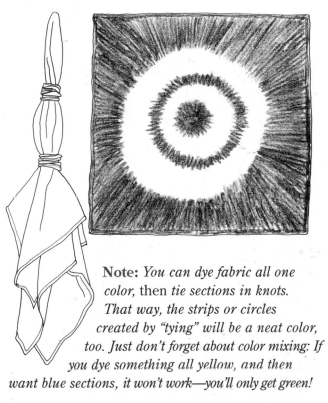

Note: *You can dye fabric all one color, then tie sections in knots. That way, the strips or circles created by "tying" will be a neat color, too. Just don't forget about color mixing: If you dye something all yellow, and then want blue sections, it won't work—you'll only get green!*

Eggshell Mosaic

How easy is it?

What You Will Need:

- an adult
- Bear Essentials
- tracing paper
- cardboard (about 8" × 10")
- 7 extra-large white eggs (save the carton)
- 9 extra-large brown eggs (save the carton)
- 2 saucepans
- water
- food coloring (red, yellow, green, and blue)
- 6 mugs or small bowls (one for each color dye)
- measuring spoons
- white vinegar
- spoon
- 6 stirrers (one for each color dye)
- paper plates

Why not decorate a small box with a mosaic of your own special design?

A mosaic is a picture that's made up of lots of small, different-colored pieces. Since ancient times, mosaics have been made using tiles or stones (or bits of glass or gems or other colorful stuff) that are arranged to create a design or scene, and then fixed in place with glue, cement, or plaster. Making a mosaic is like creating a painting, only you use tiles and glue instead of paints and paintbrushes.

Mosaics can be gigantic, covering an entire wall or floor, or they can be very small, like this portrait of Fozzie. We made it with cracked eggshells instead of tiles, and you can, too! When you're finished, whip up an egg salad sandwich to munch on while you think of new eggshell mosaic projects.

PROJECT MADE BY CARMEL DUNDON

1 Trace our Fozzie pattern on page 311 onto the cardboard (see page 9 for tracing instructions). Cut the oval shape out of the cardboard.

· · · · · · ·

2 Ask an adult to hard-boil the eggs. Save the cartons—you'll need them.

· · · · · · ·

3 In a separate saucepan, have your adult boil 4 cups of water to make your dyes.

· · · · · · ·

4 To create the dye mixtures:

- Put approximately 20 drops of food coloring into each mug or bowl (see chart at right for color proportions for the Fozzie mosaic).

- Add 1 teaspoon of white vinegar to each cup.

- Have a grown-up help you fill each mug with ½ cup of boiling water.

- Stir the dyes. Use a different stirrer for each color, so they don't mix by accident.

· · · · · · ·

5 After the boiled eggs have cooled, use a spoon to lower them gently into the dyes (see chart opposite to find out how many eggs you need of each color). Let each egg sit in the dye for about five minutes; turn the eggs carefully to make sure they get evenly coated. Place them back in the cartons to dry.

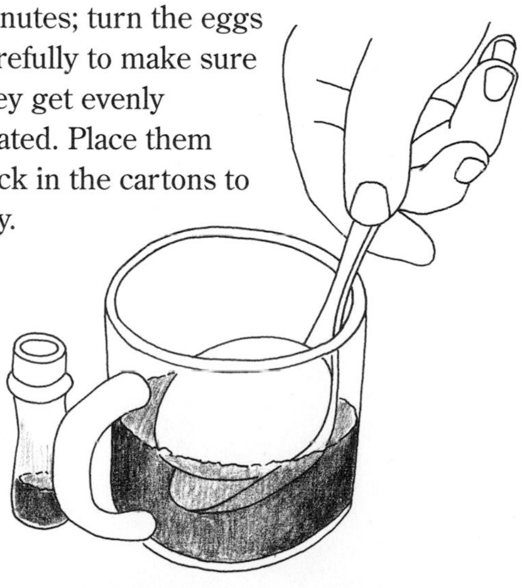

6 When the dyed eggs are dry, peel off the shells and set the eggs aside. (Be sure to peel off the egg's interior membrane—that thin, papery stuff—from the shell before it dries. This will help the shells stick better later.) Then break the shells into small bits and place them by color onto separate plates.

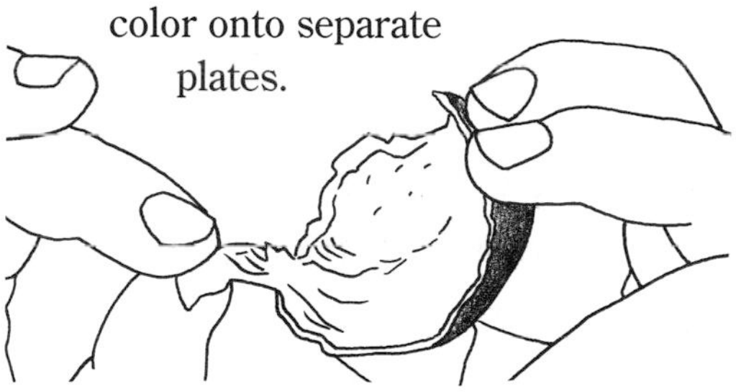

· · · · · · ·

7 Use bits of eggshell to color in the picture, following our photograph as a model: Dab a little white glue on the cardboard and press the correctly colored eggshell gently into the glue. Continue until your picture is filled in with colored shells. Let dry.

"**This mosaic really cracks me up! Wocka! Wocka!**"

EGGSHELL COLOR CHART

In order to create a mosaic that looks like our Fozzie mosaic, you'll need to know the food coloring mixtures and how many eggs of each color (brown or white) to dye. Since it's hard to re-create anyone else's work when you're using food coloring, don't be upset if yours doesn't look exactly like ours; yours is probably better!

Color / Use	# of Drops	# of Eggs
Dark Red (mouth, scarf flowers)	20 red	1 w. egg
Light Red (nose, eyelids, tongue, scarf flowers)	10 red	2 w. eggs
Blue (background)	15 blue + 5 green	3 w. eggs
Green (scarf flowers, background)	20 green	1 w. egg
Dark Brown (eyebrows, hat brim, ear centers)	20 red	1 b. egg
Medium Brown (hat, border of mosaic)	(no dye)	3 b. eggs
Orangy Brown (Fozzie's fur)	6 red + 14 yellow	5 b. eggs

Rainbow Stationery Set

How easy is it?

- Bear Essentials
- oil-based paints of different colors
- old plates (one for each paint color)
- linseed oil
- tracing paper
- construction paper in different pastel colors
- plastic tub to fit in sink or large foil baking pan
- water
- Popsicle stick or plastic straw (for dripping paint)
- Popsicle stick or fork to swirl paint mixture
- masking tape
- newspaper
- envelope (for pattern) and stickers

To make this wonderful and colorful stationery set, you'll be using a technique called marbleizing. To marbleize paper, you will first create a marbleizing solution of water and oil paints. Because oil and water don't mix, the oil paint will float on or in the water, creating a swirling effect. When paper is dipped into the solution, it picks up the paint in the same swirly, marblelike pattern. That's why this process is called marbleizing—because the swirly colors look like the swirls of color you find in marble.

Here we've dyed construction paper and cut it into some Muppety shapes to make a stationery set. But marbleizing is also the perfect technique to use when decorating wrapping paper, bookmarks, lampshades, picture frames, and more. You'll be amazed at the results once you give it a swirl!

176

1 Place a pea-sized amount of each oil-based paint on its own plate and add about 1 teaspoon of linseed oil; mix well. The consistency of the mixture should be runny so that the paint can later be "dripped" into the water.

•••••••

2 Trace the Fozzie or Kermit patterns on pages 312–313 onto your construction paper several times (see page 9 for tracing instructions), or draw your own shapes on paper. Cut out the shapes to make a matching stationery set.

•••••••

3 Fill the plastic tub or baking dish about halfway with water. Wait until the surface of the water is calm. Pick a few different colors that go well with your construction paper and, with a Popsicle stick or plastic straw, add a few drops of any or all of the paint mixtures to the water.

•••••••

4 *Gently* swirl the paints on the surface of the water, using a Popsicle stick, pencil point, or fork. Don't overdo the swirling or the colors will get too mixed.

•••••••

5 Make a little masking tape tab to hold on to while dipping your paper. Attach it to the edge of your paper and

gently and quickly dip the paper onto the surface of the "marbled" water so that one side of the paper completely touches the surface of the water. Do *not* let go of the tab or submerge the paper entirely.

•••••••

6 Carefully pull out the paper and leave it, marbleized-side up, on newspaper to dry overnight. Dip as many as you like. You can also dip the reverse side of each sheet once the first side has dried.

•••••••

7 To make envelopes, take apart an envelope from a birthday card to use as a pattern. Trace onto construction paper and cut out this shape. Use the same dipping process for your envelopes. After the envelopes are dry, fold and glue the edges and use a sticker to close the flap.

"Moi does so enjoy writing to moi's many hundreds of thousands of millions of zillions of fans...."

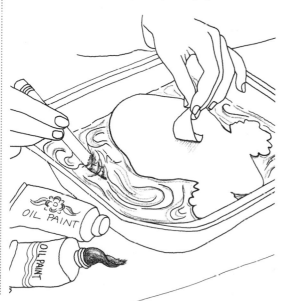

Awesome Ombré Scarf

How easy is it?

What You Will Need:

- an adult
- clothesline and clothespins
- lots of newspaper
- silk scarf (white or off-white)
- water
- mild detergent
- large stainless steel pot (to hold dye mixture)
- rubber gloves
- 1 package powdered Rit or Tintex dye
- measuring spoons
- large metal spoon
- large metal mixing bowl or plastic bin
- old towel or washing machine

Ombré is a dipping-and-dyeing technique that produces a wonderful light-to-dark shading effect, like the sky at sunset. Try making your first scarf with only one color dye that changes from very light on one end to very dark on the other end. Later, you can try this technique using many different colors of dye, say, starting at one end with orange, then shading into yellow, then shading into purple. Or choose your own color combination! These scarves make wonderful presents . . . and, if you use inexpensive fabric, they can be used as gorgeous wrapping "paper," too.

1 Hang a clothesline over a thick stack of newspapers in a safe spot near where you will be dyeing.

. . . .

2 Wash the silk scarf in hot water with mild detergent. Rinse well.

. . . .

3 Fill the pot with 2 gallons of water and have an adult heat the water to near boiling; then turn off the stove.

. . . .

4 Put on your rubber gloves. Add about ½ teaspoon of the powdered dye to the pot and mix well with the metal spoon. (You will begin the dyeing process with a small amount of dye for the lightest color and add more as you go along to get darker and darker shades. Plan to dip your scarf in four sections; each section will be a slightly darker shade of the same color.)

5 Place the first quarter of the silk scarf in the dye-bath and allow it to sit for thirty minutes.

. . . .

6 Remove the scarf and squeeze out excess dye. Place the dyed end of the scarf in a metal bowl or plastic bin so that it doesn't drip as you carry it. Hang it on the drying line until you're ready to move on to the next dipping.

. . . .

7 Add another teaspoon of dye *to the same pot* and stir (you may need your

adult to keep reheating the water a bit as you go along). This time dip all *but* the dyed quarter of the scarf into the dye, and swish it around so it's thoroughly soaked. Leave it in for thirty minutes, then repeat step 6.

. . . .

8 Add another teaspoon of dye to the pot and mix well. Dip only the third and fourth quarters of the scarf in the pot, soaking thoroughly (you may need to clip the scarf to the pot with clothespins, as shown). Let it sit for thirty minutes, then repeat step 6.

. . . .

9 For the last step, mix 1 more teaspoon of dye into the pot, and dip only the last quarter of the scarf into the dye; let it sit for thirty minutes.

. . . .

10 When all the dyeing is completed, rinse the scarf thoroughly under cold running water. Keep the light and dark ends of the scarf from touching each other. Fill your plastic bucket or metal bowl with cold water and a dash of mild detergent, and swish the scarf around for about five minutes. Rinse the scarf in cold water and squeeze out excess water. Squeeze the scarf in an old towel or put it in the washer on spin cycle by itself. Hang the scarf and let it dry thoroughly. (Remember to run the washer to clean out excess dye before you put in a load of laundry!)

Ready. Set. Accessorize!

Refresher Course:

See page 170 for general dipping and dyeing hints.

Batik Animal Skin

How easy is it?

What You Will Need:

- an adult
- stack of newspapers or brown paper bags
- scissors or pinking shears
- cotton pillowcase (standard or king size; see box on next page for colors)
- rubber gloves
- Rit or Tintex dyes (see box on next page for colors)
- water
- large stainless steel pots (1 for each dye mixture)
- metal spoons (1 for each dye mixture)
- crayons
- paraffin wax
- double boiler (for melting wax)
- old paintbrushes
- iron
- 3' length of old frayed rope or twine (for a belt)

Go wild! While wearing this wacky animal "skin," you just might hear the call of the jungle. Batik, the dyeing technique used in this project, is an Indonesian method of fabric design that uses wax and dye to create colorful patterns. In batik, melted wax is painted onto the areas of the cloth that you do not want the dye to color; the wax then blocks the dye from that area. In this project, we'll show you how to use batik to create a caveperson costume with a leopard, tiger, giraffe, or zebra pattern. Once you know how to do it, you'll think of lots of other things that would benefit from some batiking, like place mats, T-shirts, wall hangings, and many other fabric items.

Leopard

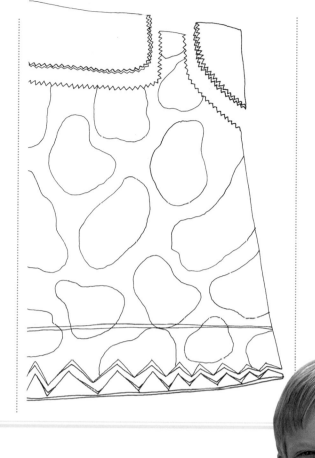

1 Cover your work area with newspaper—this project is especially messy.

· · · · · · ·

2 Cut your pillowcase to make a one-shouldered outfit as shown. Test for fit and cut the hem in a zigzag pattern to the appropriate length.

· · · · · · ·

3 To predye the pillowcase if needed (see box below): Put on your rubber gloves and prepare the dye following the package instructions. Submerge the entire pillowcase and soak for twenty to thirty minutes (see page 170 for general dyeing hints). Squeeze out excess dye, rinse with cold water until it runs clear, and spin dry in the washing machine.

WILD KINGDOM

Here are specific instructions to create particular animal skin patterns. The directions in the rest of the project are general and will tell you when to refer to this box.

Giraffe:
Predye the pillowcase light beige (or start with a beige pillowcase). Draw rounded, blobby shapes with a little space in between them (see the general illustrations for this project and the photo at right). Paint wax in the space *between* the blobs, then dye the pillowcase a rich brown.

Leopard:
Predye the pillowcase yellow (or start with a yellow pillowcase). Draw small, blobby spots that are fairly close together. Paint wax *between* all of the spots, then fill in the *center* of each spot with wax. Dye the pillowcase a rich brown.

Tiger:
Predye the pillowcase orange (or start with an orange pillowcase). Draw rows of very thin stripes that all fork and zigzag in the same direction at the same point. Paint every *other* stripe with wax, then dye the pillowcase black.

Zebra:
Start with a white pillowcase, and draw rows of thick stripes that all fork and zigzag in the same direction at the same point. Paint every *other* stripe with wax, then dye the pillowcase black.

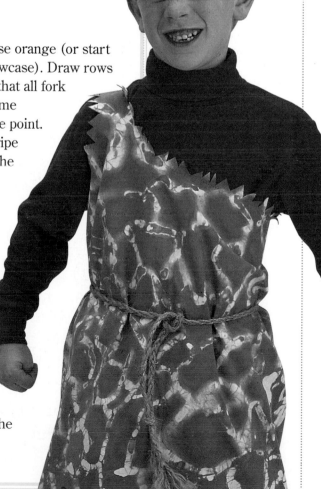

Giraffe

4 Draw the *outlines* of the animal skin pattern all over the pillowcase with crayons. *Press hard.*

. . . .

5 Have a grown-up melt paraffin wax in a double boiler (see Caution! box for warnings), following the directions on the box of wax. Prepare your pillowcase for wax painting by placing several sheets of newspaper between the layers of the pillowcase so the wax won't leak through.

. . . .

6 When you are ready to paint with wax, bear in mind that the parts of the fabric you paint will *not* receive the dye while dipping, but will stay the current color of the fabric. Have an adult help you paint the outside of the pillowcase with wax where needed (refer to the animal patterns box on page 181).

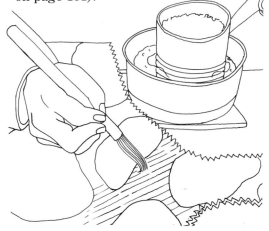

. . . .

7 Put on your rubber gloves again. Prepare the next batch of dye following the directions on the package, but use *cold* water instead of hot. *If you use hot water, the wax will melt and your batik designs will be lost.*

. . . .

8 Wet the wax-covered pillowcase with plain water, crinkle it up, and submerge it in the dye. Leave it in the dye for about thirty minutes.

9 Remove the pillowcase and rinse with cold water. Hang it above a pile of newspapers in a safe spot to dry. The pillowcase needs to be fairly dry for the next step (damp is okay).

. . . .

10 Put a stack of newspapers or brown bags in the center of the pillowcase (where the pillow goes), underneath it, and over it. Ask an adult to set the iron on a low setting, and have him or her iron over the top layer of newspaper to melt the wax off the pillowcase (the wax will be picked up by the newspaper).

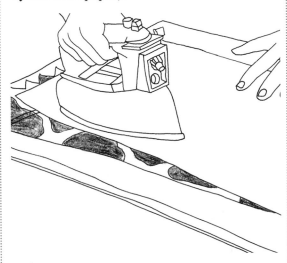

Change the newspapers often as they fill up with melted wax; adjust the iron setting, the thickness of the newspaper stack, and the position of the pillowcase to ensure that you remove all of the wax.

. . . .

11 Slip your animal skin over your head, belt it with rope or twine, and grrrrrrrowl!

CHAPTER 12 / COSTUMES AND HATS

Dress Up!

Everybody thinks about wearing costumes each Halloween, but costumes and disguises are fun *any* time of the year. Actors and actresses wear costumes to play different characters . . . and so can you. Put on a play! Or just have some fun dressing up. Wearing costumes and disguises is a great way for you to try out other personalities. In this chapter, we'll show you how to transform yourself into a whole host of characters—a furry purple monster; a caped crusader; a king, queen, or princess; a court jester; a wizard, and more.

"Jolly good day, chaps!"

"Friends, Romans, Countryfrogs . . ."

"Excellent playing is my goal."

"Batterrrrr up!"

NOT JUST VELVETEEN FOR THIS RABBIT

Here's a peek at the process we go through when designing a new costume for a Muppet.

First, the puppet (Bean Bunny, in this case) is "draped" with pattern fabric to create a pattern. The patterns, which are used only once, are pinned to costume fabric and used as a guide for cutting.

Then the costume is pinned onto the puppet so it fits just right before it is sewn.

After the costume is sewn together, the details are added. Everything is carefully crafted, from Bean Bunny's little scarf to the lining that shows on his jacket cuffs to his fingerless gloves, all shown in the far right photo below.

"Howdy, pardner."

When a regular movie is made (with human actors, that is), the costume department can usually send out for costumes: a couple hundred petticoats, or cowboy hats, or whatever they need in the right sizes. But for a movie that stars puppets, it's not so simple. Each little costume has to be made from scratch to fit each puppet, and everything is done by hand. Creating costumes for the entire cast of Muppets for photo shoots, movies, and television productions is a huge part of our work at the Muppet Workshop.

Once you've made your costume and put it on, really try to become that character. How does a king act? How silly a jester can you be? When you put on that cape, what kind of hero do you become? You may be surprised. . .

Princess and Wizard Hats

How easy is it?

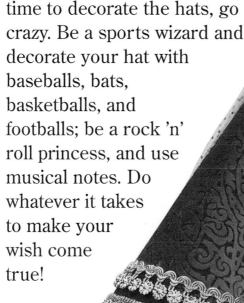

Did you ever wish you were a fairy princess? Or a powerful wizard with magical powers? Make one of these hats, add a long cape in a matching color (see "Cool Capes," page 202), and maybe your wish will come true! Each of these hats is made out of simple poster board that is covered with fabric, rolled into a cone shape, and decorated. When it's time to decorate the hats, go crazy. Be a sports wizard and decorate your hat with baseballs, bats, basketballs, and footballs; be a rock 'n' roll princess, and use musical notes. Do whatever it takes to make your wish come true!

What You Will Need:

- an adult
- Bear Essentials
- tracing paper
- poster board (18" × 24")
- velveteen (1 yard)
- iron-on fabric adhesive sheet(s) (1 yard)
- large, thick towel
- iron
- large binder clip
- 20" length of thin, round elastic cord (optional)

Decorations:

- cardboard and colored construction paper
- glitter, sequins, feathers, fancy trims
- foam sponge
- ¼ yard sheer fabric (for veil)

1 Trace, enlarge, and transfer the pattern from page 314 (see pages 8 and 9 for tracing and enlarging instructions). Cut out the pattern, trace it onto the poster board, then cut the shape out of the poster board. This is the bottom layer of your hat.

• • • • • • •

2 Smooth the velveteen out flat on a large surface. Lay the cone-shaped poster board in the center of the velveteen, and trace it onto the velveteen, adding about an additional inch *all the way around* the edge of the shape. Carefully cut out the velveteen fabric.

• • • • • • •

3 Trace the cone-shaped poster board onto the iron-on adhesive, adding about an additional inch *all the way around* the edge of the shape. Cut the enlarged shape out of the adhesive.

• • • • • • •

4 Lay out the towel as an ironing surface (make sure to lay it out somewhere scorch-proof). On top of the towel, layer three pieces as follows:

- the velveteen, centered evenly on top.

- the iron-on fabric adhesive sheet in the middle, centered evenly.

- the poster board at the bottom.

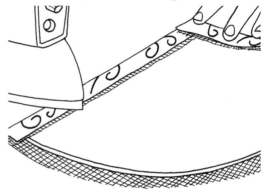

Have an adult help you iron these layers together, gluing the posterboard to the velveteen.

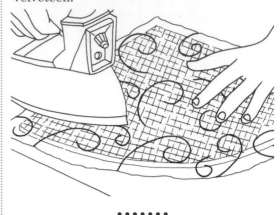

• • • • • • •

5 Fold over the extra 1 inch of the velveteen fabric and adhesive to the back of the poster board and iron down to leave a clean, "hemmed" edge.

• • • • • • •

6 Slowly begin to roll the board into a cone shape. Be patient—this takes time. When you finally get it into just the right cone shape to fit your head, place glue all along the underside of the overlapping edge to glue it down. Attach the binder clip to hold the hat together until the glue dries completely.

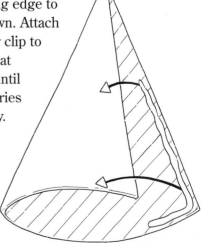

7 If you'd like to be able to secure the hat on your head, punch two small holes near the bottom edge of the hat; one over each ear. Tie the covered elastic through the holes and wear it under your chin.

•••••••

8 Decorate your hat.

For the Wizard Hat:

• From cardboard, cut out a moon and many stars of different sizes. Cover one side of each with glue and then with glitter. Let the stars dry thoroughly before gluing them onto the hat. If you want a three-dimensional effect

for your stars, glue a small square of sponge to the backs of your stars and moon. Let dry, then glue the sponges directly onto the hat.

For the Princess Hat:

• Cut out a piece of sheer fabric about 20 inches long and 5 inches wide. Gather at one end and glue it around the point of the hat.

• Glue on glitter, sequins, feathers, or any other fancy trim you like.

"Moi finds cones very slimming."

What You Will Need:

- Bear Essentials
- store-bought vest pattern (try to find an all-one-piece pattern)
- fabric scissors
- furry fabric for vest, mask, hands, and feet (about 2 yards in one color)
- poster paint and paintbrushes
- 20 to 50 Styrofoam balls (or spongy foam balls) in different sizes, and two same-size big ones for eyes
- soft tape measure
- 2 shoelaces
- white, red, and black felt (teeth, claws, toenails)
- furry fabric for eyebrows (about ¼ yard in a second color)
- paper for patterns (four 11" × 14" sheets)
- straight pins, needle, thread
- 3" strip of Velcro (both halves)
- strip of covered elastic (1" × 12")

Furry Monster Suit

How easy is it?

Monsters come in all shapes and sizes, but lots of great Muppet monsters are big and furry. With a little work, you can join the furry monster crew; all you need is some fur, Styrofoam balls for warts and eyes, and a little felt, and you're on your way.

As you can see, this costume is made up of pieces—a vest, furry hands and feet, and an ingenious headpiece that forms the monster's face. You can make all or just some of the parts of this monster costume, then use this "pieced costume" strategy to make lots of other costumes—it's much easier than making a full-body costume, and the costume will still have a strong overall effect.

But in any case, when you're done, get ready to scare your whole neighborhood. And don't forget to GGRRRRRROWL!

1 For the warty, furry vest, follow the instructions of your store-bought pattern and use the furry fabric. Most likely, you won't need to hem the vest, as the fur fabric has a pretty sturdy edge. For warts, glue some of the painted Styrofoam balls all over your fur vest. Let dry.

. . . .

2 For the monster head:

● Measure around your head with the soft tape measure. Note the measurement, then cut out a piece of fur that's 4 inches × the measurement of your head. Glue your white felt "teeth strip" to the back side of the fur so that the teeth show beneath the fur band. Glue in place.

● With your scissors, snip a tiny hole through the fur and felt layers 1 inch in from each end; thread a shoelace through each hole. (This is how you'll tie the headpiece to your head.)

● Next, glue on the eyeballs. Then glue a thin strip of the other color of fur over the eyes for bushy monster eyebrows.

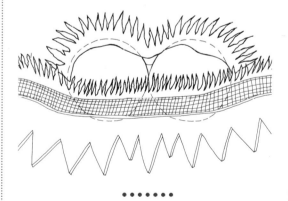

. . . .

3 For the monster hands:

● Trace one of your hands onto a large sheet of paper as though you were drawing a mitten to fit your hand, as shown below. Now enlarge the mitten shape to be about 2 inches larger all

---

BEFORE YOU START: DETAILS, DETAILS

There are a few details for this costume that you'll need to prepare in advance.

● Paint all your Styrofoam balls bright colors and let them dry. If you prefer, buy already-colored spongy foam balls.

● Cut the red felt into twenty claw-shaped triangles for your finger claws and toe claws.

● Make eyes out of two large Styrofoam balls. Paint them, let them dry, and glue small black felt circles on as pupils.

● Cut out a 1 foot × 1½-inch rectangle of white felt. Cut a pointy tooth pattern all the way along one long edge.

Put all the pieces aside for the moment.

---

the way around. Cut out the pattern, flip it over (so the thumb is pointing the other way), trace, and cut out.

● Place the fur on the table with the fur-side down. Pin both patterns to the fabric and cut out each of the mitten shapes. Pin one mitten piece to the other, fur sides together. Leaving the wrist side of the mitten open, sew all along the remaining edges using a running stitch (see page 143 for stitch information).

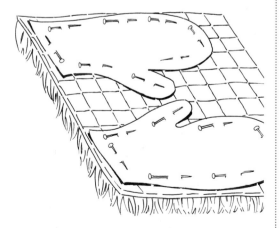

● Turn the mitten right-side out.

● Repeat the steps to make the second mitten.

- For warts, glue the colored Styrofoam balls on top of each mitten. Glue red felt triangles along the top edges and on the tips of the thumbs for claws.

· · · · · · ·

4 For monster feet:

- First you'll need to make a paper pattern: While wearing shoes, place your right foot in the middle of a piece of 11 × 14-inch paper and trace it. On the paper, mark the back center of the heel (the "heel spot"), as shown above, right. Add about 3 inches (no need to

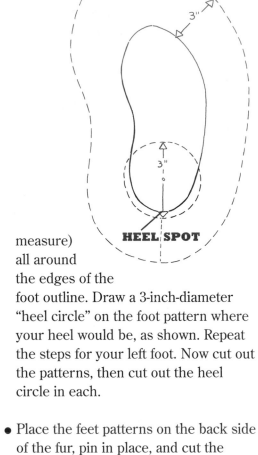

HEEL SPOT

measure) all around the edges of the foot outline. Draw a 3-inch-diameter "heel circle" on the foot pattern where your heel would be, as shown. Repeat the steps for your left foot. Now cut out the patterns, then cut out the heel circle in each.

- Place the feet patterns on the back side of the fur, pin in place, and cut the pattern shapes out of the fur. Mark the

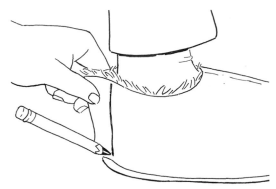

heel spot directly on the fur and cut on that spot, straight into the fabric until you reach the heel circle. Cut out the heel circle. This cutout will enable you to open the fur foot and drape it over your shoe, as shown above, to check the size. If the fur is dragging a bit on the edges, trim to fit.

- To make an adjustable heel seam, trim both halves of the Velcro to fit the

"Mmmmmm, tasty."

"Ah yes, another satisfied customer."

length of the heel seam. Using a running stitch (see page 143 for stitch information), sew one Velcro half to the fur side of the left side of the heel seam, and the other Velcro half to the nonfur side of the right side of the heel seam, as shown.

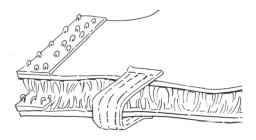

- To hold the monster feet onto your shoes, cut a length of elastic (about 5 inches) and sew each end to opposite

sides of the foot piece (on the nonfur side), in the position shown. Repeat for the other foot.

- Glue on Styrofoam balls for warts and red felt triangles for toenails.

Now you're ready to go scare up some fun!

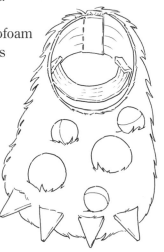

MUPPETS ON PARADE

When Kermit was a part of Macy's Thanksgiving Day Parade, the people who handled his balloon wore special Kermit headpieces. The headpiece of the "Furry Monster Suit" is based on the same design concept.

**MUPPETS
BIG BOOK
of CRAFTS**

Spiky Creature

How easy is it?

What You Will Need:

- scissors
- an old baseball cap that you can cut up
- brown paper or brown paper bags
- white glue
- broom bristles or dried reeds
- 15 to 20 plastic straws (bendable)
- paint and paintbrush (acrylic paint works best)
- pipe cleaners
- masking tape
- foam (for nose)

We've made a lot of spiky and ancient-looking creatures in the Muppet Workshop over the years, from the Sinclair family on the television show *Dinosaurs* to Hans the Hedgehog on the *Jim Henson's The Storyteller* series. Depending on how you paint it, this spiky, quill-covered headgear can turn you into a hedgehog, a porcupine, or a prehistoric creature that walked among the dinosaurs.

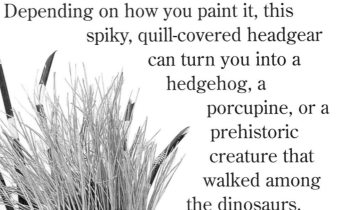

192

PROJECT MADE BY VICTORIA ELLIS

1 Cut off the brim of the baseball cap and cut half circles above both ear areas, as shown.

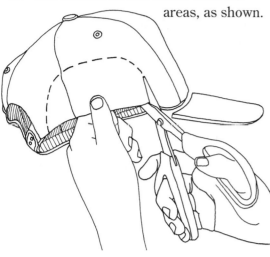

2 Cover the whole hat with papier-mâché (see page 6 for the recipe, but use brown paper instead of newspaper). Extend the papier-mâché down the front of the cap and turn up slightly, as shown,

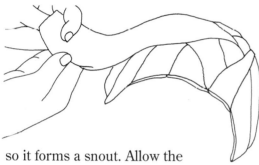

so it forms a snout. Allow the papier-mâché to dry.

3 Glue two long "aprons" of brown paper to the outside of the back of the cap, one above the other, as shown. Cut the bottoms of these aprons into a spiky pattern.

4 To add bristly hair, cut lengths of bristle from reeds or a broom. Lay bunches of them flat against the front of the cap so that they stick up above the crown. To attach them, glue or papier-mâché small pieces of brown paper over the ends, as shown. Start from the top of the cap and work your way down toward the nose.

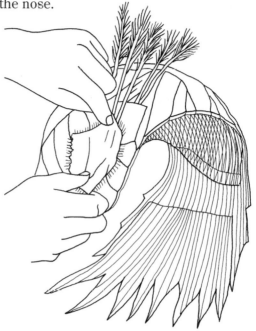

5 To create a spike, cut off the top of each plastic straw at a sharp angle. Paint the straws any way you like. Insert a pipe cleaner into the straw with about 1 inch sticking out from the bottom. Bend the pipe cleaner end into a right angle and use masking tape, as shown below, to secure the straw to the cap. Repeat until you have about fifteen or twenty spikes on the hat.

THE FINAL TOUCH

Wait until everything has dried, then:

● Paint the hat and apron any way you like.

● Make a small foam nose and paint it black. Glue the nose to the tip of the snout.

● Dab some glue on the "apron" and add sequins as scales.

● Practice acting prickly!

What You Will Need:

- **Bear Essentials**
- **Feather Fabric** (choose one or more):
  - thin plastic party tablecloths, 84" round
  - clear plastic tablecloth protectors, 60" × 90"
  - shiny or colorful fabric tablecloth
  - blue recycling bags
- old pair of panty hose
- little bells, ribbons, feathers (from a craft shop), sequins, glitter, lace (for boa beautification; optional)

Glamour Girl Boa

How easy is it?

Feather boas are very glamorous, but where's a girl to find that many feathers outside of a turkey farm? (Of course, Miss Piggy is a notable exception—she has special turkey feather buyers at her disposal!) Luckily, with our help, you won't need to find any willing turkeys. You'll be as glamorous as Miss Piggy herself when you wear these beautiful boas—and they're made out of things you might otherwise throw away. What becomes a glamorous boa? A most unglamorous plastic tablecloth or garbage bag!

Since these boas are so easy to create, why don't you make a whole wardrobe of them for your dress-up trunk, then share them with your friends when they come over to play.

PROJECT MADE BY CHRISTINE MOYES

1 Choose the material you are going to use for your boa. Cut the material into "feather" strips that are approximately 1 inch wide × 8 inches long and set aside.

· · · · · · · ·

2 Cut the top off a pair of panty hose about 5 inches down from the waistband. Discard the top part.

· · · · · · · ·

3 Spread the panty hose legs apart so that the toes are at opposite ends. Tie each toe to something sturdy at either end, making sure the panty hose are stretched out as much as possible. Now you're ready to tie on your feathers.

4 Start at one end of the stretched panty hose and tie on a feather strip with a tight knot, keeping the ends even. Continue to add strips, tying each one as

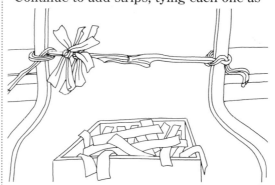

It's not a constrictor—but this boa is long and slinky and wraps around your neck just like the snake it's named after.

close to the next as possible. Every few ties, push the tied strips tightly together and twirl them around so they fluff out evenly and the ends aren't all pointing in the same direction (see illustration on previous page).

● ● ● ● ● ● ●

5 When the boa is completed, untie the panty hose toes and make a big double knot at each end so the strips won't fall off. Cut off the excess toe on each end.

6 If you like, decorate your boa by tying on little bells and ribbons or gluing on a few feathers. Add sequins or glitter with small spots of glue. Tie on a little lace for extra prettiness.

"Sometimes a girl just can't find a single thing to wear!"

HOG COUTURE

Often the Workshop's costume designers work from sketches like the one you see here by Michael Frith. Miss Piggy eventually wore the finished costume in the movie *The Great Muppet Caper.*

Funky Jester's Cap

How easy is it?

Remember the jokers from your deck of playing cards? Back in the Middle Ages, many kings and nobles employed real jokers, called jesters. A jester's job was to wear funny clothes and hats, tell jokes, and keep the king's court laughing (things in the Middle Ages could get pretty grim). The word *jest* actually means *joke*. If you've ever heard the expression "Surely you jest," then you already know that it means, "You've got to be joking!"

But we're not jesting when we suggest that you make a jester's cap of your very own. You'll just have to use some basic cutting, pattern-making, and sewing skills. When you're finished, you'll have the perfect hat to wear while telling jokes. You could also make a whole set of them for your family and stage a joke-telling contest!

What You Will Need:

- soft tape measure
- tracing paper and pencil
- scissors
- straight pins, needle, thread
- polar fleece (for a 2-color hat: ½ yard of each; for a 1-color hat: ½ yard is also sufficient)
- 2 or more bells (or any dangly object), googly eyes (optional)

Note: Use heavy- or medium-gauge fleece to ensure a proper fit.

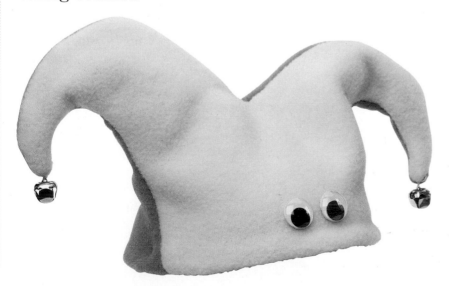

197

1 With the tape measure, measure the size of your head all the way around at ear level. Add 2 inches to that amount and divide the sum by two. (Example: If your head measures 20 inches, add 2 inches, which gets you to 22 inches. Then divide 22 inches by two. The measurement you'll need is 11 inches.)

• • • • • • •

2 Trace and enlarge the hat pattern on page 315 (see pages 8 and 9 for tracing and enlarging instructions) so that the *bottom edge* of your enlarged pattern is the same length as—or as close as you can get to—your measurement from step 1 (in our example, that measurement is 11 inches).

• • • • • • •

3 Cut out your pattern and pin it flat onto *one* of the two colors of fabric. If you're using only one color fabric, do the same but be careful to leave enough fabric to repeat this step.

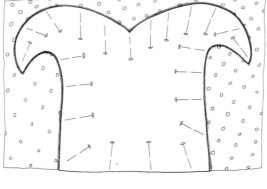

4 Carefully cut the shape out of the fabric. Remove the pins. Repeat steps 3 and 4 with your second fabric (or with the rest of the first fabric, if you're only using one color).

• • • • • • •

5 Lay one fabric shape directly on top of the other fabric shape. (*If you are not using polar fleece, and your fabric has a "right" and "wrong" side, make sure that you place the right sides together before*

"Fozzie, do you know what this strange ringing in my ears could be?"

"Gee, no. But hum a few bars and I'll fake it! Wocka! Wocka!"

pinning and sewing!) Be sure both pieces line up. Smooth in place and pin all the edges together, except the bottom edge (where your head will go).

• • • • • • •

6 Using a chain stitch, as shown below (inset), sew the two pieces of fabric together along the cap edge, about ¾ inch in from the edges (don't sew the bottom edge!).

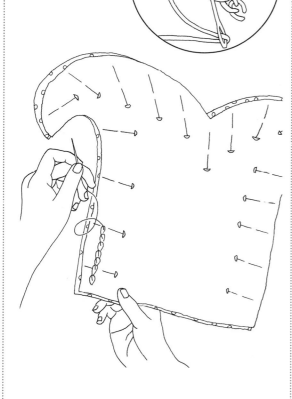

• • • • • • •

7 To hem the hat, fold about 3 or 4 inches of fabric up and pin in place, as shown top right. Try on your hat (be careful of the pins!) and adjust the length of the hem, if necessary. Pin the hem securely and sew it using a hemming stitch (see page 143 for stitch information). Turn your hat right-side out, gently pushing out the corners with your finger or with a pencil's eraser.

• • • • • • •

8 Sew bells on the dangling ends of your hat if you like. Glue on googly eyes if you've got them.

Now go make people laugh!

JUST JESTING

In the olden days, European court jesters entertained royal and noble families in lots of silly ways. You can try some of the things they did to make their audiences laugh:

● Juggling

● Silly pet tricks

● Singing songs with funny lyrics

● Reciting rhyming poems

● Acrobatics, such as somersaults and back flips

● Puppet shows

● Acting out skits

● Magic tricks

● Humorous dances

● Imitations of well-known people

Golden Crown

How easy is it?

What You Will Need:

- **Bear Essentials**
- **soft tape measure**
- **poster board or thin cardboard (1 piece, at least 9" × 12")**
- **masking tape**
- **water**
- **old or disposable plastic container (for mixing glue solution)**
- **paper towels**
- **gold or silver paint and paintbrushes**
- **fake jewels**
- **feathers, fake fur, or gold braid (for decorative border)**

Crown yourself King of Quetzlevania (or wherever) . . . or Queen of the Soccer Field! Just make this simple golden crown and start ruling.

If you'd like to complete your royal outfit, you can make a cape with a fake-fur collar from the "Cool Capes" project (see page 202). Then make the "Funky Jester's Cap" (see page 197) and the "Princess and Wizard Hats" (see page 185) and you and your friends can stage a play starring a king or a queen (or both), and the entire royal court.

1 With the tape measure, measure around your head and make a note of the measurement. Then measure and cut a piece of poster board or cardboard that's *1 inch longer* than your head measurement and about 9 inches high. Draw a flattened crown shape down the length of the cardboard, as shown below, keeping in mind that your crown should be about 8 inches high at its highest points and the lower rim of the crown (the part that grips your head) should never be thinner than 1 inch.

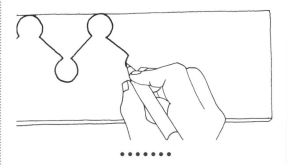

• • • • • • •

2 Cut out the crown.

• • • • • • •

3 Curl the cardboard so that it fits around your head and tape the two ends of the crown securely together.

• • • • • • •

4 Mix equal parts of white glue and water in a plastic dish. Dip strips of paper towel into the mixture and cover

the entire crown with several layers, inside and out. Smooth the strips as you go along, then allow the crown to dry.

• • • • • • •

5 When the crown is dry, paint it gold or silver and let it dry again.

To decorate:

• Glue on the fake jewels in a pattern.

• Glue on a strip of feathers, fake fur, or gold braid as a border.

Go forth and rule.

YOU RULE!

If you'd like to set up your own kingdom, here's what you need to do, more or less:

• Find a location

• Secure the rights to the area

• Name it

• Hold a coronation in which you are crowned

• Build a castle

• Designate the people in your court and your subjects

• Make up the laws

• Do business with other kingdoms to secure wealth

• Protect your borders

• Rule

"It's only a short hop from frog prince to frog king."

Cool Capes

How easy is it?

Capes can be made out of all kinds of materials for all kinds of costumes, whether glittery and elegant or batlike and downright creepy. These simply patterned and sewn (or glued) capes are just the beginning. Once you've mastered one of them, you can make capes for all occasions—be a vampire or a princess on Halloween, a magician for a birthday party, or maybe even the master of ceremonies in a three-ring circus!

PROJECT MADE BY APRIL ASHER

1 Cut your fabric into a large rectangle (approximately 45 inches × 50 inches).

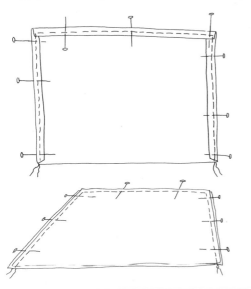

● If you are using only one layer of fabric:
Turn over the rough edges of fabric on all sides except the bottom and press down with your hands (or press with an iron, if you have an adult to help). Pin and sew a hem with a basting stitch (see page 143 for stitch information), or place a strip of fabric adhesive in the hem fold and have an adult iron it.

● If you are using two layers of fabric:
Cut a 45 × 50-inch rectangle out of the second fabric. Place both rectangles on the tabletop or floor with the "right sides" of the fabric together; pin as shown left.

DECORATING YOUR CAPE

The Glittery Cape:

1 Lay the fabric flat on your work surface and use chalk to draw small scallops along the bottom, unsewn edge of the cape. Cut along the chalk line.

• • • • •

2 Glue large sequins, rhinestones, glitter, shells, or beads all over the outside of the cape.

• • • • •

3 Glue sequin trim along both side edges and along the bottom, scalloped edge of the cape, as shown.

The Bat Cape:

1 Lay the fabric flat on your work surface and use chalk to draw big scallops along the bottom, unsewn edge of the cape. Cut along the chalk line.

• • • • •

2 Glue black sequin trim (or other black trim) onto both side edges and the bottom, scalloped edge of the cape.

• • • •

3 To make a bat on the back, draw the bat outline on the center of the back of your cape with chalk. Glue a length of yarn or other trim all along the chalk line. Glue a small red button to each of two little black pom-poms to make eyes.

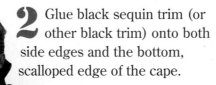

For the Glittery Cape:

● 2 yards shiny or filmy fabric (min. width 45")
● large sequins, rhinestones, glitter, tiny shells, shiny beads, sequin trim
● 1/4 yard brocade or satin fabric (for collar)
● big sparkly button (for collar closing)
● 6" length of ribbon

For the Bat Cape:

● 2 yards of dark shiny fabric (min. width 45") (optional: 2 yards of iridescent or net fabric for top layer)
● black sequin trim
● black yarn, 2 small red buttons, black pom-poms
● 1/4 yard of dark-colored satin (for collar)
● black jewel-like button (for collar closing)
● 6" length of ribbon

FABRIC EFFECTS

You can make your cape out of one layer of fabric, or use two layers for a more interesting effect—a dark shiny one on the bottom and a filmy, net, or iridescent see-through one on top. Just buy two yards of this "top fabric" when you buy the rest of the fabric.

Using a basting stitch, sew the two pieces of fabric together along *three* sides, leaving the bottom edge open. If you prefer, use iron-on fabric adhesive and have an adult help you with the iron. When finished, turn the fabric right-side out.

. . . .

2 Decorate your cape (see box on previous page).

. . . .

3 To prepare the top of the cape for a collar, with your needle and thread, sew large basting stitches (about 1½ inches each) along the top edge of the cape. Pull the loose end of the thread to "scrunch" the fabric into folds; the top of the cape should be about 12 inches wide. This is where you will add the cape's collar.

. . . .

4 To create the collar, cut a piece of brocade or satin into a 12 × 8-inch piece. Fold the two raw edges under and glue to create a 1-inch hem for each.

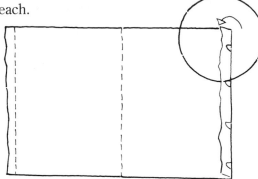

Fold it in half lengthwise and glue it to make a 10 × 4-inch collar piece.

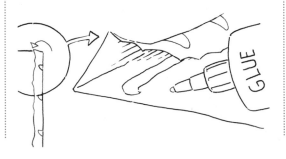

"Poultry in motion!"

Using a running stitch, sew the collar to the *outside* top of the cape and decorate it (see page 143 for stitch information).

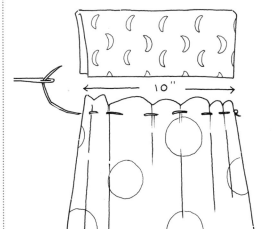

. . . .

5 Sew a big jeweled button on one of the bottom corners of the collar and a 6-inch loop of ribbon on the other bottom corner for a closure.

Now put on your cape and swoop it around yourself theatrically!

About Face

For thousands of years, people all over the world have been making and wearing masks. Some masks are silly or pretty and are worn during celebrations and holidays; others are somber or scary and are worn for more serious events, such as religious rituals and battles. Sometimes these masks look like animals, and sometimes they look like people. Other times, they look like fantastic creatures you've never seen before—except possibly in your dreams.

Masks can make you laugh, or enchant you, or even frighten you. Masks can be powerful . . . mysterious . . . or simply fun. At the Muppet Workshop, we've made lots of masks for Muppet

"Guess who?"

TURN THE MASK AROUND

Back in 1978, Harry Belafonte wanted to perform a traditional African musical number on *The Muppet Show.* So the Muppet Workshop made these beautiful mask puppets, and puppeteers had them perform a traditional African dance to Belafonte's song "Turn the World Around."

productions. We've also used just about every material you can think of: wood, foam, felt, cardboard, plastic, feathers, beads, molded papier-mâché, latex, even aluminum foil! In this chapter, we'll teach you how to use many of these materials to make some masks of your own.

You can make a mask as part of a costume, as a disguise, or as a decoration to hang on your wall. Make your masks scary or silly. Make them big or small. Make them for your friends and have a masked ball!

African Shield Mask

How easy is it?

In various parts of Africa, people have traditionally made ceremonial masks of carved wood, then decorated them with shells, feathers, beads, paint, and raffia (a straw-like fiber from a special kind of palm tree).

This African mask is made from materials you probably already have around your home. It starts with a big piece of corrugated cardboard and, with the addition of some papier-mâché, tape, and paint, it becomes a giant mask that you can wear, carry as a shield, or hang on the wall. Would you like to make one large enough to hide your entire body? Well, you can . . . as long as you find a piece of cardboard that's big enough!

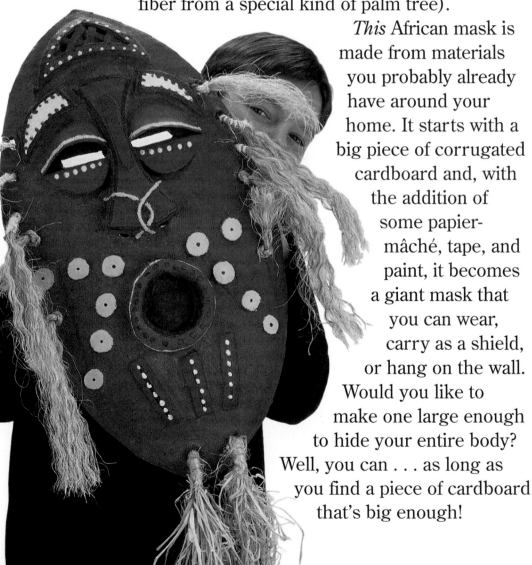

PROJECT MADE BY RON BINION

1 Draw a basic mask shape on the cardboard and cut it out. You can make it oval, like ours, or you can make it a big diamond, square, or triangle. You can even give it spiky edges, if you like. Our oval mask is about 30 inches high by 20 inches across. Keep the remaining cardboard scraps . . . you'll need them later to make some of the features on your mask.

• • • • • • •

2 To give your oval mask a curved shape like a shallow bowl, you need to make four little tucks in the cardboard called *darts*. Draw the cutting lines for your darts on the inside of your mask, as shown below (they will look like skinny triangles). Now, cut out the triangles. Pull together the two cut edges of your darts (the two long edges of each triangle) and attach them securely with several pieces of strong masking tape as shown. As you do this, the center of your mask should pop up, making your shield mask curve.

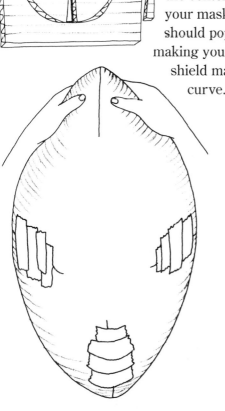

3 To make the face for your mask:

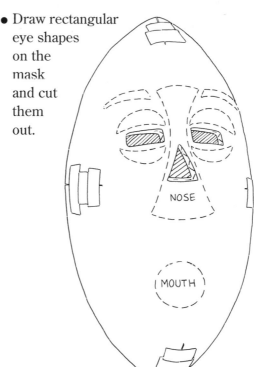

• Draw rectangular eye shapes on the mask and cut them out.

• Cut four semicircular eyelid shapes (two for the top lids and two for the bottom) and two curved, tapering eyebrow shapes out of the remaining scraps of corrugated cardboard. Tape each piece in place, curving it slightly as you do, so it will be raised off the mask. This gives the eyes and eyebrows a more realistic, slightly bulging shape, as shown above.

• Draw a triangular shape where the nose will go. Poke your scissors through the cardboard and cut out the triangle.

• On a large scrap of cardboard, draw an "hourglass" nose shape big enough to fit over the nose hole. Cut it out. In order to give the nose a three-dimensional look, cut a long, thin strip of

---

TAPING TIPS

• Use plenty of tape when attaching pieces.

• To keep everything in place and create a smooth finish, be sure that every seam on the mask (where you attach the features to the cardboard) is fully taped. Smooth the tape carefully with your thumb.

cardboard that's ½-inch wide and long enough to wrap around the entire edge of the nose. Tape the thin cardboard strip around the nose, so that the hourglass shape stands ½-inch off the mask, as shown.

- Tape the nose unit securely over the nose hole and between the eyes, reaching up into the middle of the forehead, as shown (refer to the photograph and the illustration for positioning).

- For the mouth, twist a piece of newspaper tight to make a "rope." Form the rope into a circle and tape it into place where you want the mouth to be.

- For face decorations, cut out cardboard circles, thin rectangles, and other shapes, then tape them to the mask in designs and patterns of your own creation (or refer to the photograph of our mask for ideas).

• • • • • • •

4 To make handles, find the widest part of your mask going from side to side. Measure in 2 inches from each side and mark this spot with an X. Measure 3 inches below each X and mark with another X. Use your pencil to poke a hole through each X. Now, cut two 12-inch pieces of twine. Thread one piece of twine through the top left hole from front to back, then back out the bottom left hole; the handle will be on the back of the mask, and the loose ends in front. Knot the loose ends with a double knot on the front side of your mask so the twine won't pass back through the holes. Unravel the loose ends in the front for a hairy effect. Repeat to create a handle for the right side.

**Camilla,
incognito.**

5 To give your mask more hair, punch a few more holes above your handles on each side of your mask's forehead, and on its chin. Thread a short length of twine through each hole, and knot in the back and front. Unravel the twine in front.

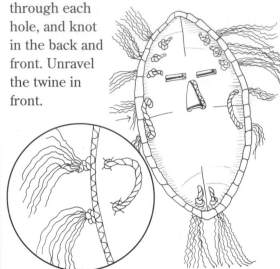

• • • • • • •

6 Mix ¼ cup of white glue with ¾ cup of water in a small bowl. Tear up the paper towels into 2-inch strips and small bits. Cover the entire mask with the strips and bits of paper towel, then gently paint over it with the glue mixture. Be patient; the paper towels may slip around a bit. This papier-mâché will form the mask's hard shell.

• • • • • • •

7 Let the paper towels dry thoroughly, then paint your mask. (We chose brown paint to make the mask look like wood, and bright colors for the facial features and decorations.)

• • • • • • •

8 Add a few final touches:

- Tape bead strings across the mask like necklaces, or dangle them from the edge like fringe.

- Glue feathers or shells to the mask or tie them to twine and attach as above.

- Glue on dry pasta or twisted newspaper to make great facial features.

Mexican Festival Mask

How easy is it?

For centuries, people in Mexico have been making masks to wear at festivals and celebrations. Oftentimes, the mask represents an animal or a mythical creature from folklore; at the festival, the wearer of the mask will perform a dance or a skit based on a legend that features the creature.

Some Mexican masks are carved from wood, but many are made from papier-mâché . . . just like the one shown here! To make this festival mask, you'll be casting a face mold . . . and guess whose face you'll be using as a model? Your own! Professional mask makers use this casting technique because they know its advantages: For one, the proportions of the mask are realistically human. For another, the mask is comfortable for the model to wear.

At the Muppet Workshop, we've used this technique while making masks for such films as *Labyrinth* and *The Witches*. Once you learn the basic process, you can make millions of masks: creatures, favorite characters, friends, relatives, pets. . . . Or make something fanciful, like we did here.

What You Will Need:

- aluminum foil
- damp sand or potting soil
- baking sheet or plastic tray
- papier-mâché glue mixture (see page 6 for recipe)
- bowl and newspaper for papier-mâché
- scissors
- newspaper
- egg cartons
- masking tape
- cardboard scraps
- poster paints or acrylic paints and paintbrush
- acrylic varnish (nontoxic) and paintbrush
- 2' of ribbon or two 1' lengths of ribbon

1 To make a cast of your face, take a long sheet of aluminum foil and fold it over three or four times to create a multi-layered square that's just large enough to fit over your face. Gently press the foil over your face, making sure to push in the small crevices and corners around features like your eyes and nose. Remove the foil from your face and roll the outside edges to make a rounded, even rim.

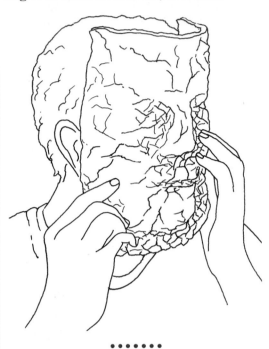

· · · · · · ·

2 To maintain the cast of your face while you work on the mask, gently hold the mask facedown in one hand and firmly pack the back of the mask with

damp sand or potting soil (be careful not to dent the mask). Once the mask is full, place the empty baking sheet upside down over the back of the mold and turn the whole thing over so that the mask is faceup on the tray.

Refresher Course:

You can read more about molding and casting in Chapter 4.

3 Mix the flour and water for papier-mâché (see page 6 for instructions and hints). Dip newspaper strips into the papier-mâché paste and cover the foil mold in three layers, letting each dry before adding another layer. As you work, be careful to gently but firmly press papier-mâché into the impressions of your mold so that it keeps its shape. It's especially important to press and smooth the paper into the recessed areas of the face, such as the eye sockets.

· · · · · · ·

4 Once the papier-mâché is completely dry, lift the mask from the foil cast. You may need to peel away excess foil. Cut eye-holes and nose holes in the mask so you can see and breathe.

· · · · · · ·

5 To make the facial features:

• **Eyes:** Cut out two individual egg holders from an egg carton to make "bug eyes." Poke sizable holes in the bottom of each one so you will be able to see. Tape in place.

- **Horns:** Roll dry newspaper into horn shapes and wrap with masking tape to help hold the shape. Tape in place on the forehead as shown, smoothing the tape with your fingers.

- **Nose and Mouth:**
  Twist, bunch, or roll newspaper to form nose and mouth shapes. Tape in place.

- **Ears:** Cut ear shapes from cardboard. Cut a slit into the bottom of each shape. Bend the tabs to create a slot for slipping the ears onto the mask. Tape in place.

········

6 Cover the entire mask and all features with papier-mâché to hide the tape and blend the features into the mask. Let it dry, then punch "seeing holes" through the eyes and "breathing holes" through the nose again, if needed.

········

7 Poke one hole for the ribbon tie just below each ear.

·······

8 Cover the entire mask with white paint. Let it dry, then paint your mask with beautiful bright colors. Let it dry.

········

9 For a shiny finish, add a coat of acrylic varnish and let it dry. Add another coat if you wish.

10 To make ties for your mask, thread a 12-inch length of ribbon through the hole under one ear. Tie the ribbon to itself with a knot at the back side of the hole as shown. Repeat for the other side.

CASTING CALL

These masks were specially made for the masked ball scene in Jim Henson's film *Labyrinth*. Using a process that's similar to the one in this project, each mask was cast to fit a particular actor's face.

Mysterious Masks

How easy is it?

Here's an easy way to make a mask that's perfect for your next masked ball: Simply buy a plastic or cloth eye mask, then glue on the glitteriest, featheriest, sparkliest stuff you can find!

These masks are great to wear on Halloween, and they make fun party favors. Why don't you make a bunch and send them out as invitations to your next costume party?

What You Will Need:

- basic store-bought plastic or cloth eye mask

Decorations:

- sequins and other fancy trims
- bits of felt or fabric
- netting or tulle
- beads
- ribbon
- straws
- feathers
- pom-poms
- glitter
- scissors
- white glue or masking tape
- paper clips
- Popsicle stick or chopstick

"I shall wear this mask to hide from my millions and zillions of adoring fans! No one will ever recognize moi."

1 Decide how you want your mask to look. Lay out all of the decorations you need so you can make sure they fit on the mask.

• • • • • • •

2 Glue (or tape) decorations onto the front of the mask from the bottom layer up. For instance, do a base layer of feathers, then glue pom-poms onto the feather "bed," then sequins onto the pom-poms, and so on. Make sure you glue lots of stuff near the bottom edge of the mask so that it hangs over the lower part of your face; that way you'll be really well disguised. Use paper clips to hold things in place while the glue sets. Let the glue dry thoroughly.

3 To add a mask holder, glue or tape a Popsicle stick or a chopstick to the back side of your mask, then decorate it with ribbon streamers.

Animal Noses, Horns, and Ears

How easy is it?

Basic Items You Will Need for All Animal Projects:

- **Bear Essentials**
- 1 headband for each mask
- clear cellophane tape (such as Scotch tape)
- masking tape
- poster board
- tracing paper

I t's amazing how a few simple features can define a character. Just put on a pair of ears, a nose, some horns . . . and suddenly, you're transformed!

Each of these simple but effective animal masks begins life as a headband. Once you learn the basic techniques of creating horns, ears, and beaks, you can experiment with other animal designs. Make a whole menagerie for your family! Or, add one to a colorful outfit to make a Halloween costume!

214

To make the Unicorn:

1 If you wish to decorate your headband "base," place glue on the headband and wrap it evenly with ribbon. Let the glue dry.

. . . .

2 Cut the poster board, as shown. Roll the cutout shape into a cone about 17 inches tall and 3 inches in diameter at the base and glue down the overlapping edge. Paint or glue on some glitter for decoration.

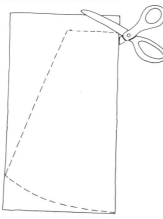

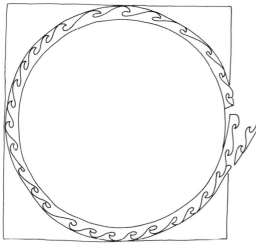

. . . .

3 Place glue on the back of some pretty ribbon and wrap it around the horn; glue down the ends. Or, trace the outline of a dinner plate onto yellow construction paper. Place a smaller plate in the center of the circle and trace another circle. Draw a wave pattern within the narrow band created by the tracings, as shown above. Cut out the narrow band, then cut out the wavy design. Wrap it around your horn, as shown, and glue at the ends.

4 Bend two paper clips into right angles and tape them to the inside bottom of the horn on opposite sides. Using clear tape, tape the paper clips to the headband, as shown.

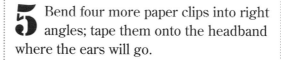

. . . .

5 Bend four more paper clips into right angles; tape them onto the headband where the ears will go.

. . . .

6 Turn to the ear pattern on page 316; cut it out and trace it onto the white poster board twice (see page 9 for tracing instructions). Cut out both poster board ears and decorate them with paint or glitter and glue. Fold the ears as shown below, and tape them to the paper clips with clear tape. Wrap a piece of tape around the base to secure.

. . . .

7 Tie or tape curled ribbons to the headband so that they dangle down over your ears. To hide the paper clips, place glue on the back side of some short lengths of white ribbon and wrap each length around a clip.

What You Will Need for the Unicorn:

- white and gold ribbon
- two 12" × 17" pieces of white poster board
- glitter, paint, and paintbrush
- dinner plate and dessert plate, yellow construction paper (optional)
- paper clips

To make the Toucan:

1 Lay out a 10-inch length of masking tape. Lay a row of feathers as shown, down the full length of the tape. Lay on another piece of tape, sticky-side down, to secure the feathers in place.

• • • • • • •

2 Cut a 2-inch piece of cardboard tubing. Flatten the tube in half, then carefully cut wide horizontal slits on opposite sides of the tube. Squeeze and roll the tube until it's round

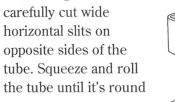

**What You Will
Need for the
Toucan:**

- assorted colorful feathers
- cardboard tube (from bathroom tissue)
- acrylic paint and paintbrush
- shiny red wrapping paper (optional)
- flour, water, and bowl (for papier-mâché glue mixture)
- newspaper
- elastic cord

again, then slide the tube onto the center of your headband, as shown below. Glue the feather tape around the tube base, wrapping and overlapping as you go. Paint the base or wrap shiny paper around it and glue in place.

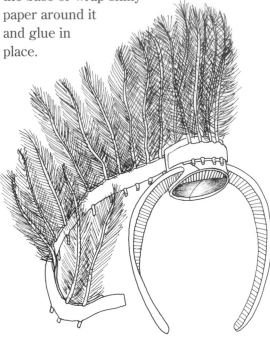

• • • • • • •

3 Trace the beak patterns on page 317 onto cardboard. Cut out the bottom piece and the two side pieces. Tape the pieces together with masking tape to make the beak.

• • • • • • •

4 Prepare the papier-mâché (see page 6 for recipe and instructions). Cover the beak with a smooth layer of newspaper and papier-mâché. Let dry.

• • • • • • •

5 Poke a tiny hole on each side of the beak, then attach elastic, as shown below. Paint the beak.

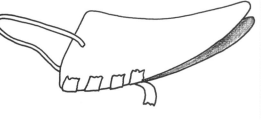

To make the Elephant:

1 Tape the middle of a straightened wire hanger firmly to the center of your headband so that the wire sticks out evenly on both sides like antennae.

. . . .

2 Wrap newspaper around the wire ear supports until they're each about 1 inch thick, then wrap them in masking tape.

. . .

3 Trace and enlarge the ear pattern on page 318, then transfer it to the brown paper bags four times. Cut out the four ears. Sandwich one of the antennae between two paper ear pieces, keeping the antenna near the top edges of the ear shapes. Glue the paper ears together and let dry. Repeat for the other ear.

4 Paint the ears.

. . . .

5 Trace and enlarge the trunk pattern on page 319, then transfer it to lightweight poster board. Cut out the shape and the shaded areas. Roll the cutout into a tube shape that tapers slightly at one end and tape it together firmly on the inside.

. . . .

6 Carefully poke one small hole into each side of the base of the trunk. Cut a little curve for your nose. Paint the trunk and let it dry. Knot on a piece of elastic and adjust it around your head.

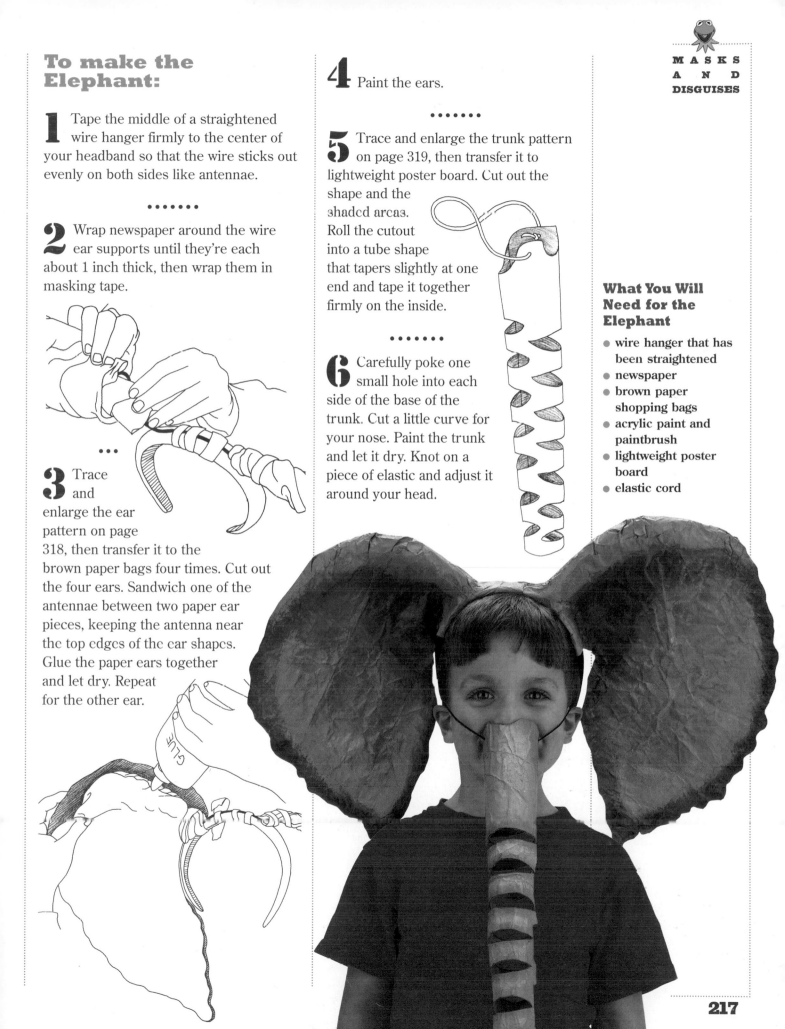

What You Will Need for the Elephant

- wire hanger that has been straightened
- newspaper
- brown paper shopping bags
- acrylic paint and paintbrush
- lightweight poster board
- elastic cord

217

Totem Pole Mask

How easy is it?

What You Will Need:

- scissors
- corrugated cardboard box, about 36" tall and 24" square (or a few smaller boxes to tape in a stack)
- pencil
- cardboard
- cardboard bathroom tissue tubes (at least 6)
- pint-size milk carton (empty and clean)
- masking tape
- colored construction paper
- poster paint (make sure you have a lot of white poster paint) and paintbrushes

Totem poles are tall, carved, painted wooden posts that were traditionally created by Native Americans in the northwestern United States and southwestern Canada. The poles usually depicted "totems"—animals that had tribal or cultural significance, and referred to a legend or represented an event.

In the Northwest, Native Americans usually had rituals and celebrations that surrounded the creation and installation of totem poles. Maybe you and your friends would like to make totem pole masks together and start your own rituals and celebrations: Have a totem pole party!

1 Cut off all flaps on both ends of the cardboard box. Squeeze and roll the square sides of your box so that it becomes a rounded tube as shown.

2 To reinforce the tube you've made and to keep it round, place the end of the rounded box on top of another flat piece of cardboard. Trace around the end and cut out the circle.

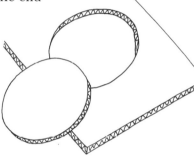

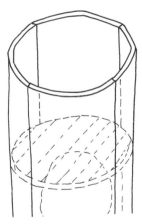

Push the cardboard circle at least two-thirds of the way up into the tube. Repeat this step, but set aside the second circle; it will become the "lid" for the top of the totem pole.

3 Mark semicircles on either side of the bottom of the tube and cut out notches for your shoulders.

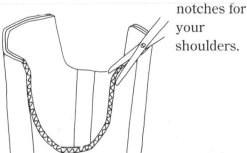

Cut out a bit at a time, checking to make sure the mask sits snugly on your shoulders.

4 Decide on the order of your totems on your "pole," then work from bottom to top. Sketch out the placement of beaks, ears, or horns on the pole. Divide the tube into fairly even sections, depending on how many characters you are making, and mark off each section (three or four characters are probably enough). Remember to plan eyeholes for yourself at the right height and width in the face of the lowest creature on your pole. To make round eyeholes, trace circles on your big tube using a bathroom tissue tube, then cut out circles. You can leave eyeholes plain, or to make bulging eyes, you can insert a 2-inch length of cardboard tube into each eyehole as shown. For directions for other features, see page 220.

5 When all the eyes, noses, mouths, horns, and other features are in place on your totem mask, cover any rough spots or gaps with tape and rub all tape down so that it is smooth. Tape the lid onto the top of the mask.

6 Paint the entire totem pole white; this creates a good base for bright colors. Let dry. Then paint your animals any colors you choose. Let the paint dry completely before wearing your mask.

"Be careful when you've got your totem pole mask on—remember, you're a lot taller!"

219

CREATURE FEATURES

Cut out, fold, and attach cardboard pieces to create the features of the totem animals. Have fun experimenting with different shapes and sizes. Here are a few useful construction methods that we used.

For beaks:

● Unfold the top end of the milk carton and cut away or unfold the bottom end. Cut away sections of the carton, as shown below, and fold to form a triangular box (sort of an elongated pyramid with a point at one end). Tape the carton back together, as shown.

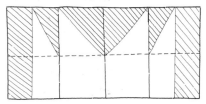

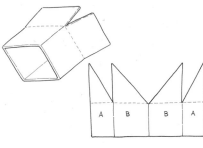

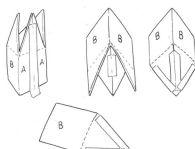

Trace the base of the beak onto the front of the mask, then cut a snug opening into which the beak can be fitted. Tape the inserted end of the beak to the inside of the mask.

For horns:

● Cut darts into cardboard tubes, as shown.

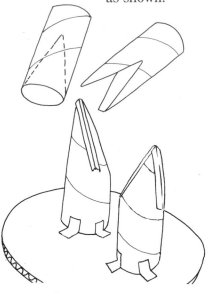

Push together the points and tape them into a horn shape. Tape them onto the mask or onto the cardboard lid you cut out earlier.

For wings:

● Draw two wing shapes on the cardboard that look like the ones shown. Cut them both out and tape the edges so they look smooth.

To attach them to your mask, cut thin slots into opposite sides of the mask, insert the wing pieces, and tape them in place.

For other features:

● Use cardboard tubes for eyes, snouts, and ears. Trace the end of the tube onto the mask where you want the feature to go. Cut the circle out of the mask, insert a tube, then tape the tubes in place from inside the mask. If you want the end of a nose or eye to be closed, trace the tube on scrap cardboard, cut out the circle, then tape it onto the end of the tube.

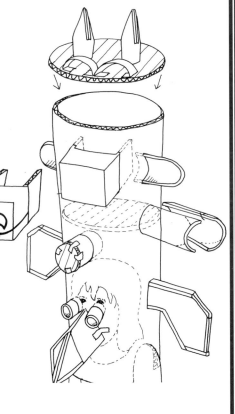

● For "stick-out ears," cut a tube in half lengthwise, then cut semicircular slits in the mask and slide the tube halves into place. Tape them in place from the inside of the mask.

● To add hair, cut strips of colored construction paper and tape on as you wish.

Glamorama

Miss Piggy is a very big fan of jewels, especially diamonds . . . and pearls . . . and rubies . . . and emeralds. . . . So, at the Muppet Workshop, we often create special made-to-order jewelry for the Divine Miss P. (When Miss Piggy gives you an order, you'd better obey . . . or else.) For instance, we made special bracelets and fancy headdresses for her role in *Muppet Treasure Island.* For that film, we also made the seashell and bone necklaces worn by the wild boars, tiny necklaces and bracelets for Rizzo the Rat and his friends, and a miniature treasure chest overflowing with tons of small-scale jewels.

CAMEO ROLE

Cameos are small pins or ornaments that feature a "relief" carving, with the relief in contrasting color to the background (read more about relief carving on page 67). Traditionally, cameos featured carved profiles of loved ones. Miss Piggy's lovely cameo pin was specially made for this shot, a spoof of a classic painting, *American Gothic,* by Grant Wood. The cameo was first carved out of wood and then painted.

"Diamonds are a pig's best friend!"

In this section, we'll introduce you to some Muppet Workshop jewelry-making techniques. You can make jewelry out of almost anything. Start to look at everything around you and think *jewelry.* How would that flower look hanging around your neck, from your ears, around your wrist, or attached to a pin?

Seasonal Necklaces

How easy is it?

Basic Materials You Will Need for All Necklaces:

- silk cord, shoelace, ribbon, string, nylon thread, or yarn (for stringing)
- scissors
- large needle (make sure it fits your thread or cord)
- hole puncher
- cardboard
- white glue

Seasonal necklaces are made using objects that you might find or collect during a particular season; look at the photographs below and see if you can identify spring, summer, fall, and winter.

Start your own seasonal necklace by hunting for materials in your backyard or at the park. You can buy out-of-season items and fun add-ons at a craft store or florist, or look through your collection of odds and ends for doodads to attach.

Like many of the crafts shown in this book, handmade jewelry is a great gift to give to family members or friends. So string up a seasonal necklace to give to someone, and give it a theme based on the time of year it's given; make a spring necklace for a May birthday, for instance. Or make a summer necklace for someone born in cold December to remind her of the balmy August days to come.

PROJECT MADE BY BARBARA DAVIS

1 Collect all the things you want to string onto your necklace and lay them out on a table. Arrange them in a line, imagining how they'll look when they are on your necklace. Think about patterns and how to sequence or repeat various items along the string. Choose one very large item like a starfish, a bell, or a shell as the necklace's centerpiece.

"Do me a favor, leaf me alone until after summer's over, okay?"

· · · · · · · · · ·

2 Hold a piece of cord or ribbon along the line of things you want to string, and cut the string so it's a few inches longer than the line of items. Be sure that the cord is long enough to slip comfortably over your head or the head of the person for whom you are making the necklace. Tie a big knot about 2 inches from one end of the cord.

· · · · · · ·

3 Thread your needle with the cord (you don't need to use one if your objects have large enough holes) and string your objects onto the cord (see "The Skinny on Stringing" on the next page).

4 When you've threaded everything onto your necklace, tie a big knot at the end. Then tie both ends tightly together with a double knot, making sure the necklace still fits over your head. Trim the ends of the cord so that they can't be seen.

What You Will Need for Each Necklace:

Spring
- fresh or dried flowers—buds, stems, and leaves
- ribbons
- lace

Summer
- seashells
- fake pearls
- green leaves or dried seaweed
- little starfish (you can make some out of clay, if you like)

Fall
- autumn leaves
- horse chestnut seed-pods
- nutshells

Winter
- pine needle stems
- pinecones
- cranberries
- rickrack
- tiny red bells

THE SKINNY ON STRINGING

Flowers

● To string flowers, thread a needle and carefully push it through the thickest part of the blossom (usually the spot just before the stem starts).

● If you want, tie little ribbon bows or bunches of lace onto the cord between bunches of flowers.

● If you'd like your fresh flower necklace to last longer, store it in the refrigerator.

Leaves

● Use a hole puncher or a needle to poke holes in leaves or stems.

● Poke the needle through the stem of a little pine branch, or tie the necklace cord right around the stem to attach.

Shells

● Any shell that has a hole in it can be strung on your necklace, but be sure that anything you use is clean and doesn't have any animals living in it. You may need to dry your finds in the sun before you can use them.

● Glue fake pearls or seaweed into seashells as decoration or to hide flaws in the shells.

Nuts, Pods, Fruit

● Glue clusters of acorns and other nuts, pods, and seeds together on a small bit of cardboard and thread cord through a hole in the cardboard.

● Thread dried cranberries onto the cord with a needle (make sure they're completely dry—you don't want a juicy necklace!).

Miscellaneous

● Tie tiny jingle bells to ends of gold rickrack pieces. Tie rickrack bows onto the cord.

Edible Necklace

How easy is it?

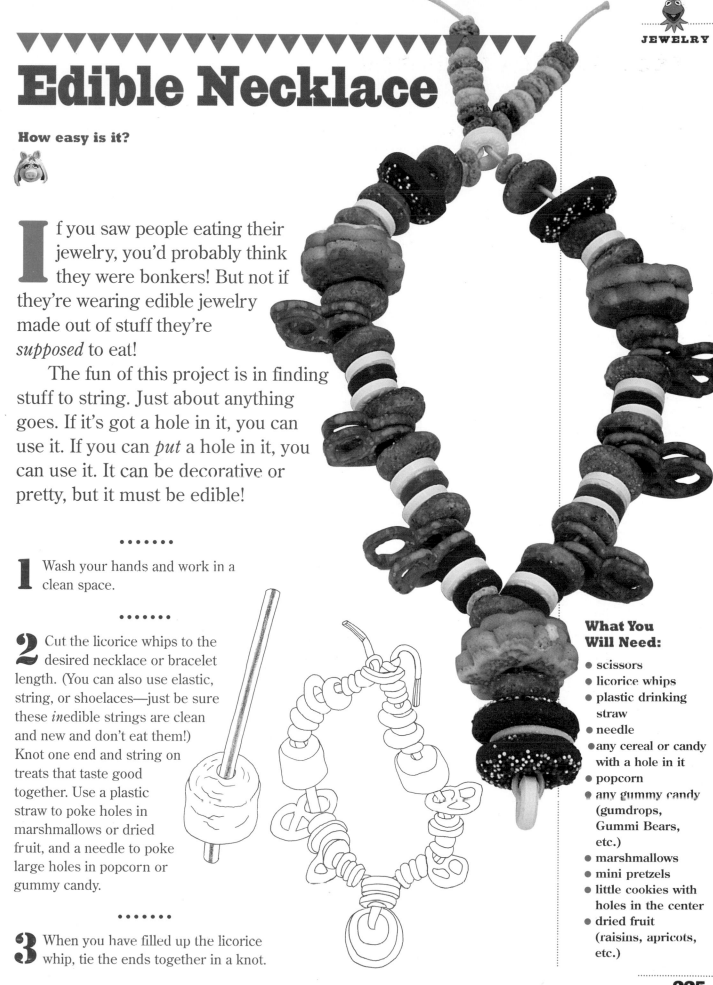

If you saw people eating their jewelry, you'd probably think they were bonkers! But not if they're wearing edible jewelry made out of stuff they're *supposed* to eat!

The fun of this project is in finding stuff to string. Just about anything goes. If it's got a hole in it, you can use it. If you can *put* a hole in it, you can use it. It can be decorative or pretty, but it must be edible!

1 Wash your hands and work in a clean space.

2 Cut the licorice whips to the desired necklace or bracelet length. (You can also use elastic, string, or shoelaces—just be sure these *in*edible strings are clean and new and don't eat them!) Knot one end and string on treats that taste good together. Use a plastic straw to poke holes in marshmallows or dried fruit, and a needle to poke large holes in popcorn or gummy candy.

3 When you have filled up the licorice whip, tie the ends together in a knot.

What You Will Need:

- scissors
- licorice whips
- plastic drinking straw
- needle
- any cereal or candy with a hole in it
- popcorn
- any gummy candy (gumdrops, Gummi Bears, etc.)
- marshmallows
- mini pretzels
- little cookies with holes in the center
- dried fruit (raisins, apricots, etc.)

PROJECT MADE BY BARBARA DAVIS

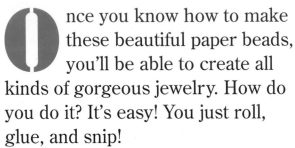

Rolled Paper Beads

How easy is it?

Once you know how to make these beautiful paper beads, you'll be able to create all kinds of gorgeous jewelry. How do you do it? It's easy! You just roll, glue, and snip!

Be picky when selecting the paper to use in this project: Look for thin paper that's easy to roll and glue (avoid thick paper since it's difficult to roll). Gift wrap rolls well, and its bright colors and bold designs make colorful beads that look great together. You can use gold, silver, or printed gift wrap, or try origami paper, marbleized writing paper, white or colored copier paper, brown-bag paper, magazine pages, comic book pages, and so on. Set up a box to store used paper that you would usually throw away, then turn that paper into beads when you have the time.

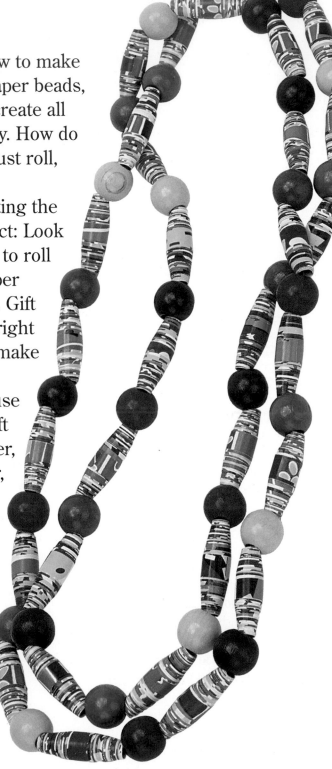

PROJECT MADE BY JANET KUHL

1 Cut long triangles out of different papers, and snip off the tips so that they're blunt and not too pointed (our bead strips were about 23 inches long, and the bases of the triangles each measured about 1½ inches across). Each strip will make one bead.

. . . .

2 Lay the paper strip out flat (if there's a "pretty side" to the paper, it should be face*down*). Glue the base of the triangle onto the middle of a straw and roll the straw and paper toward you, as evenly and tightly as possible.

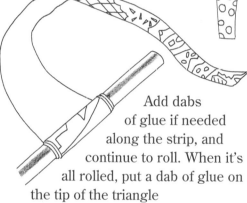

Add dabs of glue if needed along the strip, and continue to roll. When it's all rolled, put a dab of glue on the tip of the triangle and press it onto the bead to finish it. (You can roll two or three beads on each straw.)

. . . .

3 When you've rolled all your beads onto straws, cut the straws into sections, bead by bead. Trim excess straw away from the edges of the beads if necessary.

. . . .

4 If you wish, paint the beads with a light coat of glaze mixture made from 2 teaspoons white glue and 1 teaspoon water. Let the glaze dry.

5 Make jewelry with your beads:

- Make necklaces, anklets, or bracelets by stringing beads on elastic cord or dental floss. Add store-bought beads in between your paper beads if you like. Tie a knot in the cord to finish. Or, if you want to make your jewelry fastener really fancy, use needle-nose pliers to add "findings" you've bought in jewelry or craft stores (findings are the different kinds of clasps, hooks, or backings you see on most jewelry).

- Make earrings by stringing a few beads together on dental floss or an "earring pin" (available at bead or crafts stores). Hook the end of the floss or pin onto an earring wire or clip, as shown here.

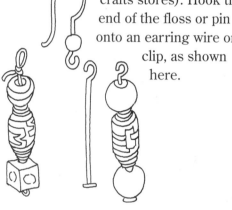

"Tangled up in jewels . . ."

ROLLING AROUND

When you roll your beads, the *wider* the strip of paper you use, the *longer* the bead will be. The *longer* the strip of paper you use (giving you more paper to roll around the straw), the *fatter* the bead will be. Try making a gorgeous giant bead for a necklace centerpiece by cutting a *really* long strip of beautifully colored paper. Try using beads of different lengths in a necklace or bracelet.

Fancy Clay Beads

How easy is it?

What You Will Need:

- an adult (to help with the oven and knife)
- Fimo, Sculpey, or other brightly colored, oven-hardening clay
- wax paper
- rolling pin
- sharp, non-serrated kitchen knife
- small-diameter aluminum knitting needle (1/16" diameter is good)
- cookie sheet covered with aluminum foil

To Make Jewelry:

- nylon thread or silk cord
- findings (clasps, hooks, ear wires, barrette backings, and pin backings available at craft stores)
- white glue
- needle-nose pliers (optional)

These clay beads are made to look like beautiful glass *millifiori* beads, which are created by master glassblowers in Venice, Italy (*millifiori* means "a thousand flowers" in Italian). To create *millifiori* beads, glassblowers first heat glass rods of different colors, then wrap them together in a sheet of heated, softened glass. This process creates long logs of multicolored glass that are then cut into beads (it's a lot like making "slice-and-bake" cookies).

Our beads look like they would be difficult to make, but they're not; you just roll and slice clay and the next thing you know, you've got a pile of beautiful beads. Once you've made an assortment of beads, you can string them together to make necklaces, attach them to safety pins to make pins, or dangle them from ear wires for earrings. Keep a bunch on hand to make beautiful and fashionable presents for your friends.

MAKING CLAY LOGS

Here's how to make the clay logs from which your beads will be sliced.

For beads with swirls:

Choose two or more colors of clay and roll them out flat between sheets of wax paper. Stack the different colors one on top of another (pile the colors so that they are a little bit staggered, as shown below) and roll them up. Chill the log in the freezer for about twenty minutes, then move on to step 1.

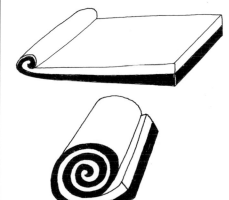

For rainbow beads:

Choose as many colors of clay as you like. Take the first color and roll it into a skinny log. Take the next color and roll it out flat into a rectangular sheet. Wrap the sheet around the log. Continue wrapping rectangular sheets around the growing tube until you are satisfied with your rainbow.

(If you'd like to imitate the colors of a real rainbow, they are: red, orange, yellow, green, blue, indigo, violet.) Chill the log in the freezer for twenty minutes, then move on to step 1.

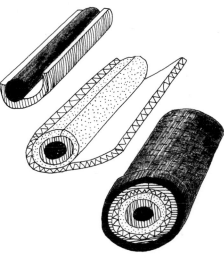

For flowery starburst beads:

Take one color and roll it out into a skinny log. Take another color, roll it out flat into a rectangular sheet, and wrap the sheet around the log.

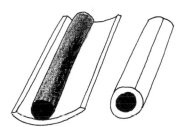

Now take small amounts of another color and roll them out into four *very* skinny little rods, the same length as the first log, but much smaller in diameter. Take yet another color and roll out four more

very skinny rods. Now, position all of the smaller rods around the larger log, alternating colors, and gently press and roll everything

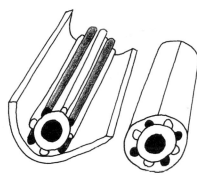

together. Take a final color, roll out a large, flat rectangular piece, and wrap it around the whole log and rod group. Roll the log gently and evenly with your hands until it is the diameter of the bead you want. Repeat these steps to create a multi-log roll as shown below. Chill the rod in the freezer for twenty minutes, then move on to step 1

"Roll 'em up!"

"**When making jewelry, one must always be fully accessorized. You never know who might show up to help!**"

1 Once a log is chilled, have an adult help you use a sharp kitchen knife to slice the log into beads, as shown. If the clay gets too warm to cut smoothly, re-chill the log as needed.

2 Gently poke a hole through each bead using a small-diameter aluminum knitting needle. Lay the beads out on cookie sheet that's covered in aluminum foil. Ask an adult to bake the beads in a 265°F oven for twenty to thirty minutes. Take the beads out and

let them cool for about thirty minutes.

3 To make jewelry from your beads:

● String them on nylon thread or silk cord. For bracelets and necklaces, tie the ends in a knot or add a clasp from the craft store. For dangling earrings, hang them from earring hooks.

● Glue them together in clusters and attach a cluster to an earring or pin backing, or barrette.

CLAY TIPS

● Before working with this type of clay, you should knead it a little to make it soft. Roll it into a ball, then into a long snake, then back into a ball.

● Wash your hands between colors to prevent color mixing—unless you *want* to experiment by mixing two or more colors together.

● Each bead is cut from a long log of clay. You can cut thin or thick slices for beads, but it's harder to poke holes through the thinner slices. Remember that the diameter of the log will be the diameter of the bead, so try

making some logs with large diameters and some with small diameters.

● When making logs, be sure to smooth any seams in the clay, then roll the logs very well to get rid of any air pockets or bubbles in the clay. You want all of your clay pieces to be smoothly joined or you'll end up with holes in your beads.

● Beads will not shrink, grow, or melt when cooked; they just harden.

● Clay logs can be shaped into squares, triangles, or other shapes

so that bead slices will have different shapes. (See the square beads in our necklace photo on page 228. They came from a square log.)

● For variety, you can gently roll bead slices into balls, or gently flatten them with a rolling pin.

● Be sure to place clay between sheets of wax paper before rolling.

● If you want to use a bead to glue onto a barrette or an earring stud, you don't have to poke a hole in it before you bake it.

CHAPTER 15 / SET AND MODEL SHOP

Big and Small Stuff

At the Muppet Workshop, we spend a great deal of time imagining, designing, and building the special little worlds where our puppets perform. Specially sized sets featuring detailed rooms, houses, buildings, towns, and other kinds of fantastical scenes are built for Muppet television shows, photo shoots, and movies, and each set is specifically designed to accommodate the Muppets and their puppeteers. (Often, sets are built very high off the ground so the puppeteers can stand upright below the set, performing their puppets over their heads. This is a lot easier than having to lie on their backs or in other contorted positions, which they often do when they're shooting "on location" out in the real world.)

Once you learn a few set-building concepts and terms, you can re-create just about anything or any place you

"Ouch! Was that a building I just crushed, or is it my bunion acting up again?"

like. Good sets and scenery are really visual magic, because they trick the eye into seeing things the way they *aren't.* For example, the *scale* is the size relationship, or proportion, of objects to one another. In our minds, we have a good basic idea of "human scale": how tall a person is in relation to human objects, like a toothbrush or a bus or a house. But if scale is manipulated, there can be unusual (or funny or scary) results: A normal-sized character in a miniature set will look like a giant, like the blue monster on the previous page. On the other hand, a normal-sized character in an oversized set will look tiny. If you want to build a miniature world for a miniature character, you have to take care that things—like cups, chairs, even pets—are in proportion there, too. These kinds of details are very important because they make a scene look richer and more realistic; they help fool the viewers' eyes even more. So think about scale and detail as you add items to your "Treasure Island Diorama," your "Dollhouse Deluxe," your "Model City," or your "Snow Globe Scene."

Also, in thinking about *props* (the freely moving objects and furnishings in a set or a scene), bear in mind that you can use certain items or materials and make them appear to look like something else. Soap flakes can be snow, a doll can be a baby, and so on. In the "Tepee" project in this chapter, you'll see how grocery bags can become animal skins. And when you're putting on performances, whether they're filmed or staged, you must bear in mind that the audience doesn't see things as close-up or for as long as the actors do. You can use this to your advantage when you're trying to pass one thing off as another.

Another important thing to think about is *perspective,* which is the audience's view of the scene and how near or far away things appear to be. As the creator of a scene, you can manipulate the perspective. If you want the background in your set to appear far away, you should paint a background where things appear to get smaller in the "distance." You should also make the colors of those things fainter and their outlines less distinct, since this gives the impression of distance (people's eyes get fooled into thinking that things are too far away to see them clearly).

Another helpful feature is a *vanishing point,* which is a point at which a line, after getting thinner and thinner, seems to disappear in the distance. Check out our "Fairy Tale Stage Set" project in this chapter and look at the photograph. See how the brown road appears to wander off into the distance? That's because we ended it in a vanishing point. Cool, huh?

False backgrounds also add depth to scenes, as do freestanding structures in the *foreground* (which is the area that's nearer to the audience than the background). Both the "Fairy Tale Stage Set" project and the "Treasure Island Diorama" employ these techniques. You'll see how it helps once you try it.

The thing that's neat is, as a set or model builder, you only have to build a little bit of a scene or add a few props in the right scale, and the viewers' brains fill in the rest.

A MINIATURE WORLD IS BORN

This wonderful miniature-scale set was made for the opening sequence of *The Muppet Christmas Carol*, in which it seems as if the viewer is flying over the city of London. The basic forms of the buildings were made from wooden orange crates and cardboard boxes, with details like little handmade "bricks" and "shingles" added. There were real lights on inside the buildings so it would look like a real nighttime city.

When the set was finished, all the people who worked on it wrote their names on the bottoms of the buildings.

What You Will Need:

- Bear Essentials
- newspaper
- masking tape or duct tape
- ball of string
- chalk
- 6 thick wooden dowels (about 6' tall, ½" diameter)
- 2 or 3 elastic bands (large and thick)
- 24 big brown paper grocery bags (or use brown mailing paper)
- 1 shank button (a smooth button that has a loop on the back instead of holes in it)
- poster paints and paintbrushes
- feathers

Tepee

How easy is it?

Did you ever wish you had a special place that was all your own, where you could get away from your pesky siblings, hide from homework, or just have a few minutes to think quietly? Make this tepee and you'll have your own portable hideaway; it's big enough to hold a friend, too—in case you get lonely. The Native Americans who invented the tepee made it lightweight and portable, so it could be picked up and moved as they migrated over the course of each year. Their tepees were made from animal skins, so they were warm as well as wind- and rainproof. As you make your tepee, you'll learn how to make structures that are balanced and sturdy. You'll also learn how to trick the eye by using easy-to-find materials that imitate other materials like animal skins and branches.

234

1 Lay out newspapers on the floor to cover a 6-foot-square area, overlapping them slightly and taping them onto each other in place.

• • • • • • •

2 Cut a piece of string 36 inches long and tie a piece of chalk to the very end. From the chalk end, measure out 33 inches. Have a friend hold the chalk-free end of the string at the 33-inch mark, just at the center of your newspaper "island." You hold the chalk. Pulling the string tight as you go, begin to move in a circle around your friend, as shown below, drawing a chalk circle on the paper as you go. Be careful not to pull the string out of your friend's grip. When you've completed the circle, mark the center of the 66-inch circle, right where your friend's hand was.

• • • • • • •

3 Gather your dowels together and secure with one or two thick elastic bands placed about 6 inches from the top of the gathered ends, as shown here. Space the bottom of the dowels out evenly around the edge of the circle.

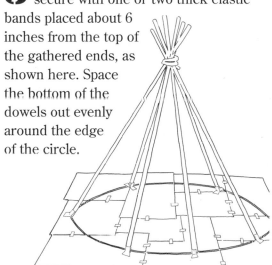

Rearrange them until they're balanced and not wobbly. Tape the ends of the dowels down onto the newspaper with duct tape.

• • • • • • •

4 To make the tepee "skin": rip or cut open brown paper bags to make flat "skins" of paper (cut off the bottoms of the bags and discard). Scrunch up the bags, then flatten them out again to give them the appearance of rumpled skins. Tear a tiny bit of paper off along all edges of the bags to eliminate straight edges.

• • • • • • •

5 Lay three bags out at a time, long edge to long edge, each slightly overlapping the next. Tear a fourth bag in half and position each half, one on top of the other at the top of the three long bags, as shown below. Put glue on the seams and glue the bags in place. Repeat to make six separate panels.

• • • • • • •

6 Draw a triangle onto each panel, with a base measuring 33 inches across and the other two sides each measuring 65 inches (have the two sides meet at a point directly above the midpoint of the base). Carefully tear out the triangle.

"Keep your tepee in a dry place like your bedroom or garage."

Repeat to make a triangle from each of the other panels.

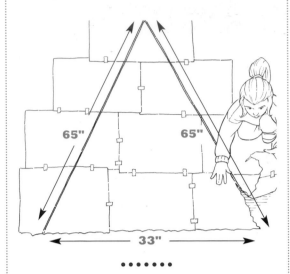

65"   65"

33"

• • • • • • •

7 Arrange the six triangular panels on the ground so they form a half-circle, as shown below. Overlap slightly and glue the panels together. Let dry.

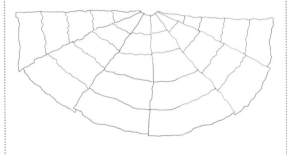

• • • • • • •

8 Wrap the whole paper-bag skin all the way around the tepee's frame, leaving the top 6 inches of the dowels exposed. Overlap one of the skin edges over the other a little and adjust them to fit. Glue securely at the seam, and use masking tape to hold it in place while it dries.

• • • • • • •

9 To make a door flap, pick a location for your door that's directly opposite the big seam where your tepee skin is glued. Make two long tears—the two long sides of your door—in your tepee skin between two dowels. Do not tear the top edge of the door (you may want to close the door later). Just above the door, glue a small reinforcing strip of brown paper bag.

10 From the outside of the tepee, poke the metal loop of a shank button all the way through the reinforcing strip about 6 inches above the top of the door flap (you may need to use a pencil to poke the hole). Thread a 12-inch length of string through the button loop on the inside of the tepee and knot it, as shown. To keep the door open, roll up the door flap and secure by wrapping the string around the button.

• • • • • • •

11 If you'd like to strengthen the tepee structure, glue or tape at least three rectangles of brown paper over each length of dowel inside the tepee, spacing them evenly, as shown.

• • • • • • •

12 When all the glue is thoroughly dry, the tepee is ready to be painted and decorated. Stick feathers in the rubber bands near the dowel tops. Carefully tear a window opening if you'd like.

• • • • • • •

13 When the whole tepee is dry, carefully peel the taped dowels from the newspaper floor cover and discard the newspaper.

Have some friends over for a camp-in!

Snow Globe Scene

How easy is it?

Did you ever wish for snow in the middle of summer? Well, you can make it snow anytime you want with your very own snow globe! Creating a snow globe scene is like creating a set for a play or a diorama or even a dollhouse. You need to think about the scene, the props, the scale, the perspective, and even the star! But the best thing about making a snow globe is adding water and making the scene come to life!

What You Will Need:

- an adult (to hammer a nail)
- Bear Essentials
- glass jars with interesting shapes and watertight lids
- soft plastic lid from an ice cream pint, margarine, or take-out container

(continued on next page)

What You Will Need continued:

- empty plastic thread spool
- glue (waterproof)
- acrylic paint (we used gold) and paintbrush
- hammer and nail
- tacks or straight pins (optional)
- plastic waterproof toy figurines
- glitter or glitter confetti (don't use paper confetti—it will fall apart in the water)
- distilled water (this is a *must* to avoid mold growing in the globe)
- liquid dish detergent
- Teflon thread sealing tape

Optional:

- decorations for the base, such as beads, trims, bows, pebbles
- 1 jar lid that is bigger than the mouth of the jar you are using
- air-dry clay (Crayola Model Magic Lightweight Modeling Compound is a good choice)

1 Trace the glass jar opening on the soft plastic lid and cut out the plastic circle. Mark the center of the plastic circle. It will become your globe's base.

2 To make a pedestal base for the figurine, paint an empty plastic thread spool with acrylic paint and let it dry. Center the plastic circle over the spool and ask an adult to hammer a nail through the plastic lid and through the spool. Glue the figurine to the other end of the spool.

Note: *The spool helps the figurine stand taller in the jar. If you don't want to use a spool, position the figurine on the center of the plastic circle and have an adult help you stick tacks or straight pins through the plastic and into the bottom of your plastic figurine to keep it in place.*

3 Glue the underside of the plastic circle to the underside of the jar lid. Let the glue dry.

4 Place about 2 tablespoons of glitter in the jar. Pour distilled water in slowly until the jar is filled to the top. Add a small drop of detergent to help the glitter float.

5 Gently put the figure upside down into the jar and water. Some water will seep out, but make sure that the jar remains as full as possible to prevent air bubbles in the globe. Put the jar lid on and screw it shut very tightly.

6 Carefully wrap Teflon tape smoothly around the lid edge and glass jar about three times to prevent leaks.

7 Decorate the outside of the jar with bows, beads, or trinkets, if you like.

· · · · · · ·

8 Add special features to your snow globe. To make a base for the globe:

• Fill an empty jar lid that is bigger than the base of your snow globe with air-dry clay (the lid will be a temporary mold). Place your sealed globe in the clay-filled lid, as shown below.

• If you like, continue to add clay to form a sculptural base, as shown.

• Decorate the clay with whatever else you like—stick sequins, beads, even pebbles or tiny shells directly into the clay. Or paint the clay once it dries and glue the objects on later.

• Once the clay is dry (approximately twenty-four hours later) remove the outer lid holding the clay.

Shake it up, baby!

**"Oh Kermie,
isn't the snow
romantic?"**

**"BRRRRR...
can we go
inside now,
please?"**

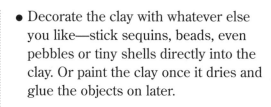

Fairy Tale Stage Set

How easy is it?

A stage set, props, and scenery are important parts of any kind of performance because they tell us a lot about the characters—where they live, how they live, in what era they live, and sometimes what their personalities are like.

This scene was made using a refrigerator box, but you can make your set even larger by adding more boxes; it all depends on what kind of show you're putting on.

1 Using heavy-duty scissors, cut off the top flaps of the large cardboard box. Leave the bottom flaps on. Then cut open one corner seam and flatten the box. Stand the box up, with the bottom flaps turned to the front and overlapped slightly. The box's two sides will fold in slightly, enabling the box to stand up straight.

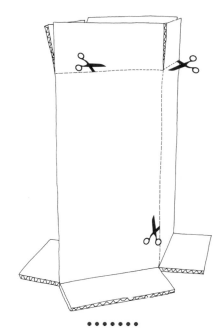

• • • • • • •

2 To secure the overlapped bottom flaps in position, reinforce them with masking or duct tape. (You may want to reinforce the stage with triangular cardboard supports that are similar to the support on the back of a picture frame. To do so, cut right-angled triangles from cardboard, then tape them to the back of the scene at the bottom, so they stand on the floor, as shown above. Bend and adjust as necessary.)

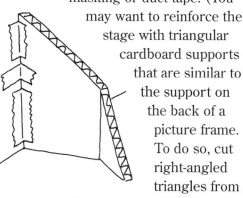

• • • • • • •

3 To add depth to the scene as we did, cut out a small section from the scene you've built, and create another scene to stand behind it (following the directions in steps 1 and 2, but using a smaller box). Later, when you paint them, you should paint the "far background"

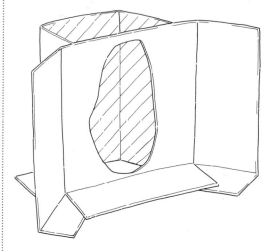

scene to blend in with the foreground set, as we did (see in our photograph how it makes it look like the forest keeps on going into the distance?).

• • • • • • •

4 If you want to add doors and windows to your set:

• Sketch designs directly onto the set (make these openings small enough so they don't weaken the structure of your stage). Cut out your doors and windows on three sides only, leaving one side uncut to make the "hinges," so you can open and shut the door or window if you like (you may have to ask an adult to use a utility knife to do this cutting).

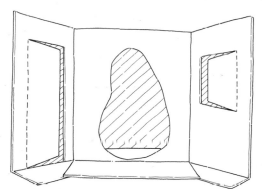

• To create a "view" out the door or window, paint the view onto a flat piece of cardboard then tape it to the back of the set, facing toward the audience. You could make a few different views, then have your "stagehands" change them

What You Will Need:

• an adult (if you use a utility knife)
• Bear Essentials
• heavy-duty scissors
• very large, corrugated cardboard box (wardrobe or appliance box)
• wide masking tape or duct tape
• other cardboard: boxes, gift wrap and tissue tubes, corrugated sheets, etc.
• utility knife (optional; must be used by adults only)
• poster paints and paintbrushes
• paper plates
• twine and small bucket

SCENIC ROUTE

The possibilities for scenery themes are endless; it all depends on the theme of your performance. Some of the following scenery ideas may help you get started:

- City skyline
- Ocean with an island
- Oasis in the desert
- Ship
- Planet in outer space
- Amusement park
- Circus tent
- Candy store
- Pet shop
- Interior of a rocket

as the performance progresses (this way you can open the window and have it be rainy "outside," then sunny, then rainy, and so on).

•••••••

5 Paint the set. Refer to the introduction of this chapter for a few tips.

•••••••

6 Design extra scenery pieces.

Movable sky elements:

- Cut shapes—such as the sun, moon, clouds, stars, and rainbows—out of extra cardboard, paint them, and tape each one to a cardboard tube. To create "holders" for these sky elements, tape a strip of cardboard to the back of the set, fitting it snugly to the size of the tube.

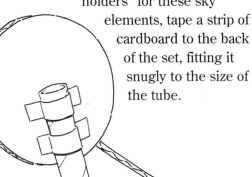

Mushrooms:

- Cut a long, skinny triangle "dart" out of a paper plate, then overlap the two edges of the plate and tape, as shown, so that the plate is umbrella-shaped.

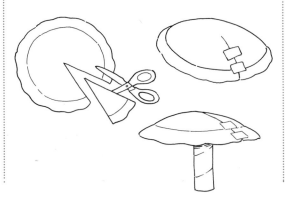

Tape a bathroom tissue tube to the underside of the plate and paint the whole thing to look like a mushroom. To attach it to the floor of your set, cut slits into the bottom of the tube on opposite sides. Bend out and tape the resulting tabs to the floor.

Wishing well:

- Cut an 8 × 14-inch rectangle out of cardboard, then cut 1-inch tabs into either end, as shown. Paint a stone design on the front of the rectangle and let it dry.

Cut a 6 × 8-inch semicircular window in the set where you want the well to go. Cut two slits into the set on either side of this window.

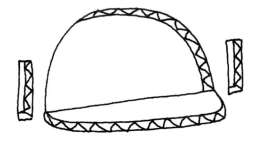

Insert the tabs of the well's "stone" rectangle into the slits (it will curve to fit) and bend the tabs behind the set. Tape the tabs to the back of the set to secure.

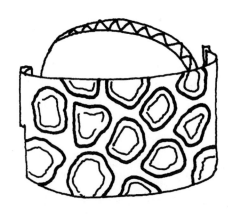

PROPPING UP PUPPETS

When you see the Muppets in photographs or on film, it's easy to forget that almost all of their props had to be specially made to scale for them. Remember—many of these puppets are only about two feet high! The Workshop makes these tiny props look so real that no one thinks about the fact that they are not life-size.

"Hey! We're from the moooooooving company. Did somebody order some scenery?"

• Paint the wooden crossbars directly onto the set background. Poke a small hole over the center bar and thread through a 12-inch length of twine from behind the set. Knot at the back to secure. Tie on a small bucket and adjust the twine so that the bucket passes through the window and sits behind the set.

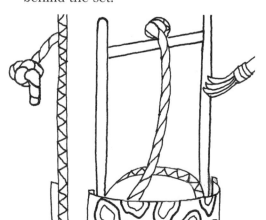

Other movable scenery:

• To create freestanding trees, bushes, flowers, cars, buildings, furniture, and animals, cut them out of flat cardboard, paint the front, and tape a support to the back (see step 2 to make supports).

Now add some props, a few actors, and break a leg!

Sound Effects Set

How easy is it?

Sound effects are a key part of Muppet productions since we don't always film in the actual place where something appears to be happening. For example, a movie script may have a scene that takes place outside. But because it's easier to control light and sound indoors, we would film the scene in a studio that's decorated to give the illusion that it's outside. We add the background noises later, back in the sound studio, where we can control the sounds so they remain in the background—and don't drown out what a Muppet is saying.

However, by the time we get into the sound studio to add or "dub" in sounds, we're really far away from real-life noises. At that point, the sound effects experts—known as Foley Artists—step in and create realistic noises out of unexpected and unusual items. Here they share some of the tricks of their trade.

Practice each one till you get it right, then record your sounds on a tape recorder. Think about the ways you can use your sound effects behind the scenes during a play or in a video.

PROJECT MADE BY FRED BUCHHOLZ

SOUNDS GREAT!

Horse's hooves (two plastic yogurt containers without lids): Clap the open ends on a flat surface or over gravel to make hoof sounds, varying the speed for walking, trotting, or galloping. For a different effect, try clapping containers with the closed-side down.

Crashing sound (two cardboard boxes, odds and ends like metal pipes, cans, bottle caps, lids, old silverware): Put everything in one box, then pour the contents into the empty box to make a loud crashing sound.

Rustling in the bushes (bristle broom): Hold a small bristle broom in one hand and twist the bristles to make the sound of something rustling in the bushes.

Train (sandpaper, two cans, tape): Wrap sandpaper around each of the cans and tape in place. Rub the cans together to make a chugging train sound. Whoo-whoo!

Walking in the snow (a full box of cornstarch): Squish a full cornstarch box hard with alternating thumbs in a walking rhythm.

Crackling fire (crinkly plastic wrap): Bunch up plastic wrap to make the sound of fire crackling.

Walking feet (shoes with different types of soles): Put your hands into old shoes and tap heel to toe, slowly for walking, faster for running. Try walking shoes on tabletops. Try walking shoes on top of gravel or dry pasta or bread crumbs in a box to make crunchy sounds.

Ripping (Velcro strips): Pull apart Velcro strips to make a ripping sound.

Slapping sound (2 strips of wood, duct tape): Stack two strips of wood and tape together at one end with duct tape to create a hinge. Open the sticks and snap them shut quickly to make a loud noise, like the sound of a baseball being hit. Watch your fingers!

Prisoner in chains (a chain): Shake the chain gently, then lift and drop it repeatedly for the sound of a prisoner walking in chains.

Megaphone (big plastic juice or milk container): Cut the bottom out of the container. Experiment by making different noises through the spout of your "megaphone"— whistling, screeching, screaming, deep low laughing, howling wind.

Rattlesnake (dried peas, plastic water bottle): Put about 1 inch of dry peas into a plastic water bottle. Hold at the top and shake to make a rattlesnake sound.

Model City

How easy is it?

PROJECT MADE BY CINDY FAIN

**What You
Will Need:**

- Bear Essentials
- lots of empty, clean cans with lids, boxes, and milk cartons, in different shapes and sizes
- large, flat, heavy cardboard or Masonite board (for base of city)

(continued on next page)

If you'd like to create a model city for your action figures to live in or your toy cars and trains to travel through, this is the project for you. The more boxes, cans, and tubes you can find, the more buildings you can create.

But the most important thing is to remember that this is *your* town. When the Muppet Workshop built the "Planet Koozbane" set for a zany *Muppet Show* comedy sketch, no one told *us* what the right color or style was; no one indicated the scale of the objects on zany, alien Koozbane. We got to make it up, limited only by our imaginations and creativity. After all, who was going to tell us what Koozbane *really* looks like?

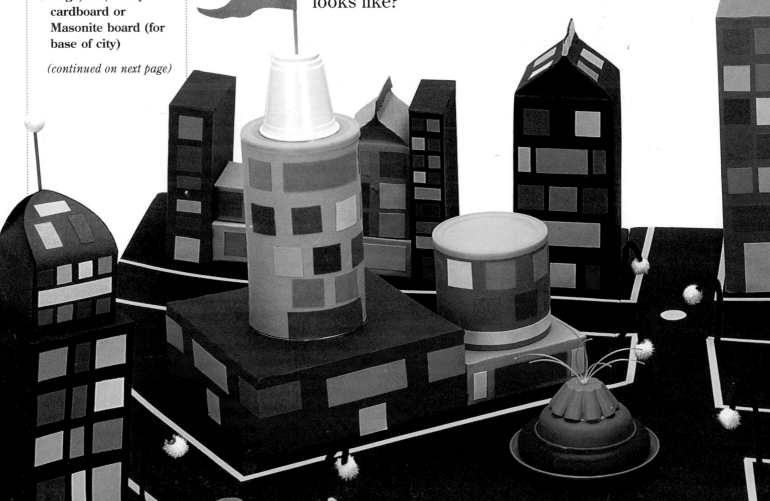

1 Stack cans, boxes, and cartons on the board base until you find an arrangement you like. Trace them in place so you can remember where they go.

• • • • • • •

2 To cover your buildings with construction paper:

● Fold paper around the buildings and trim to fit. Crease folds as flat as possible before gluing.

● For tops or awkward shapes, trace the area you want to cover onto construction paper and cut out the shape. Glue in place and smooth well.

Just as Koozbane was "our" planet, you are about to build your own city; so make it the city of your dreams.

● To cover cans, remove the lid, roll the can in construction paper, and mark a line where the paper begins to overlap itself. Trim along that line. Trim along the top and bottom edges, remembering to leave room for the can's lid to fit back on. Glue in place and replace the lid.

● To cover milk cartons, open the top carefully, cover the entire carton with paper, refold, and glue shut into the original shape, as shown below. These carton tops will form interesting roofs for your buildings.

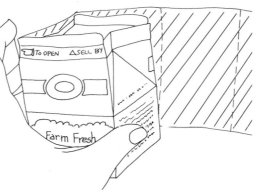

**What You
Will Need
continued:**

● colored construction paper
● white chalk
● paint and paintbrushes (optional)
● pom-poms
● pipe cleaners (glittery ones if possible)
● wooden curtain rings
● paper or plastic cups
● plastic straws, toothpicks, or bamboo skewers
● cardboard
● masking tape
● moss and small branches
● Styrofoam packing peanuts

SCALING YOUR CITY

Think about scale in the real world, and how big normal cars are in relation to normal buildings. (See this chapter's introduction for a description of scale.) If a normal car is about 4 feet tall, and a normal floor of a building is about 12 feet tall, then each floor is three times as tall as each car. To figure out a scale for your city that's based on cars, make the "floors" of each building (which are designated by the placement of the colored "windows") at least three times as tall as the cars you plan to use. So if your car is 1 inch high, each floor of a building should be about 3 inches high.

If you want to add "people," think about the fact that most people are between 5 feet and 6 feet tall, so they're a little less than half the height of a floor of a building, and they're almost a third taller than cars. Therefore, if your cars are 1 inch high, your people should be about 1⅓ inches high.

"Moi finds city life tres romantique."

3 Cut windows out of additional pieces of construction paper in contrasting colors and glue them into place on the covered buildings.

• • • • • • • •

4 Cover the large, flat, cardboard city base with construction paper and glue your buildings on top, in the approximate layout you created and traced on the cardboard.

Make up a name for your city (why not name it after yourself?), add the "people" and cars, and have fun!

FIXING UP THE STREETS

● Make roads and sidewalks by cutting then gluing gray or black construction paper to the base; add white lines with white chalk or paint.

● Cut thin strips of yellow paper to mark off lanes in the roads.

● Make streetlamps by gluing pom-poms to the bent "necks" of pipe cleaners. Bend the pipe cleaner bases and glue to the sides of roads.

● Stack wooden rings to make a shallow fountain. Use glittery pipe cleaners to create a water spray effect.

● Glue on paper or plastic cups as towers. Use straws, toothpicks, or skewers as flag poles, building spires, or antennae.

● With blue construction paper, create a river passing through your city. Build a bridge from a thin strip of box cardboard and tape it in place so it straddles your new river.

● If you want to make it look like summertime, glue moss or other greenery to small branches, then glue the branches to the base.

● If you prefer a winter scene, you can scatter crumbled Styrofoam packing bits or paint the rooftops white (also, craft stores often sell fake snow in bags).

Dollhouse Deluxe

How easy is it?

Please Turn the Page to See What You Will Need

Every house has a unique personality that reflects the personalities of the people who live there. After all, we don't all have the same taste or all the same stuff that our neighbors do. So, when we make sets for our characters at the Muppet Workshop, we have to concentrate on the little details that give a room personality.

When you make this home sweet home, you'll want to think about the same things that we do at the Workshop. Is it a firehouse or a mansion? Is it for your favorite dolls or action figures? Ask yourself these questions, pick a theme, then decorate along the theme. It could even be the house you'd like to live in someday!

**What You
Will Need:**

- **an adult (to help you
  with cutting)**
- **Bear Essentials**
- **2 same-sized, long,
  narrow cardboard
  storage boxes with
  lids (such as file
  boxes)**
- **heavy-duty scissors**
- **craft knife (for adult
  use only)**
- **corrugated cardboard
  sheets (for walls and
  other parts of the
  house)**
- **origami and/or
  wrapping paper (for
  wallpaper)**
- **strong masking tape**
- **tracing paper**
- **8½" × 11" sheet of
  thin cardboard**
- **poster paint and
  paintbrushes**
- **bits of lace or fabric,
  construction paper
  (optional)**
- **clear tape (Scotch
  tape is good)**

1 Set aside the lids from your two boxes and turn the boxes on their sides. Don't immediately attach the first floor to the second because it is easier to work on them separately.

• • • • • • •

2 Decide where you want windows and doors. Ask an adult to help you cut them out using heavy-duty scissors and/or a craft knife. You can make doors that open and close by taping them back in position on the box, using tape "hinges" on the inside, as shown below.

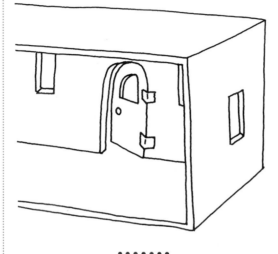

• • • • • • •

3 Trace the end of each box onto a piece of cardboard and cut two cardboard walls to divide the upstairs and downstairs into two rooms each. Cut a doorway into the top-floor partition. Trace each wall onto the reverse side of your various "wallpapers," cut out the resulting shape, and glue to each wall. Decorate the floors and ceiling with paper or paint.

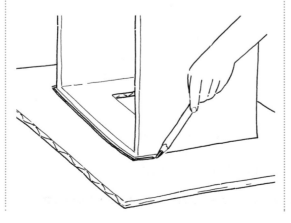

Attach the walls with tape, as shown below.

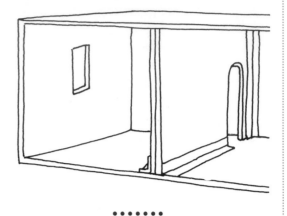

• • • • • • •

4 To make stairs:

- Decide where you want the stairs. Ask an adult to cut a square hole in the ceiling of the first story. Have the adult cut a corresponding hole in the floor of the second story, tracing the first hole onto the second box so the holes fit together when the second story is placed on the first.

- Trace the stairs' side pattern on page 320 and transfer it to corrugated cardboard (see pages 8 and 9 for tracing and transferring instructions). Cut out the shape.

- Trace the stairs' steps pattern on page 320, transfer it onto thin cardboard, and cut it out. Fold back and forth along the lines into an accordion-like shape. Tape the steps to the staircase side.

- Position the stairway against the wall and tape or glue the stairway to the downstairs floor and to the back of the hole in the ceiling.

5 Tape your two stories together, one box on top of the other. Run the tape all the way around your house.

•••••••

6 To form the two attic walls, measure the width of your box, then measure a triangle onto cardboard, making sure that the bottom side of the triangle matches the width of the box. Extend the triangle sides up at whatever pitch (slant) you like, but make both sides equal in length. Cut out the triangle, trace it onto the cardboard, and cut out a second

identical triangle. Have an adult help you cut out windows in them if you like. Then tape them securely to the top of your house, as shown.

•••••••

7 To make a roof:

● Measure the length of one of the sides of the attic triangles (not the base); double the number and add 4 inches.

● Measure across the front of your house and add 4 inches. Take a ruler and mark off a rectangle of exactly these measurements on a piece of cardboard. Cut out the rectangle and fold it exactly in half so that the fold rests on the points of the triangular attic walls with approximately 2 inches of overlap on all sides, as shown, left. Glue on permanently, or hinge in place by taping the underside of the back of the roof to the back edge of the attic walls.

● To shingle the roof, cut out cardboard "shingles" that are approximately $\frac{1}{2} \times 1$ inch. Draw parallel lines on the rooftop as guidelines, and glue the shingles in place as shown. Shingle from the bottom up, overlapping each row slightly as you go. Trim the top row of shingles to fit if needed.

"This pad needs a splash of color."

DECORATING TIPS

Here are a few decorating suggestions:

● Paint the outside of your house, (we used a brick pattern).

● Cut cardboard strips for window frames, windowsills, or shutters. Paint them and glue in place. Glue on lace curtains.

● Use cardboard to make furniture or a railing to go around the stairwell landing. Decorate furniture with fabric scraps and wrapping paper.

● Do some landscaping: Place the house on a large, cardboard base, then add a lawn with paths, trees, bushes, maybe even a pool!

● Make a family of clothespin people to live in your house. Use fabric scraps and markers for details.

Find a moving truck and move in your miniature family!

Treasure Island Diorama

What You Will Need:

- Bear Essentials
- shoe box (discard the lid)
- thin sheet of cardboard (approximately 24" × 12")

(continued on next page)

How easy is it?

You may have seen dioramas at a museum or made them in school. Besides depicting animals or historical scenes, dioramas are also good for illustrating scenes from stories; this diorama features the island from *Muppet Treasure Island.* As you make this project, think about *perspective.* Are the things in the background in proportion to the rest of the scene? Does it look as if the view goes on forever? Do you get the feeling that this is really an island? We hope so!

1 To create the foreground/hinged door, put the shoe box facedown on the thin cardboard, trace around it, and cut the traced rectangle out of the cardboard. Stand the shoe box on its long side, facing you, and match up the long, bottom front edge of the shoe box flush with the long edge of the cardboard. Join them with masking tape on top of the seam, as we did, then underneath, to create a "hinged door" that opens out toward the viewer. Bend a pipe cleaner into a loop and tape it to the front edge of the hinged door. Paint the inside of the door so it looks like sand and water, using our photograph as a model. Cover the outside of your box by gluing on paper. Glue a bead to the top of the diorama, near the front; this will be the clasp to keep the diorama closed.

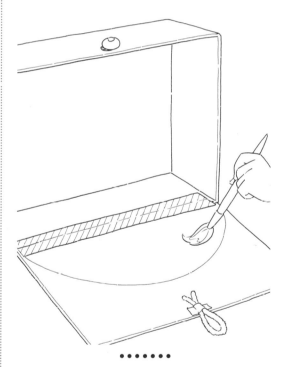

· · · · · · · ·

2 Place the box on its back on a piece of sky blue construction paper and trace it; extend the resulting rectangle so it's about 6 inches wider than the tracing. Cut out the rectangle.

· · · · · · · ·

3 Cut a strip of blue acetate or plastic recycling bag "water" to cover the bottom third of the sky blue rectangle. Glue it onto the rectangle. Glue cotton

ball "clouds" onto the upper two-thirds of the sky blue rectangle.

· · · · · · · ·

4 Put glue on the back of both short sides of the sky blue rectangle. Slide the rectangle into the box and glue it to the inside edges at the front of the box so that the construction paper curves into the box, as shown below. Trim the rectangle to fit if needed.

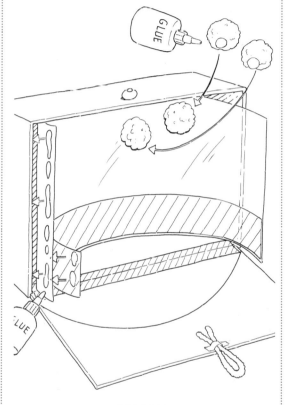

· · · · · · · ·

5 Paint glue on the "floor" of the shoe box and sprinkle sand onto the glue to begin forming an island. Cover the portion of the island that you painted on the hinged door in glue and add sand, too. To build up a hill, glue in a piece of cardboard or a small box. Cover with glue and continue to add sand until you're happy with the look of your island.

· · · · · · · ·

6 Fill up the island scene any way you like. Here are some suggestions:

• For a palm tree, cut green construction paper to look like palm leaves. Cut

What You Will Need continued:

- masking tape
- pipe cleaner
- poster paint and paintbrushes
- colored construction paper (including sky blue and green)
- bead
- clear blue plastic sheet of acetate (or blue recycling bag)
- cotton balls
- sand
- pencils (for tree trunks)
- wooden beads (or anything else that looks like small coconuts)
- corrugated cardboard (small sheet)
- small box with lid (for treasure chest)
- gold or metallic confetti or glitter, rhinestones, or small pearls
- flour and water for papier-mâché glue mixture (See page 6 for recipe)
- bowl and newspaper for papier-mâché
- 20 oz. plastic bottle (for papier-mâché mold)
- leaves, moss, or other vegetation
- feathers, string, and straight pins

THINK ABOUT IT

These directions will tell you how to copy our diorama, but you could always design your own. Pick a scene from one of your favorite books, or imagine a place you'd really like to be, then make your own diorama from scratch. Yours might contain a city scene, or an underground cave, full of beautiful crystal formations . . . or the red rocks of Mars. Anything's possible!

narrow strips into each side of the leaves to make a leafy fringe, as shown. Wrap masking tape around a pencil

"tree trunk," then tape the leaves in place near the top of the trunk. Paint the tape brown to look like bark. Glue coconuts (wooden beads) onto the leaves at the top of the trunk. Cut a small disk base out of corrugated cardboard. Poke the pencil point through the cardboard disk and glue onto the sandy island. Cover the disk in sand and glue leaves or moss as "shrubs" around it.

- For a treasure chest, paint a small lidded box brown with black streaks to make it look like a wooden chest. Paint on a clasp or glue on a button, then fill the box with glitter, rhinestones, and strings of beads. You can drape or glue some of the strings of beads so

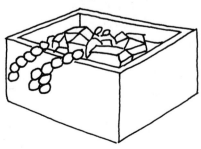

they look like they're overflowing from the chest.

- For a beach hut, dip newspaper strips in papier-mâché glue (see page 6 for recipe and instructions) and mold them around the top half of a large soda bottle (but don't cover the spout). Make sure that the bottom of the hut is flat, so it can stand evenly on the island. When the outside of the hut is dry, remove it from the bottle by lifting it over the bottle top. Add a little more papier-mâché to the top of the hut to cover the hole in the roof. Let dry, then cut a door into the front. If you wish, place the treasure chest in the hut. Glue vegetation around the outside, then string feathers onto a thin thread and hang above the door using straight pins on either end.

Imagine yourself on a desert island: If you could only take three Muppet Crafts with you, which ones would they be?

No Strings Attached

Y ou can turn just about anything into a puppet: a piece of wood, a chunk of foam, even a kitchen utensil. All you need is an idea, a technique, and a little creativity.

In the beginning, we made Muppets using the simplest of materials: spare bits of fabric, old socks, Ping-Pong balls. These days, we still use these materials, but we've also added state-of-the-art plastics, resins, fibers, and electronics to the Muppet mix.

We're about to show you a bunch of different ways to make puppets, and some original ways to use them. Did you ever think of taking a bath with a puppet? Do you know how to use light and paper to make a puppet show? Well, you will when you've finished reading this chapter.

Make the "Talking Sandwich," and you'll learn about working with thin sheets of foam. The "Finger Puppet" project will teach you all about latex and moldmaking. You'll learn how to make a flexible fabric "Bath Mitt Puppet." The "Shadow Puppets" will help you think about shape and form in a whole new way. The "Wiggly Worm" project will give you practice in making and operating an easy rod puppet.

And the "Portable Theater" project will teach you how to make a simple stage that's adaptable for many different puppet shows.

Once you've built a puppet, a different kind of fun begins. It's time to make that puppet come "alive," by giving it a personality, a voice, and its own way of moving.

As you look at your puppet, think about what kind of personality you'd like it to have. It's fun to choose unexpected character traits. A big guy with a mustache, for example, can turn out to be a scaredy-cat. A tiny fair-haired girl could be a fearless daredevil.

Movement is another good way to make your puppet unique. Naturally, the way your creature moves will be determined by the sort of puppet it is. You'll need to experiment with your hand movements for a hand puppet, or the rods for a rod puppet, or the strings for a marionette. But once you've got the basics down, you can start adding individual quirks to your puppet's movements. Think, for instance, about the way Kermit scrunches up his mouth when everything's going wrong; it's a simple gesture that has become one of his trademarks. Some movements can be subtle; some can be broad, but they can all be indelible.

Voices, too, are fun to play with. Try out every kind of sound you can make—high or low, gruff or nasal, animal or human, imaginary or not. Practice every sort of accent. Fool around with voices you'd never expect from your puppet—a high, squeaky voice from a big bruiser, for example. Keep in mind that being a puppeteer gives you a chance to pretend to be somebody different. You might normally be soft-spoken, but as a puppet, you can shout, be gruff, and act short-tempered. You might be the serious type, but as a puppet, you can tell funny jokes. And if anyone wonders—well, it wasn't really you; it was the puppet!

A Muppet trick: Practice all this stuff with your puppet while you're looking in a mirror. It'll give you a good sense of how the puppet will look in front of an audience. When you're ready, you'll be able to put on a show for your family or friends. Or take your show on the road and visit the children's ward of a local hospital; or perform at a little kid's birthday party. With our help, you'll look like a professional!

Gonzocchio
This puppet of a puppet is a real working marionette version of Gonzo. It was made especially for this spoof photo of Pinocchio. All its joints work, but it was never really used as a marionette.

Talking Sandwich

How easy is it?

Next time you invite a friend over to lunch, why not serve something totally different—like a sandwich that tries to bite back? This sandwich looks good enough to eat, but it's actually a puppet made out of foam. As you work on it, you'll learn a lot about foam construction—including pattern making, cutting, piecing together, and sewing a foam puppet.

Give your sandwich character a voice and a personality, then create a puppet play based around him or her. Maybe you could call it "Lettuce Entertain You!"

What You Will Need:

- scissors
- ½"-thick white foam (for bread slices only)
- brown acrylic paint and paintbrush or brown colored markers
- foam glue or rubber cement
- old glove or mitten
- Foamies (layers of thin foam found at craft stores, sold in different colors) or felt
  - green (for lettuce)
  - yellow and orange (for cheese)
  - pink (for bologna)
- 2 beads (for eyes)
- paper or Styrofoam plate

"Yeah? Well, you're full of baloney!"

PROJECT MADE BY ROLLIE KREWSON

1 Cut out two bread shapes from the white foam. Make them quite a bit larger than real bread slices, so your hand will fit comfortably inside the sandwich. Paint the crusts brown or color them with a marker.

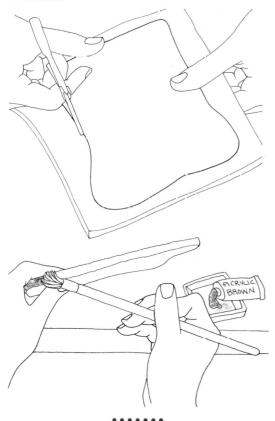

. . . .

2 Glue the top part of the glove fingers to the underside of the top piece of bread, as shown below.

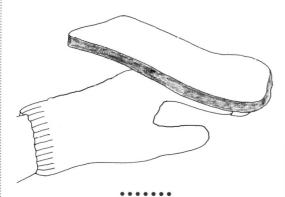

. . . .

3 Cut sandwich-sized lettuce leaves from green foam or felt. Cut sandwich-sized slices of cheese and bologna from foam or felt (orange squares for American cheese, yellow rectangles with different-shaped holes for Swiss, and pink circles for bologna). Cut a slit that's

as wide as your glove in the center of each "ingredient," and slide the ingredients, one by one, up over the glove. Glue in extra smaller pieces to hide any parts of the glove that are still showing.

. . . .

4 Cut one last slice of bologna, fold it in half, and glue it into the front of the sandwich as a mouth.

. . . .

5 Cut a slit in the bottom slice of bread that's big enough to stick the bottom of the glove through. Glue the thumb to the underside of the bottom slice of bread. Let it dry.

. . . .

6 Glue the two "eye" beads into the sandwich.

. . . .

7 Cut out the center of a paper plate and place your sandwich on top so that the glove hangs down through the plate. Glue the sandwich in place on the plate.

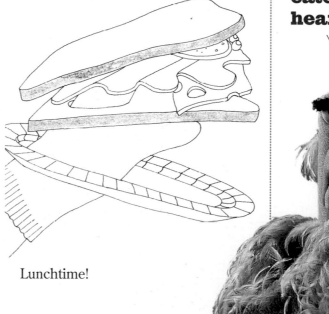

Lunchtime!

"I cannot support this project. Food should be eaten, not heard."

Portable Theater

How easy is it?

- Bear Essentials
- acrylic paint (red and yellow) and paintbrushes
- white picture mat 16" × 20" or larger (store-bought, precut for framing)
- masking tape (½" wide)
- lightweight fabric (for curtain)
- stapler
- 4 empty thread spools that are exactly the same size
- colored markers

(continued on next page)

Here's your chance to become a great director: Just construct your own miniature theater, add some puppets, and put on a puppet show. Why not do a weird take on a famous fairy tale: Maybe have the evil stepsister run off with the prince? Or pick a scene from one of your favorite books, movies, or television shows. Then practice, practice, practice!

The great thing about this theater is you can take it anywhere, anytime. So think about upcoming events that might be improved by adding a puppet show! What about a talent show at school, or a holiday dinner at some relatives' house?

PROJECT MADE BY MARK RUFFIN

1 Paint the picture mat for the front of your stage. To make stripes, paint the whole front of the frame yellow and let it dry completely. Then use masking tape to mask out the stripes, as shown below. Paint the uncovered yellow stripes red. You can go right over the yellow paint and the tape; the tape will prevent the red from going where it shouldn't. Let dry and gently remove the tape.

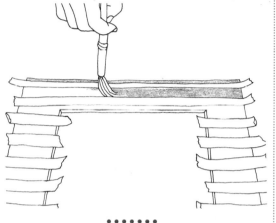

2 To make the curtains, cut a piece of fabric a few inches longer than the width of the stage, and about 6 inches wide. Gather it at the ends, and staple it horizontally to the *back* of the frame along the top edge and on the sides so that it hangs down a bit in the middle, as shown below. Glue spools to the back of the frame at the corners.

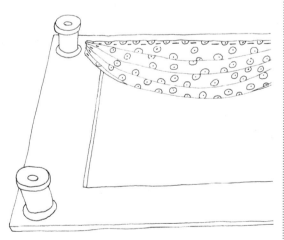

3 Draw your backdrop scene on the light cardboard or bristol board mat, and lay it faceup on the table. Dab glue on the spools, and glue the whole stage front

to the backdrop to put together the stage. Let it dry.

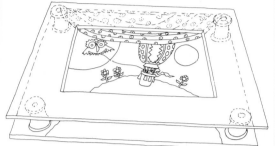

What You Will Need continued:

● lightweight cardboard or bristol board, the same size as the picture mat (this may come in the package with the picture mat)
● long paint mixing sticks (available at a paint or hardware store)

TO CHANGE SCENES

If you want to change your background, cut a piece of paper so that its width is the same as the width between the spools that hold up the stage and its height is the same as the height of the stage. Draw a new background on the paper and hang it flush against the back mat with small pieces of tape. This way, you can create as many different sets as you like.

To create characters:

● Draw the characters' outlines on thin cardboard or poster board, then paint or color them in. Cut them out.

● If you want your sticks to be less visible, paint them the color of your background and let them dry before you glue them to your characters.

● Glue the figures to the sticks. You can glue a stick on sideways to your character and move it from the side of your stage, or you can glue the stick to the top of the character, so it can be inserted into the stage from the top. See which style of performance is easier for you. (The boy in the photograph is working from the side.) Whichever way you do it, you're ready to put on a show!

261

Wiggly Worm

How easy it it?

What You Will Need:

- an adult
  (to cut the wire hanger)
- wire coat hanger
- wire cutters
- acrylic paint and paintbrush
- 3 beads (2 for eyes, 1 for nose; holes should be big enough to pass hanger wire through)
- 6" length of ½" diameter spring (it should be soft enough to wiggle when you shake it, but rigid enough to straighten itself out and not flop over)
- 24" tinsel garland
- pipe cleaners
- safety pin
- masking tape

Because it's made with a bouncy spring mechanism, this worm has a wonderful, wiggly way of moving. It's fun to see how many different ways it can twist and turn and how those twists and turns can be used to reveal or convey the worm's personality.

Make a bunch of these simple worms, then, when you're not performing with them, hang them in your room as a colorful, wiggly mobile!

1 Untwist the hanger and have an adult cut it in half with the wire cutters.

· · · · · · ·

2 Paint pupils on the eye beads and let them dry.

· · · · · · ·

3 Thread the three beads onto the end of the wire hanger. Bend the wire into two U-shapes under the eyes, with the beads between them, as shown here.

· · · · ·

4 Thread the long end of the wire down into one end of the spring, passing it through the first five or six coils of the spring, then poking it back out of the coils.

· · · · · · ·

5 Take the other piece of wire and thread it through five or six coils at the bottom of the spring, as shown below. Bend the end of the wire into a hook so it stays in place on the spring.

· · · · · · ·

6 Wrap the tinsel around the spring, wrapping in the same direction as the spring is coiled. Catch the core of the

tinsel in between the coils of the spring now and then, so it stays put on the spring.

· · · · · · ·

7 When the spring is all wrapped in tinsel, tuck the end of the tinsel into the last coil of the spring.

· · · · · · ·

8 Twist pipe cleaners onto the wire above the eyes to make antennae.

· · · · · · ·

9 Link the two wire handles to each other with a safety pin: Thread the bottom end of the head through the pin, then thread the hook end of the other handle through the pin, as shown below (pinch the hook closed tightly so it stays on the pin).

· · · · · · ·

10 Bend the bottoms of both wire handles into looped handle shapes, and wrap the handles with tape.

Now you can slide, wiggle, and twist the worm up and down the wire that holds the eyes. Make a whole army of tinsel worms and then have a wiggly worm dance party!

"Wanna dance?"

Shadow Puppets

How easy is it?

PROJECT MADE BY RON BINION

What You Will Need:

- an adult
  (to use the utility knife)
- Bear Essentials
- black electrical tape
- vellum sheet (to fit behind the mat)
- black picture-framing mat, 16" × 20" or larger (store-bought, with precut center square)
- black mat board (store-bought)
- utility knife (only to be used by an adult)

(continued on next page)

Shadow puppets are mysterious and beautiful. The black shadows on the screen are created when a light is projected from behind the screen toward the audience. Since the puppets are behind the screen, with the light behind *them*, the audience sees the shadowy puppet silhouettes as though they are appearing on the screen.

When you perform your shadow puppets, remember that your audience will never actually see your puppets—they'll only see the puppets' shadows through the screen. So when you compose each scene, think about what the audience will be seeing.

1 Use black tape to tape a sheet of vellum to the back of the picture mat, covering the opening completely. This will be your "stage." Ask an adult to cut four large, identical triangular pieces out of the other piece of mat board with a utility knife, and use black tape to tape them to the back of the stage for side supports, as shown below. Two should angle back and two should angle forward; they will hold your stage up, make your shadows show up better, and help hide the puppeteers.

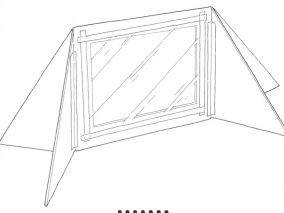

• • • • • • •

2 Draw your shadow puppet shapes on black construction paper, then cut them out. You can create jointed puppets by cutting out the puppet in overlapping pieces, then attaching the pieces with a paper fastener or grommet.

• • • • • • •

3 Cut landscape shapes (like the bridge and riverbank) out of black construction paper, and cut any bodies of water (like a pond or river) from the blue lighting gel or cellophane. Tape all the scene pieces together with clear tape, then tape them in place on the vellum on the back side of the mat.

4 Tape bamboo skewers or chopsticks to the backs of the puppet shapes (if any of your puppets are jointed, you may need to use more than one skewer to make the puppet move in segments).

• • • • • • •

5 To use your shadow puppet theater, turn on a small light behind your stage.

Turn down the lights in the rest of the room and start the show!

What You Will Need continued:

- black construction paper
- paper fastener or grommet (optional)
- blue lighting "gel" or cellophane
- clear cellophane tape (Scotch tape)
- bamboo skewers or chopsticks
- a small light

Finger Puppets

How easy is it?

What You Will Need:

- an adult (to order latex and to use the utility knife)
- modeling clay
- kitchen knife or flat-head screwdriver
- heavy-duty scissors or utility knife (for adults only)
- clean, empty half-gallon milk or juice carton
- plaster
- liquid dish detergent and basting brush or paintbrush
- rubber bands
- paper clip
- casting latex (see ordering information on page 269)
- acrylic paint and paintbrushes
- fabric
- chalk
- scissors
- needle and thread
- cardboard
- construction paper
- yarn, trim, and glue

Meet Wayne and Wanda, two lovely puppets with latex heads! Latex is a soft plastic that casts well in molds. When you do this project, you'll learn how to make a two-piece mold out of plaster, and how to mix, pour, and mold latex. You'll also get a chance to exercise your basic sewing, decorating, and designing skills.

The nice thing is, you can use this mold-making method to make molds for anything you've made out of soft clay or wax. Then make them out of latex, too!

"Oh, Wayne, you're head and shoulders above the rest!"

1 Make any kind of clay head and face you like, but be sure it will fit inside your milk carton with 1 inch to spare all around.

- Roll the clay into an oval shape for the head (about 3 inches to 3½ inches long).

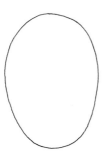

- Roll a small piece of clay into a hot dog shape and press onto the oval to make a nose. Smooth into place.

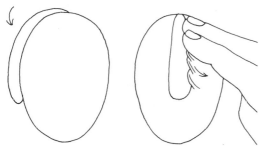

- Roll two small balls of clay for eyes and press them onto the face. You can make funny ears this way, too.

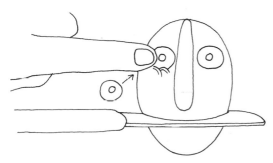

- Use a dull knife to cut one-third of the way horizontally through the oval shape under the nose to make a mouth, and rock the knife slightly so the mouth opens (don't cut all the way through).

- Smooth the clay around the features, so the plaster doesn't get into any cracks later (plaster in the cracks makes it hard to remove the clay from the plaster mold).

- Make a clay tube for the neck. Make sure you'll have enough room to insert two fingers into the neck (approximately 1½ inches wide and 1 inch long) so you can puppeteer the head later. Attach the neck tube to the head, smoothing the clay along the outside seam.

"I love a woman with a good head on her shoulders. . . ."

2 Cut the carton in half. If you use a utility knife like the one in the illustration, ask an adult to do the cutting for you.

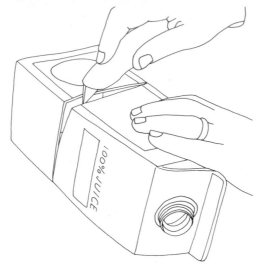

3 Mix a small batch of plaster according to the directions on the package, and fill the bottom of the carton about halfway up with liquid plaster. Paint a thick coat of liquid dish detergent onto the back of the clay head. When the plaster begins to harden, push the clay head into the plaster so that it's faceup and halfway submerged.

"Make a perfect couple!"

IMPORTANT: *Make sure that the base of the neck is placed flush against the side of the carton; the hole that this placement creates will be important later. Let the plaster set until it's hard.*

• • • • • • •

4 When the plaster is hard, reach down into the carton and dig out small holes around the edge of the dried plaster mold with a paper clip, as shown below. This will make the mold easier to open later. Brush the surface of the clay face and the plaster with dish detergent and pour in another layer of liquid plaster, until the carton is full. Let dry completely.

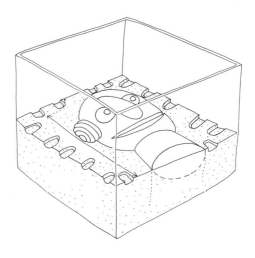

• • • • • • •

5 Peel off the paper carton. Then firmly pull apart the halves of the mold and remove the clay head.

• • • • • • •

6 Moisten the mold halves under water. The plaster will absorb water fast.

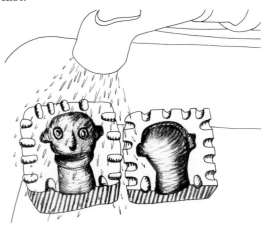

7 Close the mold and wrap tightly with rubber bands.

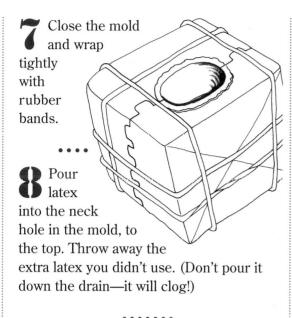

• • • •

8 Pour latex into the neck hole in the mold, to the top. Throw away the extra latex you didn't use. (Don't pour it down the drain—it will clog!)

• • • • • • •

9 Set aside the mold to dry, with the hole facing upward, for about a day. Insert a chisel or knife sideways into the seam of the mold and rock it slowly and evenly until the mold opens. Remember, you might reuse the mold, so be careful. Gently remove the head.

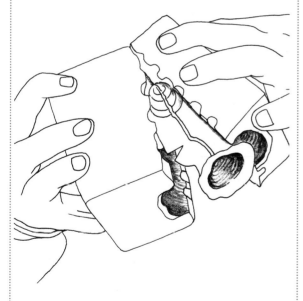

• • • • • • •

10 Decorate your puppets. Paint the head with acrylic paint.

• • • • • • •

11 Make clothes by drawing a chalk pattern onto a piece of fabric (make sure it's a big enough piece so the puppet costume will fit your hand). Your pattern will look like half a dress, with half

a neck hole (make sure the finished hole will fit your puppet's neck).

- If you want the puppet to work like Wayne, add two sleeves to the pattern; your thumb and pinkie will go in the sleeves.

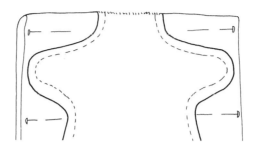

- If you want your puppet to work like Wanda, cut holes for two fingers in the front.

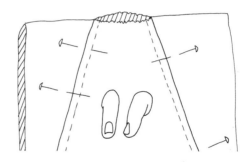

Cut the pattern out, then trace this half of the costume onto another piece of fabric and cut that out. Sew up the sides of the costume, leaving the bottom edge and the neck hole open. Fit the puppet's neck though the neck hole, and sew or glue the fabric tightly onto the puppet.

• • • • • • •

12 Use yarn to make hair, and glue it onto your puppet's head. Then, make hats from cardboard cutouts and paint them.

• • • • • • •

13 Decorate the hats and outfits with trim and construction paper, then attach the hats to the heads with glue.

Make some friends and family for your puppet, then invent life stories and personalities for each one and put on a show with them!

Sky Puppet

How easy is it?

**What You
Will Need:**

- an adult
- Bear Essentials
- heavyweight, unlined plastic shopping or trash bags (different colors)
- craft knife or small handsaw (for adult use only)
- 4 wooden dowels:
  - two 18" dowels
  - one 22" dowel
  - one 17" dowel
- spool of kite string
- tracing paper
- hot glue gun (for adult use only)

It's a bird! It's a plane! No, it's a Muppet kite! Although this kite isn't a traditional puppet, it is a cute character that you can manipulate and move. With a strong wind you can make it swoop and dive while providing your own commentary in the puppet's "voice." Maybe you can even make a video of the kite, recording your own voice as the voice of the character. When the wind isn't blowing, tack the kite to the ceiling of your room and pretend it's soaring high overhead.

As you create the "Sky Puppet," bear in mind that the secret to designing and making a good kite is using lightweight but strong materials and learning to balance them together just right.

1 Cut the plastic bags into a triangle that measures 30 inches × 30 inches × 50 inches.

. . . .

2 Have an adult cut the wooden dowels to the lengths specified. Lay the dowels on the back side of your plastic triangle, as shown below. Glue one 18-inch dowel along each of the shorter sides of the triangle, 5½ inches from the top triangle point (have an adult use a hot glue gun on a low setting—if you have one). Fold the edge of each kite side over each dowel and glue to secure. Make a crossbar for the center of the kite with the 22-inch dowel positioned vertically and the 17-inch dowel lying across it horizontally. Tie together with string at the center. Position this crossbar at the center of the kite and glue the ends of each dowel to the kite.

. . . .

3 Cut a jagged edge along the bottom of the kite, making sure to leave the dowels untouched.

. . . .

4 Trace the patterns for the eyebrows, eyes, lip, nose, and teeth on pages 321–322 (see page 9 for tracing instructions). Then:

• From plastic, cut out the eyebrows. Accordion-fold each one, like a fan, then glue them in place, curving in half circles near the point of the kite.

• Cut the eyes out of white plastic and add the pupils with permanent black marker. Glue the eyes in place over the edges of the eyebrows.

• Cut two halves of the lip from plastic. Position on the kite and glue in place.

• From white plastic, cut out the pattern for the teeth, lay over the lip (curving slightly), and glue in place.

• Attach the nose vertically down the center of the kite by putting glue along the long, straight edge of the nose piece; do not glue down the rest of the nose. Make a hole near the bridge of the nose and tie the end of the kite string through this hole. You may reinforce this hole with extra plastic if you think the wind will be extra strong.

Happy flying!

"Sigh. Moi is a star, a brilliant, heavenly star shining down from above, radiating good taste to all of vous."

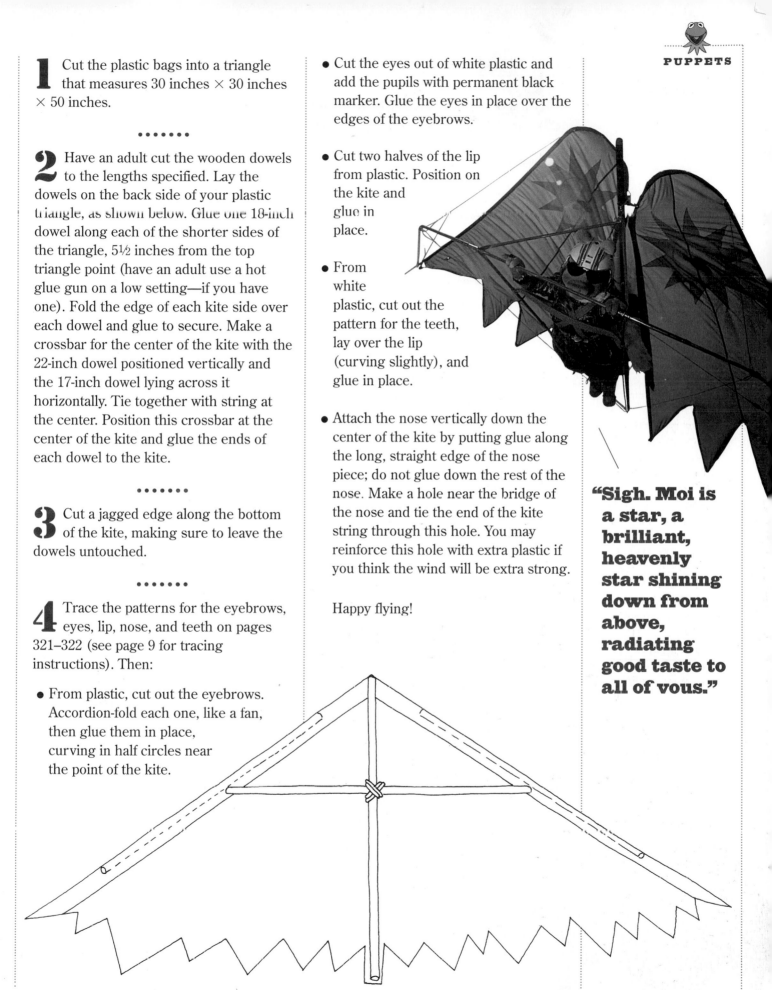

Bath Mitt Puppets

How easy is it?

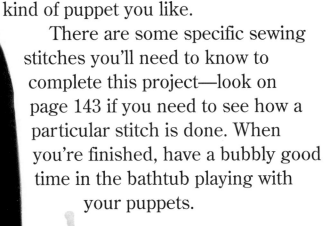

Now you can get clean and put on a puppet show at the same time. Have fun making these silly washcloth puppets while you learn a lot about basic puppet making. You'll also learn a little something about making your own Muppet characters since we used Miss Piggy and Rowlf as our models for these puppets. But the instructions are for basic puppets, and you can make any kind of puppet you like.

There are some specific sewing stitches you'll need to know to complete this project—look on page 143 if you need to see how a particular stitch is done. When you're finished, have a bubbly good time in the bathtub playing with your puppets.

PROJECT MADE BY SARAH IAMS

1 Place your hand on the center of a washcloth, sticking out your thumb and pinky finger on either side (your three middle fingers will be the head, while your thumb and pinky will be the arms). Trace around your hand with chalk, but leave extra room around your hand to sew the seam.

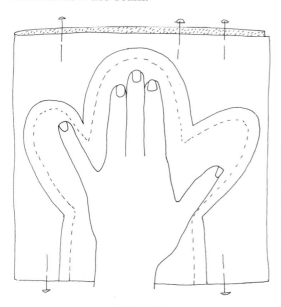

2 Cut the pattern out, trace it onto another washcloth, then cut that out, too. Sew facial details onto what will be the front of your puppet (check out "Face Facts" on page 274 for ideas). In most cases, it's easier to sew these details onto your puppet before you sew the two halves of the body together.

· · · · · · · ·

3 Place right sides of the puppet body together (the face will be *inside*) and pin the pieces together. Using a running stitch (see page 143 for stitch information), sew along the edge of the puppet body, leaving the bottom edge open for your hand.

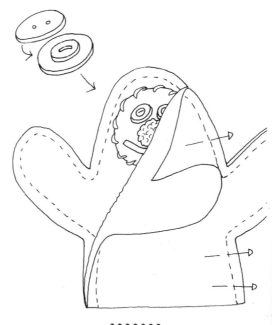

· · · · · · ·

4 Turn the body right-side out. Smooth flat.

Scrub-a-dub-dub!

"If you have to take a flea bath, you might as well have some fun!

"As vous knows, moi prefers a long, leisurely bubble bath, followed by a mud pack and full body wrap."

FACE FACTS

There are many things you can do to make your bath puppet come to life. Here are a few suggestions for making faces. You can sew the elements of a face right onto your puppet, or you can sew on a felt or washcloth circle (using a whip stitch (see page 143 for stitch information) of a different color to start the face as we did for Rowlf.

Eyes

● Cut out felt circles for eye whites and pupils. Stack them in place on a button and sew them all together. Attach eyes onto the puppet front by sewing through all of the material and through the button holes.

● For eyelids: Cut half circles of felt, place them above the eyes, and stitch around the edge.

Noses

● Sew on a pom-pom, as we did with Rowlf.

● Or sew on a circular piece of pink sponge for a Miss Piggy nose.

● Or sew on a button.

Ears

● Cut triangle shapes of pink sponge or felt for ears like Miss Piggy's, and whip stitch the ears to the puppet.

● Make floppy ears by cutting dangly ear shapes out of leftover washcloth scraps. Whip stitch the ears into place on the puppet.

Mouth, Teeth, and Tongue

● Use different colors of felt and cut out appropriate shapes. Sew them on the puppet's face.

Hair

● Wrap yarn around your fingers, as shown.

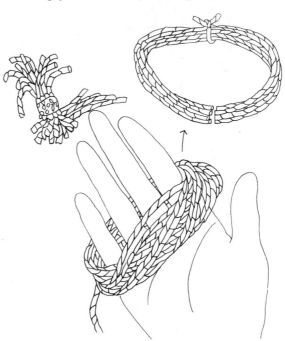

Carefully remove yarn loop from fingers and tie another piece of yarn tightly around it. Cut yarn loops apart and sew the "wig" onto the top of the head, centering it between the ears. Repeat process to create a topknot. Trim ends to make it as short and spiky as you like. Add a bead or ribbon for decoration. Sew topknot in place.

● Add tiny ribbons or barrettes for high style!

Finishing Touches

● To finish Miss Piggy, sew on a skirt around the bottom of her body. Tie a bow in a piece of wide ribbon and sew it on as a bikini top. Decorate both with trim.

● Other details: use ribbons or fabric to make bow ties, caps or other accessories and sew them on.

Bing! Bang! Bong!

"Flamenco, anyone?"

Music today is more exciting than ever because of the wide varieties of styles, sounds, and instruments that are readily available. Cable television, worldwide movie distribution, and mega-music stores have made all kinds of music accessible to almost everyone. Listeners in Chicago can hear tribal music from rural African countries, while people in Beijing can listen to Madonna. But one of the most common ways to listen to music is when it is part of a performance. Music is a key part of many performances, from radio and television shows to movies and live stage performances. Whether music is highlighted as part of the action, as in a musical, or playing in the background to set a mood, as in a movie, it adds a richness and depth to any performance. There are always musical numbers in Muppet productions— partly because the puppeteers have musical talent, but also because they simply love music. Of course, many of the popular Muppet characters are natural musicians, as well. Kermit, for example, is a fine singer and banjo player. Rowlf is a skilled piano player,

"Dum tiddly um tum— dum dum!"

STRUM AND TWANG

Since we think music is fun, we think musical instruments should be fun, too. At the Muppet Workshop, we've thought up some pretty unique ways to help Muppets make music. You'll see them throughout this chapter.

and Fozzie can hold his own on the ukulele. And let's not forget the "house" bands: Dr. Teeth and the Electric Mayhem, The Rock Lobsters, and Rizzo and the Rat Pack.

As you'll learn in this chapter, musical instruments can be made from almost any object. All of the projects in this chapter make plenty of wonderful noise, and some can even make beautiful music. And there's an added bonus: They are also works of art.

You don't need to have a ton of talent to play an instrument— you just need to enjoy it; anyone can tap out a little rhythm on any object. When you were little, you probably enjoyed banging on pots and pans—most toddlers do. You banged because it was fun and noisy, but if you think about it, you were also learning how to drum. So don't be shy now—you've been making music for years!

"Squeeze if you love the accordion."

"Okay guys... Let's take it from the top!"

▼▼▼▼▼▼▼▼▼▼▼▼▼▼▼▼▼▼

Marvelous Maracas and Cute Castanets

How easy is it?

H ere are two kinds of percussion instruments that are both used traditionally in Latin music, and are both used traditionally in pairs. (Percussion instruments are things that you strike or shake to produce a rhythm—things like drums, tambourines, and gongs.) Castanets are often used to provide a rhythmic accompaniment to Spanish flamenco dancing, while maracas are used in big band dance music as well as folk music. Maracas are usually made from dried gourds filled with rice or seeds, so they produce a hissing sound when you shake them. Castanets are usually made from wood, shell, or ivory and make a clicking sound when you clap them between your fingers and thumb.

Maracas

What You Will Need:

For the Maracas:
- balloons (long or pear-shaped variety)
- papier-mâché glue mixture (see page 6 for recipe)
- bowl and newspaper strips for papier-mâché
- dried lentils, peas, beans, and/or rice
- sandpaper
- poster paint and paintbrushes
- fur, ribbon, feathers (for decoration)

Castanets

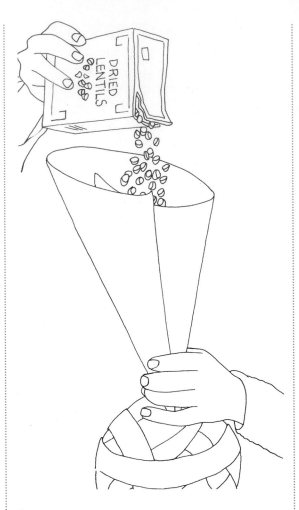

What You Will Need for the Castanets:

- **an adult**
  (to punch holes with the hammer and nail)
- **sandpaper**
- **model paint and paintbrushes**
- **4 juice bottle caps**
- **hammer and nail**
- **scissors**
- **elastic cord**
- **small white beads**
- **large colorful beads**
- **red felt**
- **white glue**

To Make the Maracas:

1 Blow up and tie two balloons.

· · · · · · · ·

2 Mix the papier-mâché (see page 6 for recipe and directions) and cover each balloon with papier-mâché-covered newspaper strips, leaving the tied balloon ends uncovered. Let dry. Cover each with a second layer of papier-mâché and let them dry completely (overnight, if necessary).

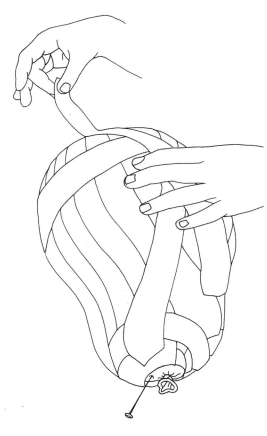

· · · · · · · ·

3 Pop the balloons. Pour rice and/or beans into each hole as shown above right, then seal tightly with papier-mâché and let dry completely.

· · · · · · · ·

4 Sand dry papier-mâché for a smooth finish. Paint and decorate your maracas to look like funny creatures, let them dry, then shake, rattle, and roll!

To Make the Castanets:

1 Sand or paint the bottle caps to get rid of any lettering or labels.

· · · · · · · ·

2 With an adult's help, use a hammer and nail to punch two holes about 1 inch apart on each of the caps, as shown below.

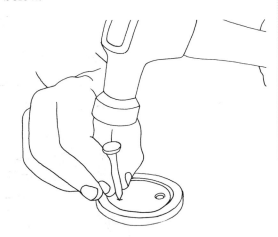

3 Cut a piece of elastic cord about 3 inches long and thread it halfway through one hole in one cap. On the underside of the cap, thread white beads onto the elastic to make the upper teeth, as shown; thread "beady eyes" onto the elastic on the top side of the cap (paint pupils on the eye beads if you like). Thread the remaining elastic through the other hole, and tie the ends together in a double knot on the underside of the cap, leaving enough room to slide your finger between the elastic and the top of the cap.

4 Repeat step 3 on the second cap, but this time thread white beads onto elastic only on the *underside* of the cap to make bottom teeth.

"Yeah, yeah, yeah...."

Tie off in a double knot on the underside of the cap, leaving room for your fingers in the elastic.

· · · · · · ·

5 For the second castanet, repeat steps 3 and 4, but if you'd like to add a tongue *instead of* bottom teeth to this second castanet, cut a tongue shape out of the red felt and glue it over the elastic knot inside the cap as shown.

· · · · · · ·

6 Wear a toothy/tongue cap on each thumb. Wear an eyeball cap on the middle three fingers of each hand. Now, clickety-clickety-clack the pieces together as fast as you can.

MINI MUSICIANS

We rarely make real, working musical instruments for the Muppets, since they couldn't really play them. Instead, we create many wonderful replicas of instruments (including these tiny rat instruments) for Muppets to "play." The real musical soundtracks are added later.

Rainbow Water Xylophone

How easy is it?

- an adult
- Bear Essentials
- large cardboard box

(continued on next page)

This isn't just a musical instrument—it's also a rainbow! The "Rainbow Water Xylophone" is easy to make, and it works well. Each bottle has a different level of water in it, so it produces a different tone or note when it is struck.

You'll need a little patience to get the xylophone tuned, and you'll need to experiment with tunes and notes. But once you do, you'll be able to play real and made-up songs with it. Then you can put on a concert for your family or friends—opening up with the Muppets' "Rainbow Connection," of course.

1 Paint the large cardboard box inside and out with light blue paint, then glue cotton balls into cloud shapes inside the box. Have an adult help you poke a hole in the center of both ends of the box, as shown below, about ¾ inch down from the top, in the center of both panels. Insert the dowel through the holes and set the box aside.

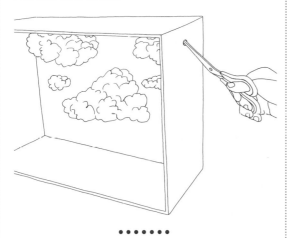

2 Have an adult help you use a hammer and nail to punch a small hole into the center of each of the eight bottle caps.

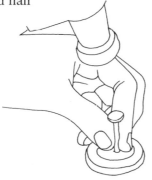

3 Cut eight pieces of string into equal lengths. Thread one string end through the hole in each bottle cap and tie double or triple knots on the inside of the caps so the strings won't pull out. Tie the other ends of the strings to the dowel so that the bottle caps hang at different lengths (copy our arrangement, or make up your own), and trim off the excess string.

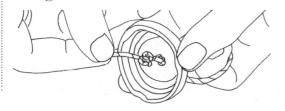

4 Fill the jars with different amounts of water, as shown in the photo opposite, to create the graduating sounds of a musical scale. Tap the bottles to hear how they sound. You might need to add a little water or take a little out to get the tones just right. If you're really ambitious and have a good ear, you can try and pitch the notes of the bottles based on a real scale. Remember this: more water = a higher note; less water = a lower note.

5 Add food coloring to the water in each bottle. We've ordered our colors as they appear in the rainbow:

- red—4 drops red
- orangy red—3 drops red, 3 drops yellow
- orange—2 drops red, 3 drops yellow
- yellow—4 drops yellow
- green—4 drops green
- blue green—3 drops blue, 1 drop green
- blue—4 drops blue
- purple—5 drops blue, 2 drops red

6 Carefully screw the filled bottles into the caps.

7 Glue a bead to one end of each chopstick to make mallets for the xylophone.

Compose a xylophone symphony and rock the house!

What You Will Need continued:

- light blue poster paint and paintbrush
- cotton balls
- ¾"-diameter wooden dowel (cut to the length of your box)
- hammer and nail
- 8 identical small glass juice bottles with caps (clean and empty)
- heavy string
- water
- food coloring (a variety of colors)
- 2 large wooden beads
- 2 chopsticks

Footed Drum

How easy is it?

What You Will Need:

- scissors
- construction paper
- rounded cardboard oatmeal box (discard the lid)
- 5 cardboard toilet paper tubes
- clear tape (like Scotch tape)
- 4 different-colored sponges
- white glue
- fake fur, feathers, beads, raffia, and other decorations
- 2 chopsticks
- acrylic paint and paintbrush

In order to tap out a cool tempo on a hip, homemade drum, you need to make it—and we're here to show you how. In this project, you'll learn how to use unusual materials to make and decorate your own snazzy, jazzy drum with feet of its very own.

You'll want at least one of these flat-footed friends in your room for those times when a drum roll is needed. But you can also make a whole family of them. If you use containers of different sizes and shapes for the drumming surfaces, you'll get a range of different drum sounds. And a collection of these drums sitting on a shelf or the floor will make anyone's room look truly beat-iful!

PROJECT MADE BY MATTHEW BROOKS

Note: *The oatmeal box will be your drum and the toilet paper tubes will be your drum's "legs." If you choose a different-sized box, you may need to use extra tubes or larger-diameter tubes to keep your legs in place (you'll see what we mean).*

1 Cut construction paper to cover the outside of the oatmeal box and four of the cardboard tubes; tape in place.

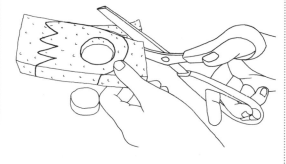

2 Cut the sponges into four separate foot shapes, as shown. Make holes through the middle of each foot (so they can slide onto the ends of the tubes), and line the holes with glue. Glue one foot onto each of four tubes.

3 Cut the remaining (fifth) cardboard tube down to 4 inches in length and glue the other four legs around it. The short tube should be in the center and the tops of the cardboard legs should be glued around the bottom third of the center tube.

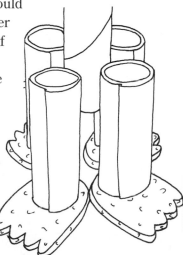

Next, fit the legs into the bottom, open end of your oatmeal box. They should wedge tightly into place.

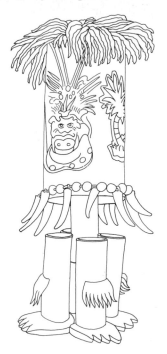

4 Decorate your drum with drawings, fake fur, feathers, or strings of beads. Our drum has cutout construction paper drawings taped to the sides and raffia coiled flat on the drumming surface.

5 For drumsticks, paint the chopsticks in bright colors and glue a bead on one end and feathers on the other.

Drum up an audience and show them your stuff!

"Nothing beat good drum!"

Rain Stick

How easy is it?

What You Will Need:

- an adult (to help cut yogurt containers)
- Bear Essentials
- extra-strong scissors
- 20 small, empty, clean, same-sized plastic yogurt containers (save 2 lids, discard the rest)
- duct tape
- 1 cup uncooked rice
- plastic googly eyes
- colored felt
- colored tissue paper

If You Use Gauze to Cover Your Rain Stick:

- rubber gloves
- 1 package fabric dye
- water
- pot or bowl (to dye gauze in)
- roll of cotton gauze
- wooden spoon
- paintbrush
- white glue solution (1 part water to 3 parts glue)

(continued on next page)

The "Rain Stick" is a wonderful instrument that makes a sound like falling rain. They were originally made in South America using the dried-out branches of dead cacti. The rain sound actually comes from tiny seeds or pebbles falling through passageways created by the dried fibers inside the cactus branch.

At the Muppet Workshop, we often have to think of creative ways to mimic or re-create a sound from nature using materials we can easily find. While we might have a hard time locating a South American cactus, we figured out a way to use empty yogurt containers and uncooked rice to make the same sounds.

We've decorated our "Rain Stick" with tropical birds and big green leaves—if you hold it up one way, it looks like a plain, leafy stick, but if you turn it upside down, you'll see big-eyed creatures peeking out from behind the leaves!

PROJECT MADE BY VICTOR YERRID AND ED CHRISTIE

1 Have an adult help you cut out the bottoms of *all* twenty yogurt containers.

· · · · · · ·

2 Cut fringe strips, as shown below, around the tops of *only* ten of the containers. Bend the fringe to the inside of the containers.

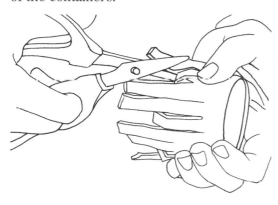

· · · · · · ·

3 Slide one fringed container completely inside each of the unfringed containers, then stack the unfringed containers, duct taping them together as you go. Alternate stacking bottom to bottom and top to top, and make sure that the containers on the very ends of the rain stick are both open-end out.

4 Place a plastic lid on one open end of the rain stick and secure with tape.

· · · · · · ·

5 Pour rice into your rain stick and put the other plastic lid on the other end of the rain stick. Secure with tape.

What You Will Need continued:

If You Use Papier-Mâché to Cover Your Rain Stick:

(See page 6 for recipe and directions.)

● bowl
● flour and water
● 1"-wide newspaper strips
● poster paint and paintbrush

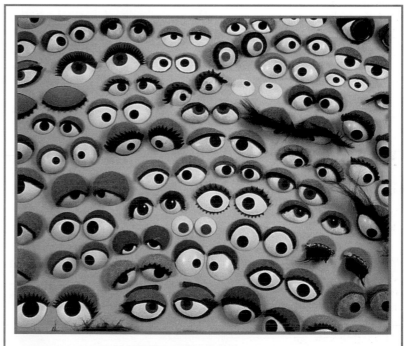

THE EYES HAVE IT

Here are some of the eyes—open and closed, happy, sad, surprised, and sleepy—that are kept around in drawers in the Workshop to give puppets different looks.

Sometimes Muppets themselves are the musical instruments, like the Mupp-a-phones (below) which yelp in different tones when bonked on the head by the unforgettable (and perhaps unforgivable!) Marvin Suggs.

6 To cover your rain stick with gauze:

● Prepare the fabric dye according to package directions. Dye the gauze, stirring with the wooden spoon for even color. Thoroughly wrap the rain stick with gauze while the gauze is still slightly damp, and tuck the ends of the gauze under the gauze wrap to secure.

● Paint a thin coat of the white glue solution all over the gauze. Do not use too much glue or it will discolor the tissue paper you'll be adding later. Allow the glue and gauze to dry a bit. Skip to step 8.

"OW-OW-Ooowwwwww!!!"

7 To cover your rain stick with papier-mâché:

● Prepare the papier-mâché mixture, then dip newspaper strips into the mixture and wrap them evenly around the yogurt containers. Let dry.

● Paint the papier-mâché with poster paint.

• • • • • • •

8 Glue googly eyes onto the rain stick, creating a "creature" on each yogurt container section. Glue on felt beaks and eyebrows.

• • • • • • •

9 Cut fringed strips of colored tissue paper to wrap around the stick, as shown on previous page (we used a dark green and a light green).

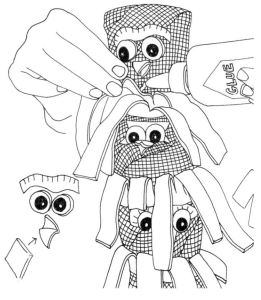

• • • • • • •

10 Glue two or more strips between each creature, as shown, then allow the rain stick to dry completely.

When finished, your "Rain Stick" will look like a tree when held one way, or a stack of birds when held the other way. Turn your "Rain Stick" upside down and imagine yourself in the rain forest, listening to the soft sound of the rain.

CHAPTER 18 / THE END

That's a Wrap

Now that you've made some or all of the projects in this book, you qualify as an honorary Muppet Workshop member. But you're probably wondering what to do with all these wonderful projects now that you've finished. We know that a lot of the fun is in making the projects, so we're going to give you some ideas for making that fun last once the project is over. Some of our ideas are obvious, while some might not have occurred to you yet, but they're all good ways to share the fruits of your labors with family and friends.

"Like, these puppets are far out, fer sher!"

PACK A PERFECT PORTFOLIO

Artists and other creative types keep a record of the work they've done by making a portfolio. A portfolio is a flat, portable cardboard or leather folder in which you can store your work—or photos, slides, or copies of your work—for safekeeping and posterity. Every time you create something new, make sure to put a photo or a color photocopy of it in your portfolio. This is a great way to keep track of the projects you've made and to see how your artwork changes over time as you learn new things. It's also a great way to show your work to people when you can't bring it along; just bring your portfolio to your grandparents' house or to the editor of the school newspaper who is looking for a new illustrator. Your portfolio will become a catalog of all your work (go ahead and include writing and other artistic works, too) and will be a handy reference tool for the future.

GIFT WRAPPING AND PERFECT PACKAGES

It doesn't take too much extra work to present your gift in a one-of-a-kind package. Try making your own wrapping paper by stamping plain paper with handmade cut-vegetable stamps; or use plain paper and draw a special picture on your package. Wrap a present in colorful comic pages from the newspaper, or paste some of your favorite stickers on unpatterned wrapping paper. Then tie on colorful or sparkly bows and ribbons, and add silk or paper flowers, a small plastic toy, or balloons. Make a handmade card to top it all off. When you're finished wrapping, think up funny ways to give your gifts: Try hiding a present in your house and writing clues that lead the way to it.

"Are these all for me? Really, you shouldn't have!"

PUT ON AN ART SHOW

Make and send out invitations so that friends and family can view the work you've done. You might want to ask friends or relatives to show their creations at the same time and make it a group art show. Pick a big, open space for your show, then have an adult help you hang things on the walls or set up displays on tables and chairs. Art galleries usually post labels next to each work, listing the name of the piece and the artist who created it. If you want to do this, you can fill out regular 3-by-5 index cards and prop or tape them in place.

PERFORM PERFECT PLAYS AND PUPPET SHOWS

If you'd like to show off any of the scenery, mini-theaters, costumes, musical instruments, masks, props, sound effects, or puppets that you've made, why not have a show? For any performance, all you really need are a stage or open space, a script, and an audience. You may want to make tickets to sell or hand out beforehand. Then, when it's time for the show, be sure you've got a comfortable place for each member of your audience to sit. Maybe make some popcorn for them to eat. Stamp and stencil playbills that tell who plays which part (or that give the names of your puppet characters). Now raise the curtain—it's show time!

FORM A FABULOUS FASHION SHOW

If you've made a lot of wearable projects from this book, you might want to show them off at your own fashion show. All you'll need is a space to hold your show and some willing models to wear your creations. Set up the space so that your models can pose against some sort of backdrop (try a mirror or a curtain). Then they can walk around a little to show off what they're wearing. You may want to narrate the fashion show as your models come "onstage." And be prepared to take orders—people may like your creations so much that they'll want you to make something for them, too!

"Moi put the 'sty' in style!"

289

▼▼▼▼▼▼▼▼▼▼▼▼▼▼▼▼▼▼▼▼▼▼▼

Acknowledgments

A very special thanks goes to Ed Christie, Project Coordinator. Lots of people helped make this book possible and I'd like to say thank you to them all: Lisa, Cheryl, Lynn, Claudia, Mom, Dad, Michael, Elizabeth, the whole gang at The Muppet Workshop, and the editorial staff at The Jim Henson Company. Thanks everyone!

—STEPHANIE ST. PIERRE

Thanks to the following people for all your help with this book: David Osser, Rosie Osser, Dan Osser, Jon Osser, Edna and Abe Osser, Irving Fleischer, Louise Slamin, Hanna and Rudy Hohenberg, Marianne Goldman, Julie Goldman, Caitlin Young, Liz Horwitz, Jessica Rubin, Carly Fishkin, Bradley Fishkin, Laura Edelman, Leah Hsu, Dunyelle Rosen, Annette and Michael Grant, Needham MotoPhoto Shop, Starr and others who came by and "lent a hand."

—STEPHANIE OSSER

The book cover and all craft projects were photographed by John E. Barrett with help from Danielle Obinger, Lauren Attinello, and Kate Jennings Foster.

Special thanks to Victor Yerrid of The Muppet Workshop; to Danielle Obinger, Lauren Bien, Karen Falk, and Catherine Meiseles of The Jim Henson Company Archives; to Jane Leventhal, Lauren Attinello, and Kiki Thorpe of Jim Henson Publishing; to former "Hensonites" Kate Foster and Mary Maguire; to Louise Gikow and Matthew Fox, the Eleventh Hour Saviors; and to Sally Kovalchick, Liz Carey, Barbara Balch, Jeanne Hogle, Rena Kornbluh, Eric Ford, Paul Gamarello, and Paul Hanson of Workman Publishing. Thanks also to Craig Shemin for his clever commentary.

Other people who helped out making crafts: Cheryl Henson, Stephanie St. Pierre, Lynn Brunelle, Lauren Attinello, Danielle Obinger, Jenny Lytle, and Mary Maguire.

Additional photography courtesy of Richard Termine.

Many thanks to the models who appeared in this book: Benjamin Schneider, Aya Gallego, Abby Maguire, Annie Maguire, Matt Maguire, Brion-ta Ayala, Celena Kopinski.

MEET THE MUPPET WORKSHOP!

These are just some of the people who build the Muppets and their world: Ed Christie, Workshop Director, Victor Yerrid, Assistant to the Director, Paul Andrejco, April Asher, Ron Binion, Mary Brehmer, Matthew Brooks, Fred Buchholz, James Chai, Bryan Crockett, Carmel Dundon, Victoria Ellis, Barbara Davis, Eric Engelhardt, Cindy Fain, Patricia Farr, Paul Hartis, Ann Marie Holdgruen, Jane Howell, Sarah Iams, Doug James, Larry Jameson, Rollie Krewson, Janet Kuhl, Peter MacKennan, Christine Moyes, Tom Newby, Elena Pellicciaro, Connie Peterson, Kip Rathke, David Roberts, Stephen Rotondaro, Mark Ruffin, Goran Sparrman, Jason Weber, Carlo Yannuzzi, Mark Zeszotek.

Crafts Weekly

Patterns

The following pages contain the patterns for many of the projects in this book. Not every pattern in this book is drawn to scale, so you'll have to adjust (usually increase) the size in order to have your designs turn out right.

The easiest way to enlarge a pattern is to use a copy machine. Ask an adult to help you set the machine to the percentage shown on the pattern. Then select the paper size, press "copy" and—presto! Your pattern is ready to go.

If you are copying the pattern by hand, remember that you don't need to include all the text shown on the page as well; just copy the grid and the design. See page 8 for more instructions on copying by hand.

Some projects in this book—like the Funky Jester's Cap on page 197—require you to custom fit the pattern to your own body. In those cases, the project's directions will tell you how to do it.

If you are confused about any part of the pattern process, just refer to the instructions that accompany every pattern or turn back to pages 7 through 9 for a refresher course.

Even if you've never worked with patterns before, our helpful hints will guide you every step of the way.

Each pattern page includes the elements shown here.

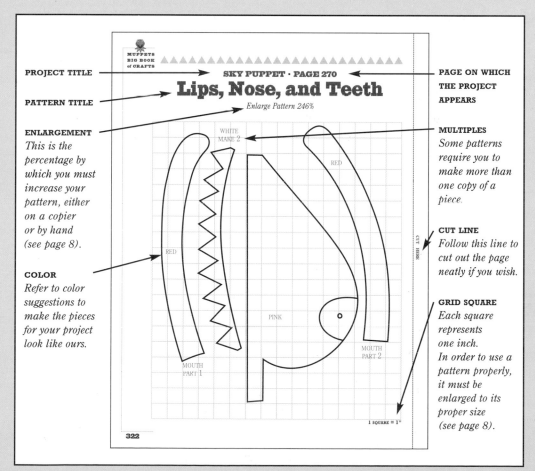

PROJECT TITLE

PATTERN TITLE

ENLARGEMENT
This is the percentage by which you must increase your pattern, either on a copier or by hand (see page 8).

COLOR
Refer to color suggestions to make the pieces for your project look like ours.

MUPPETS BIG BOOK of CRAFTS

SKY PUPPET · PAGE 270
Lips, Nose, and Teeth
Enlarge Pattern 246%

WHITE MAKE 2

RED

RED

PINK

MOUTH PART 1

MOUTH PART 2

CUT HERE

1 SQUARE = 1"

322

PAGE ON WHICH THE PROJECT APPEARS

MULTIPLES
Some patterns require you to make more than one copy of a piece.

CUT LINE
Follow this line to cut out the page neatly if you wish.

GRID SQUARE
Each square represents one inch. In order to use a pattern properly, it must be enlarged to its proper size (see page 8).

▲▲▲▲▲▲▲▲▲▲▲▲▲▲▲▲▲▲▲▲▲▲▲▲

Paper Dolls and Stand

Enlarge Pattern 145%

CUT HERE

CUT SLITS IN FEET

PAPER DOLL STAND
CUT 1 SLIT AT A SLIGHT ANGLE

FOLD HERE

1 SQUARE = 1"

PAPER DOLL SET · PAGE 12
Paper Doll Clothing
Enlarge Pattern 145%

CUT HERE

1 SQUARE = 1"

STAINED GLASS BUTTERFLY WINDOW · PAGE 23
Butterfly "Lead" Frame

Enlarge Pattern 213%

CUT HERE

1 SQUARE = 1"

GROOVY GLASSES · PAGE
Eyeglass Parts

Enlarge Pattern 188%

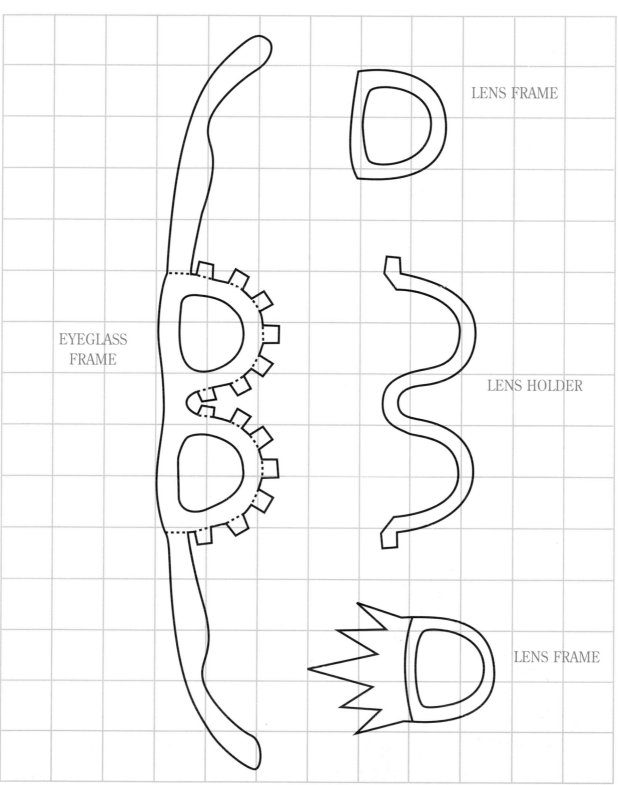

LENS FRAME

EYEGLASS
FRAME

LENS HOLDER

LENS FRAME

1 SQUARE = 1"

Spider Piñata Features

Enlarge Pattern 128%

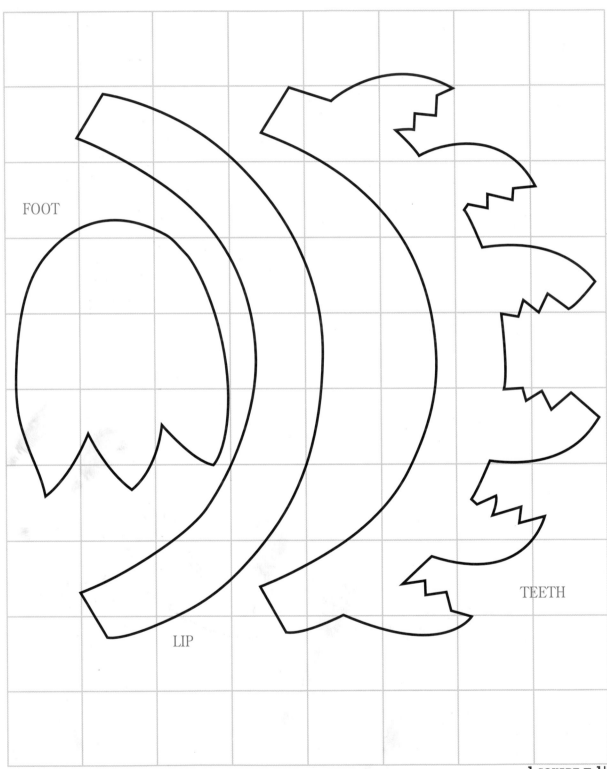

FOOT

LIP

TEETH

CUT HERE

1 SQUARE = 1"

POP-UP CHOMPER · PAGE 42
Robin
Pattern Shown Is Actual Size

1 SQUARE = 1"

Mermaid, Fish, and Octopus

Enlarge Pattern 143%

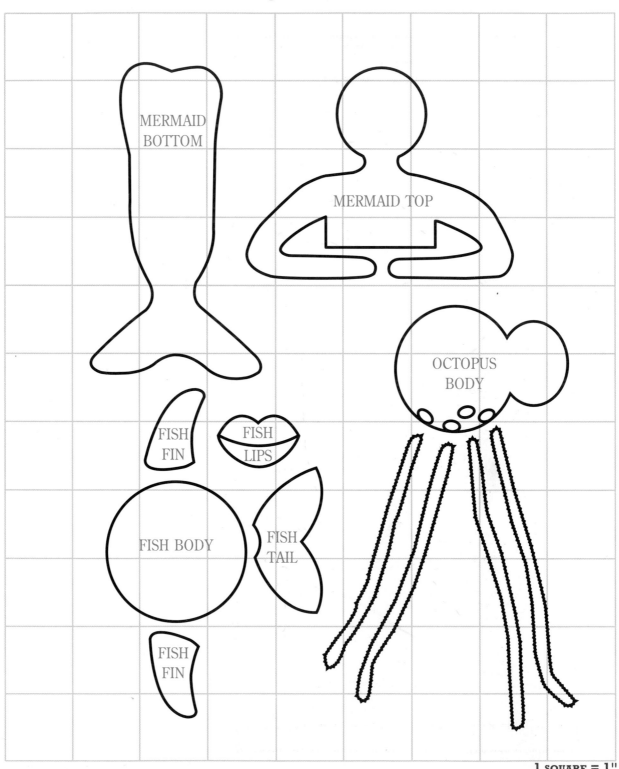

MERMAID
BOTTOM

MERMAID TOP

OCTOPUS
BODY

FISH
FIN

FISH
LIPS

FISH BODY

FISH
TAIL

FISH
FIN

CUT HERE

1 SQUARE = 1"

GARGOYLES · PAGE 76
Gargoyle I
Enlarge Pattern 229%

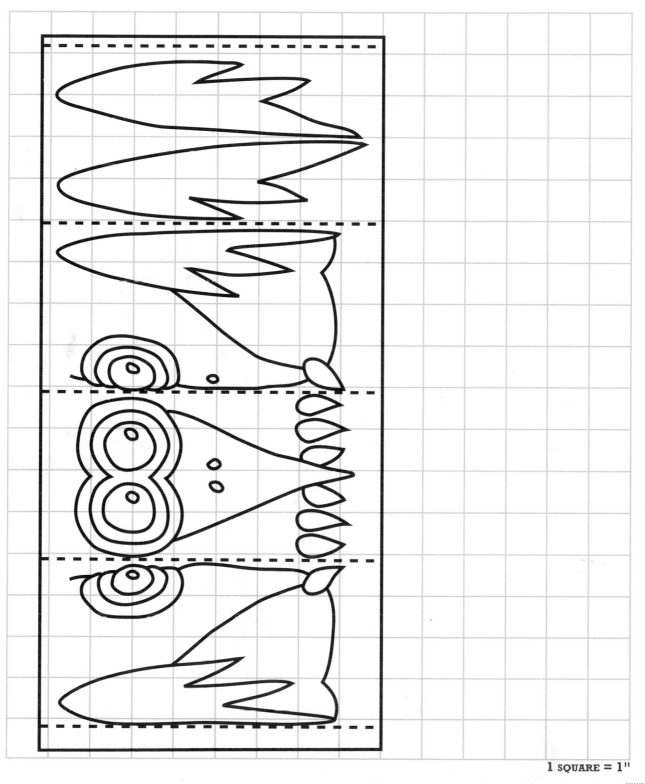

1 SQUARE = 1"

GARGOYLES · PAGE 76
Gargoyle II
Enlarge Pattern 229%

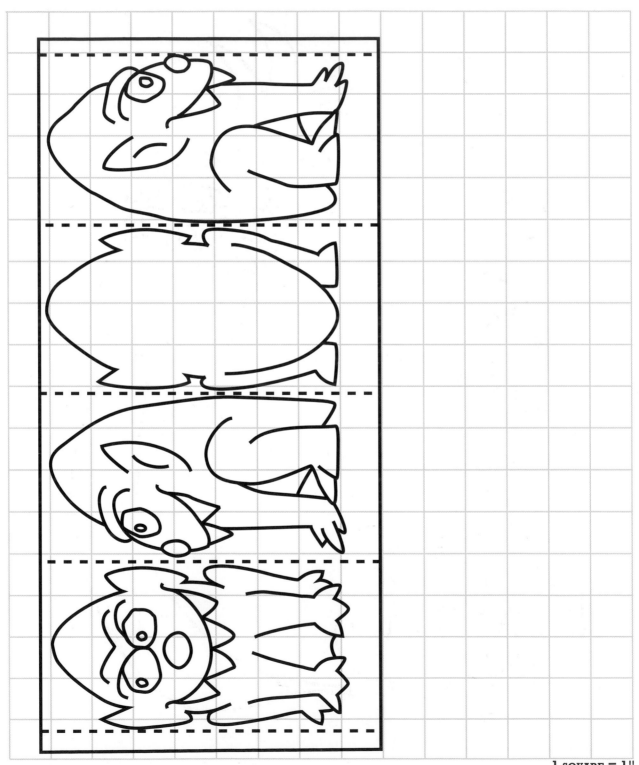

CUT HERE

1 SQUARE = 1"

▲▲▲▲▲▲▲▲▲▲▲▲▲▲▲▲▲▲▲▲▲▲▲

SUPER APRON STENCILS · PAGE 88
Fruit Shapes
Enlarge Pattern 200%

CUT HERE

1 SQUARE = 1"

WILD & WACKY PEN AND PENCIL SET · PAGE 96
Wild & Wacky Creatures

Pattern Shown Is Actual Size

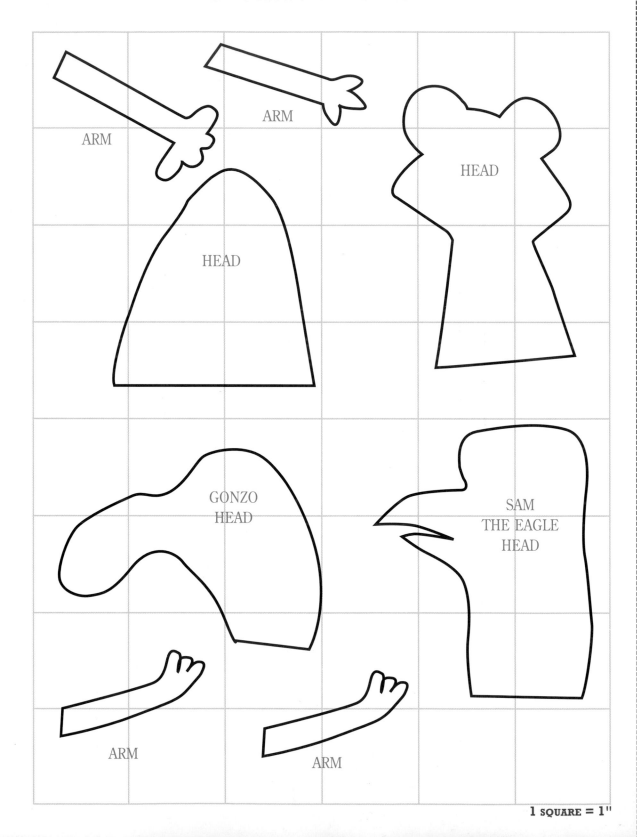

ARM

ARM

HEAD

HEAD

GONZO
HEAD

SAM
THE EAGLE
HEAD

ARM

ARM

CUT HERE

1 SQUARE = 1"

ROLLING THINGAMAJIG · PAGE 119
Egg-Shaped Wheel
Pattern Shown Is Actual Size

CUT HERE

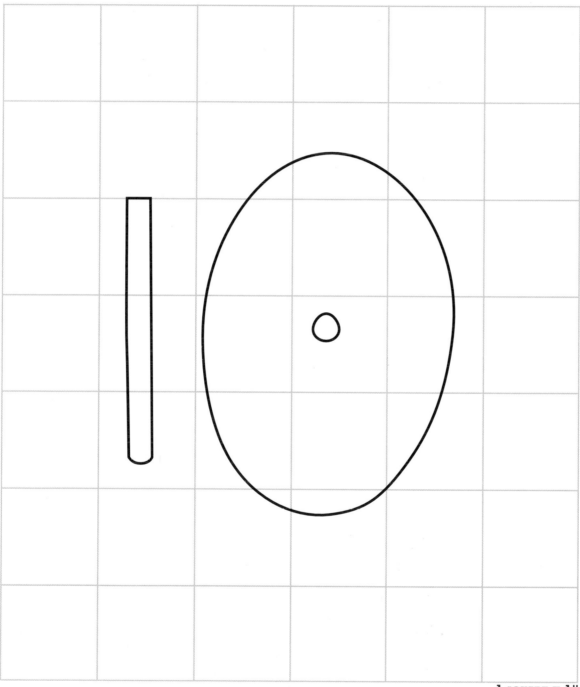

1 SQUARE = 1"

ROLLING THINGAMAJIG · PAGE 119
Bow Tie and Top Hat

Pattern Shown Is Actual Size

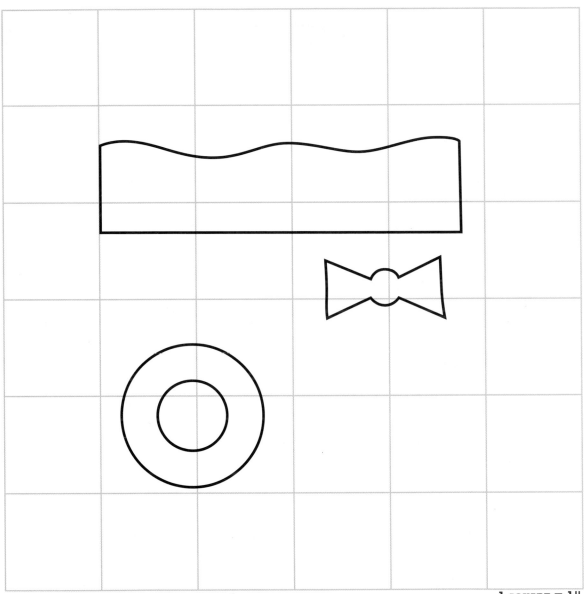

1 SQUARE = 1"

CUT HERE

STUFFED CREATURE · PAGE 146
Creature Body
Enlarge Pattern 168%

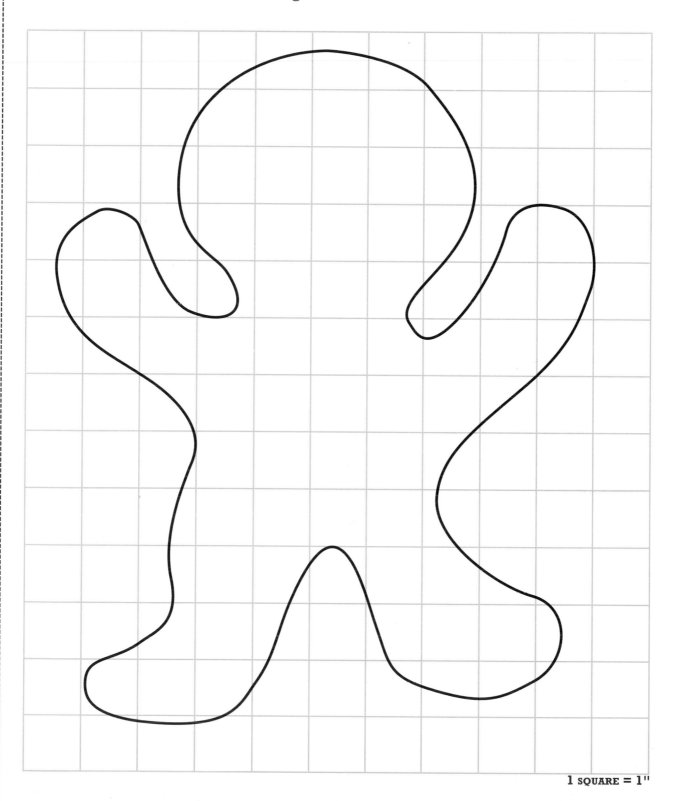

CUT HERE

1 SQUARE = 1"

Kermit Appliques

Enlarge Pattern 246%

RED

GRASS
GREEN

BRIGHT
PINK

BLACK

GRASS
GREEN

OLIVE
GREEN

WHITE

CUT HERE

1 SQUARE = 1"

▲▲▲▲▲▲▲▲▲▲▲▲▲▲▲▲▲▲▲▲▲▲▲▲▲▲▲

PETS' HOLIDAY STOCKINGS · PAGE 154
Stocking
Enlarge Pattern 246%

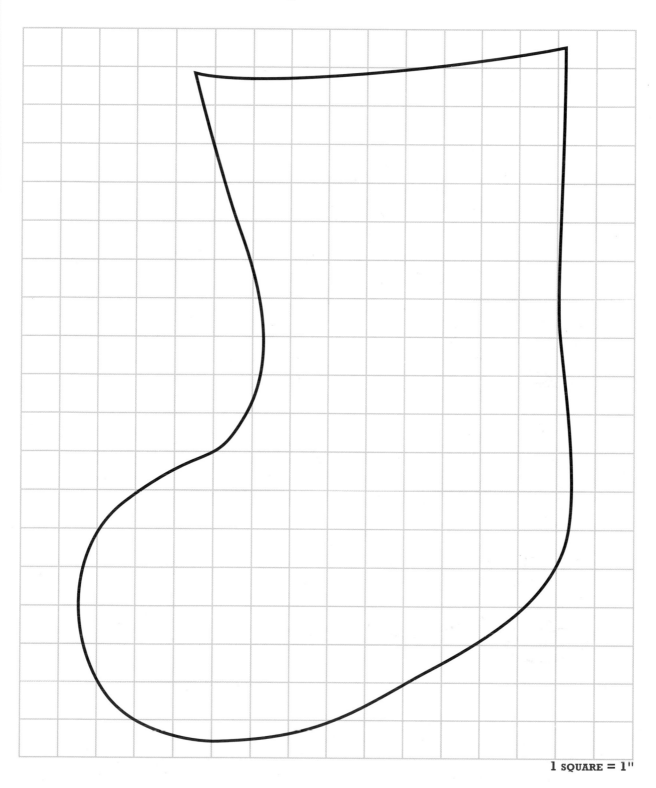

CUT HERE

1 SQUARE = 1"

PETS' HOLIDAY STOCKINGS · PAGE 154

Salamander

Enlarge Pattern 208%

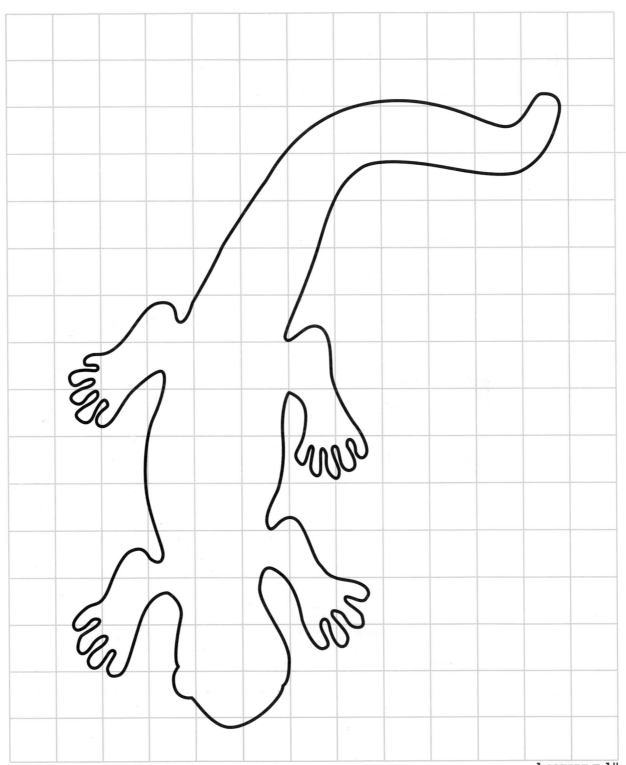

1 SQUARE = 1"

▲▲▲▲▲▲▲▲▲▲▲▲▲▲▲▲▲▲▲▲▲▲▲▲▲▲

LOOP-DE-LOOP HOOKED RUG WALL HANGING · PAGE 158

Scooter

Enlarge Pattern 188%

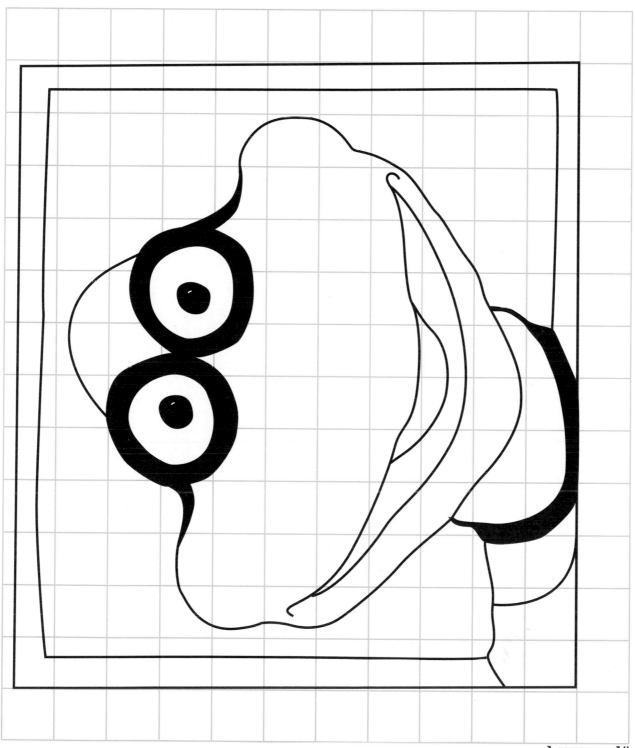

CUT HERE

1 SQUARE = 1"

Beaker

Enlarge Pattern 222%

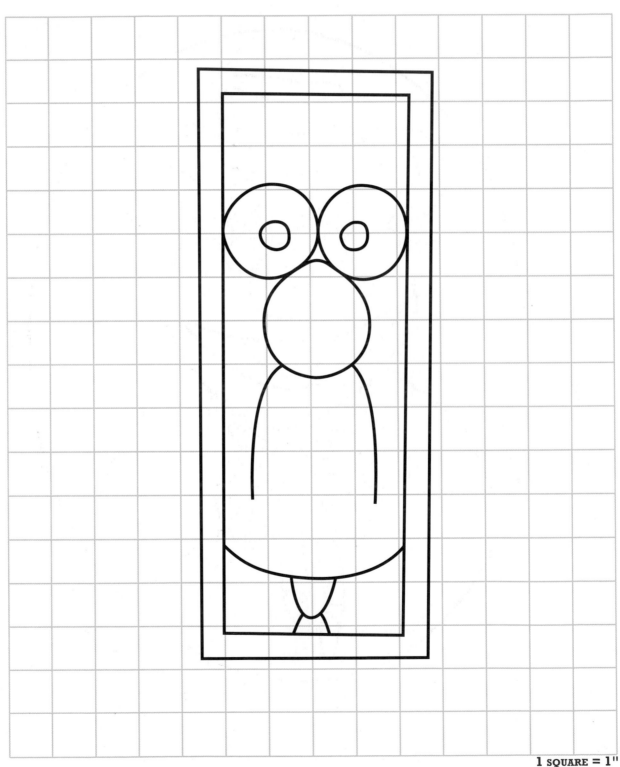

CUT HERE

1 SQUARE = 1"

EGGSHELL MOSAIC · PAGE 174
Fozzie Mosaic
Enlarge Pattern 145%

CUT HERE

1 SQUARE = 1"

RAINBOW STATIONERY SET · PAGE 176
Kermit Head

Enlarge Pattern 108%

CUT HERE

1 SQUARE = 1"

▲▲▲▲▲▲▲▲▲▲▲▲▲▲▲▲▲▲▲▲▲▲▲▲▲▲▲▲▲

RAINBOW STATIONERY SET · PAGE 176
Fozzie Head
Enlarge Pattern 139%

CUT HERE

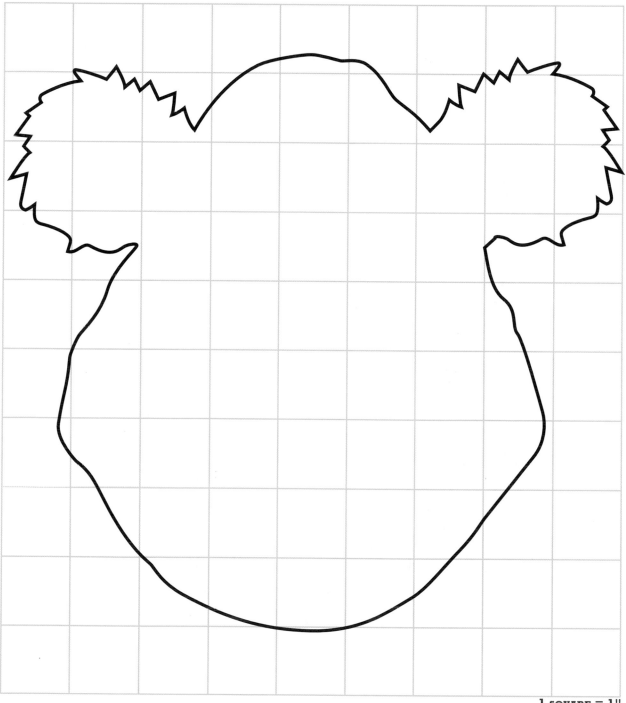

1 SQUARE = 1"

PRINCESS AND WIZARD HATS · PAGE 185
Hat
Enlarge Pattern 291%

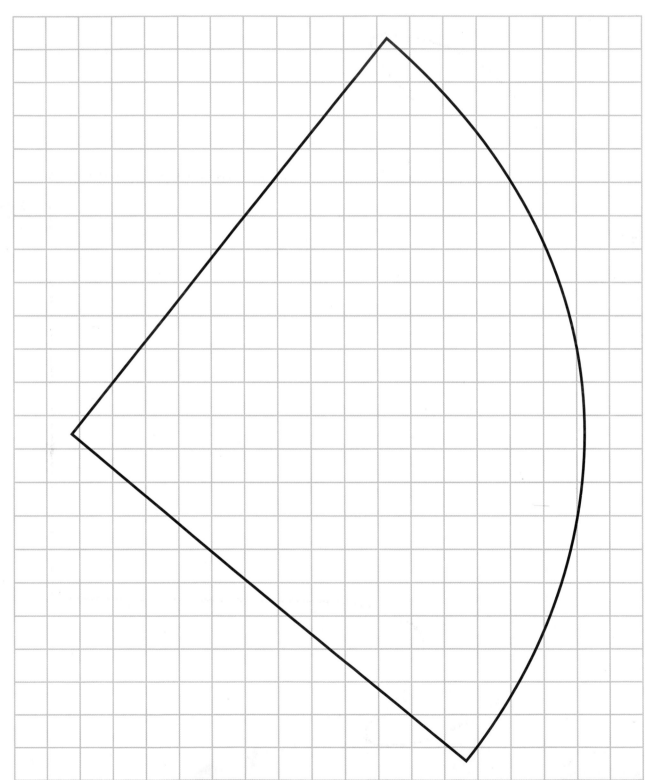

CUT HERE

1 SQUARE = 1"

FUNKY JESTER'S CAP · PAGE 197

Cap

Enlarge Pattern 216%

CUT HERE

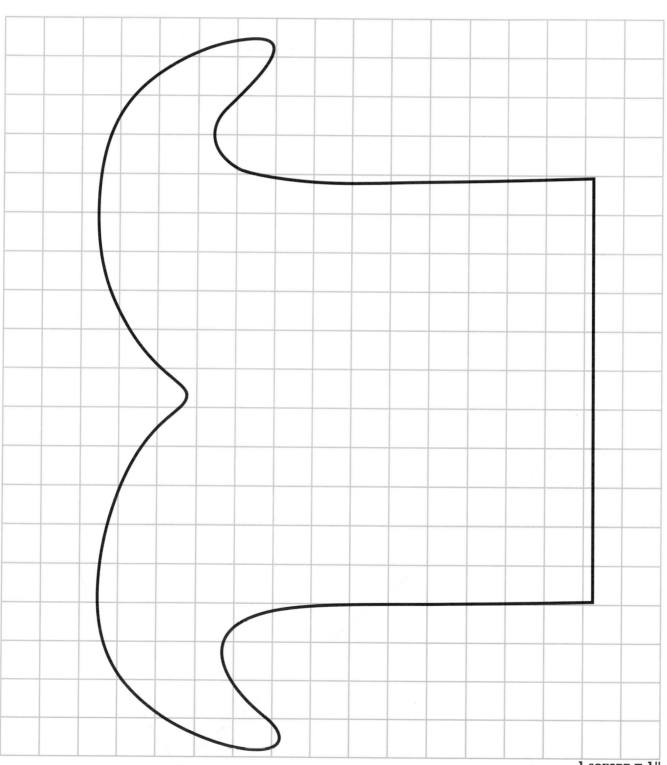

1 SQUARE = 1"

ANIMAL NOSES, HORNS, AND EARS · PAGE 214

Unicorn Ear

Enlarge Pattern 160%

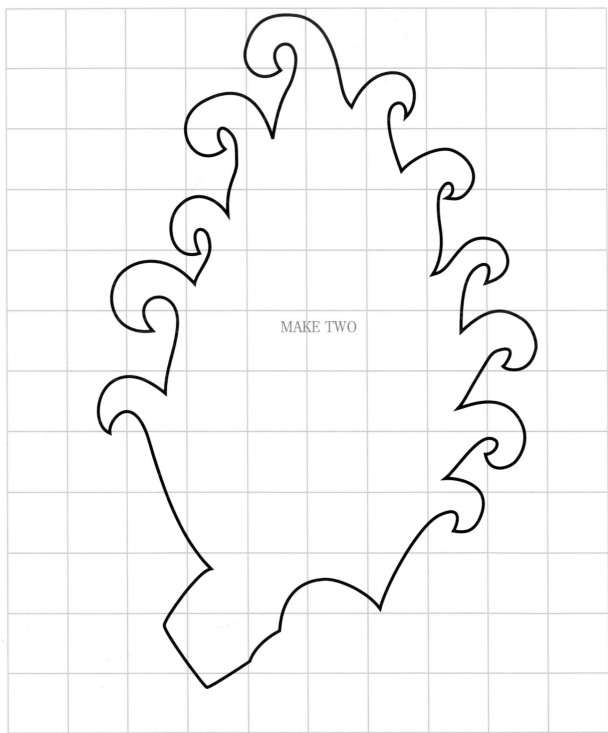

MAKE TWO

CUT HERE

1 SQUARE = 1"

ANIMAL NOSES, HORNS, AND EARS · PAGE 214
Toucan Beak

Enlarge Pattern 110%

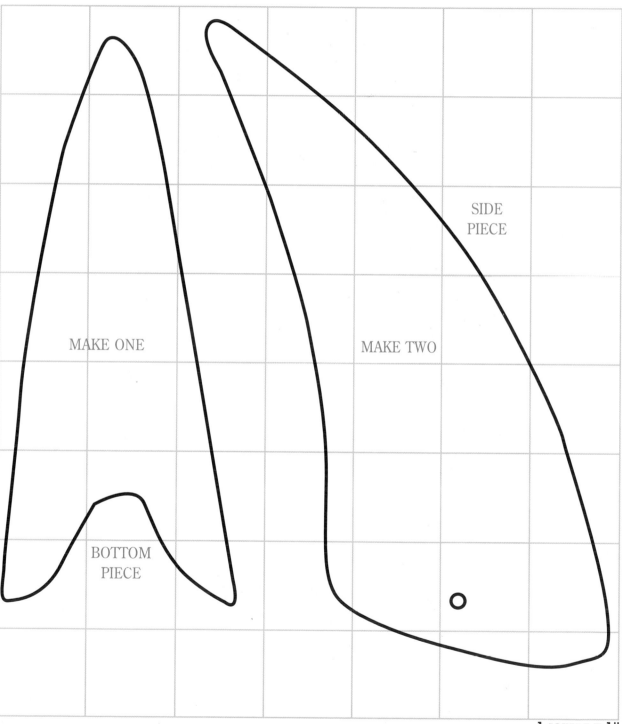

CUT HERE

MAKE ONE

SIDE
PIECE

MAKE TWO

BOTTOM
PIECE

1 SQUARE = 1"

▲▲▲▲▲▲▲▲▲▲▲▲▲▲▲▲▲▲▲▲▲▲▲▲▲▲▲▲

ANIMAL NOSES, HORNS, AND EARS · PAGE 214
Elephant Ear
Enlarge Pattern 200%

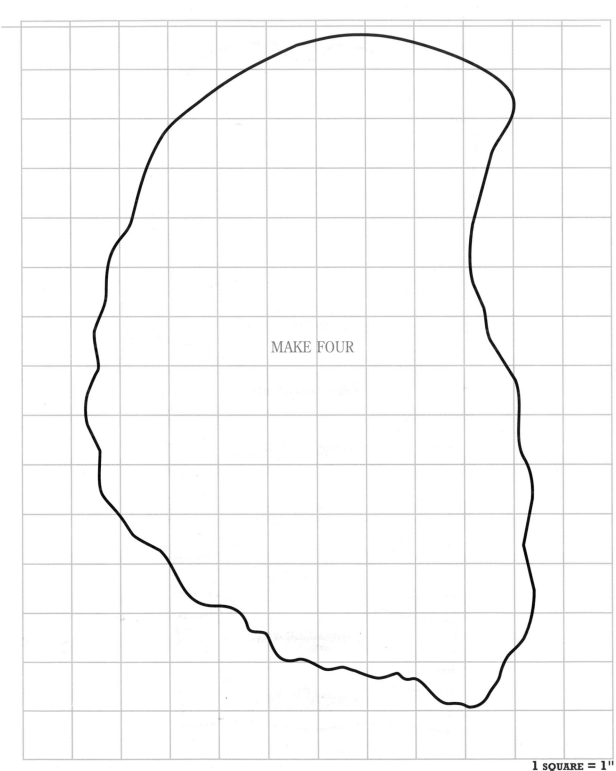

MAKE FOUR

CUT HERE

1 SQUARE = 1"

ANIMAL NOSES, HORNS, AND EARS · PAGE 214
Elephant Trunk
Enlarge Pattern 213%

CUT HERE

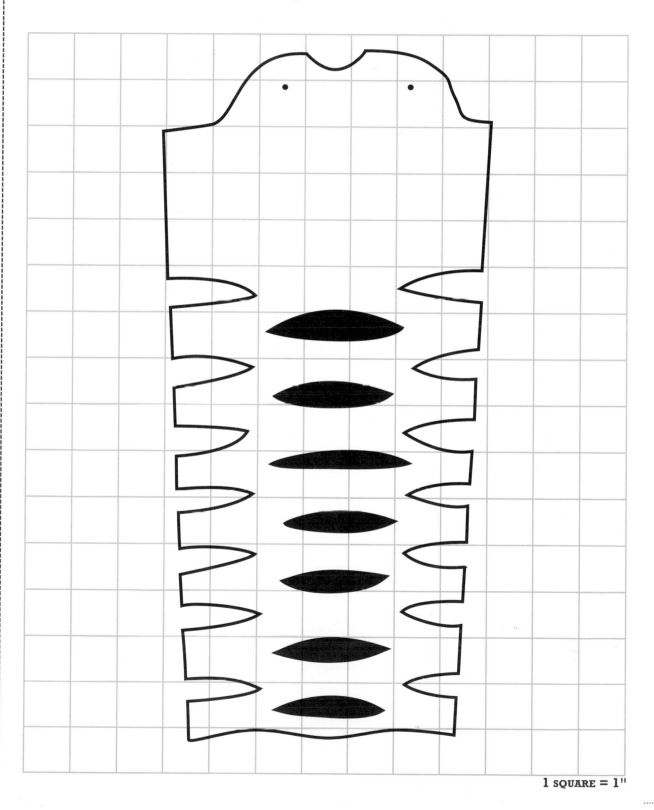

1 SQUARE = 1"

Stairs

Enlarge Pattern 291%

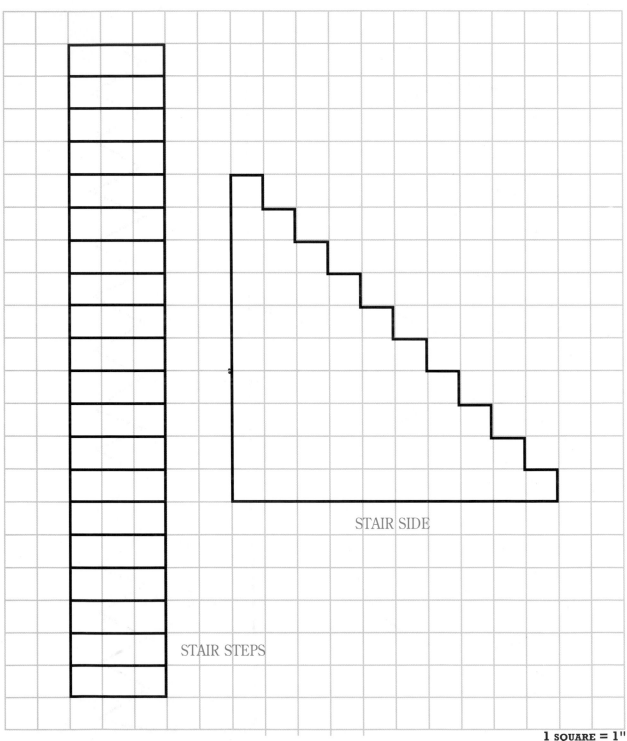

STAIR SIDE

STAIR STEPS

CUT HERE

1 SQUARE = 1"

▲▲▲▲▲▲▲▲▲▲▲▲▲▲▲▲▲▲▲▲▲▲▲▲▲▲

SKY PUPPET · PAGE 270
Eyes and Eyebrows
Enlarge Pattern 188%

CUT HERE

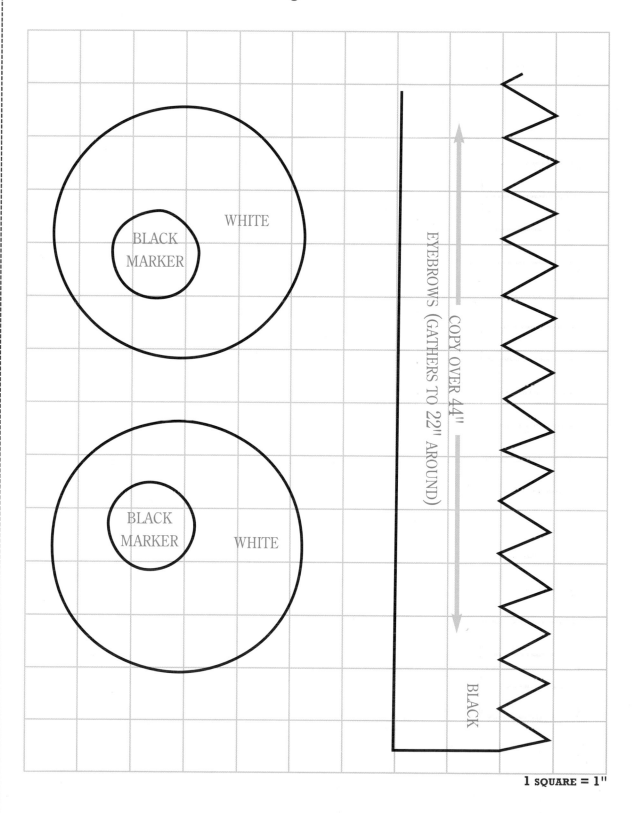

WHITE

BLACK MARKER

EYEBROWS (GATHERS TO 22" AROUND)

COPY OVER 44"

BLACK

BLACK MARKER

WHITE

1 SQUARE = 1"

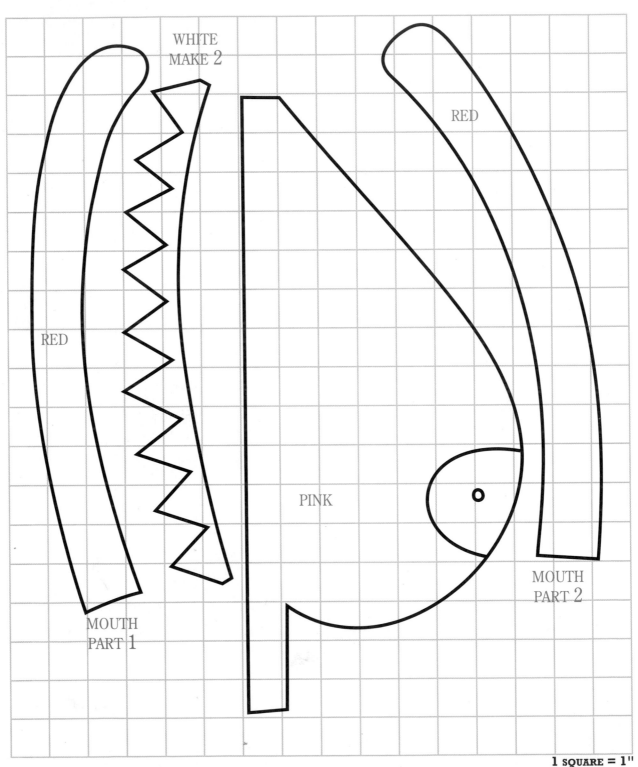

SKY PUPPET · PAGE 270

Lips, Nose, and Teeth

Enlarge Pattern 246%

WHITE
MAKE 2

RED

RED

PINK

MOUTH
PART 1

MOUTH
PART 2

CUT HERE

1 SQUARE = 1"